FALTEN
FOLDS

Herausgegeben von
Edited by

Lilli Hollein und
and Mio Wakita

VERLAG DER BUCHHANDLUNG WALTHER
UND FRANZ KÖNIG, KÖLN COLOGNE

MAK

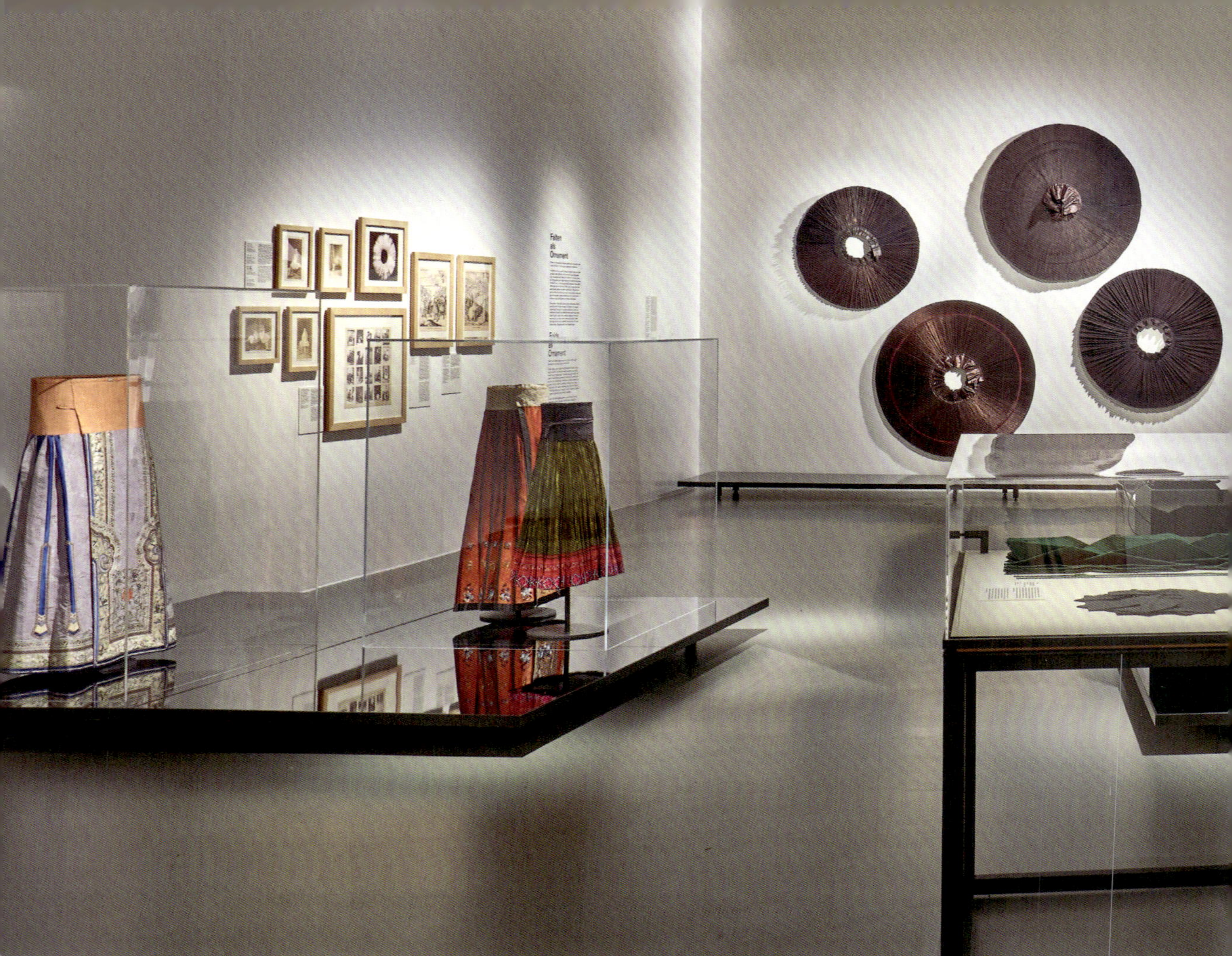

Inhalt Contents

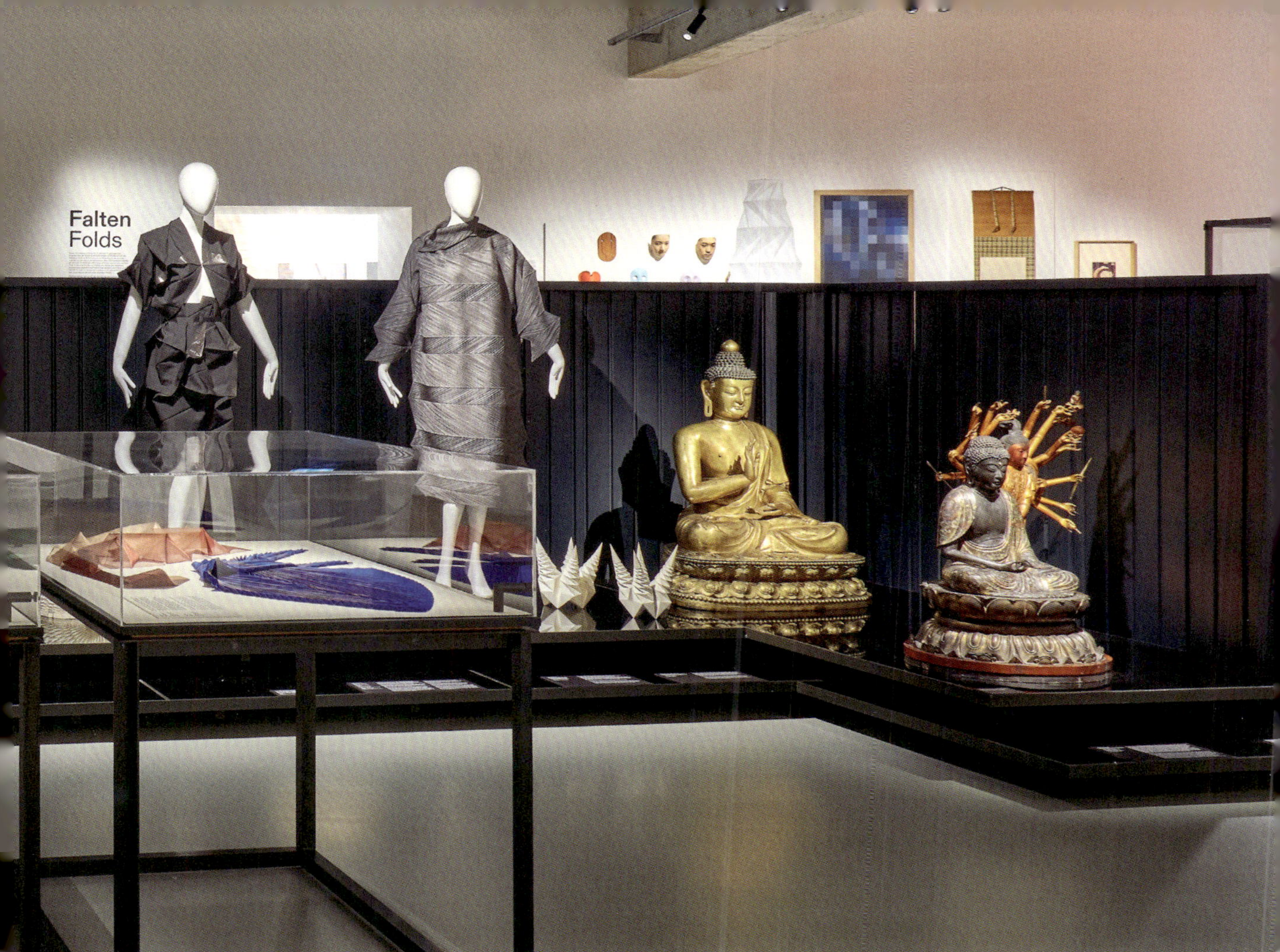

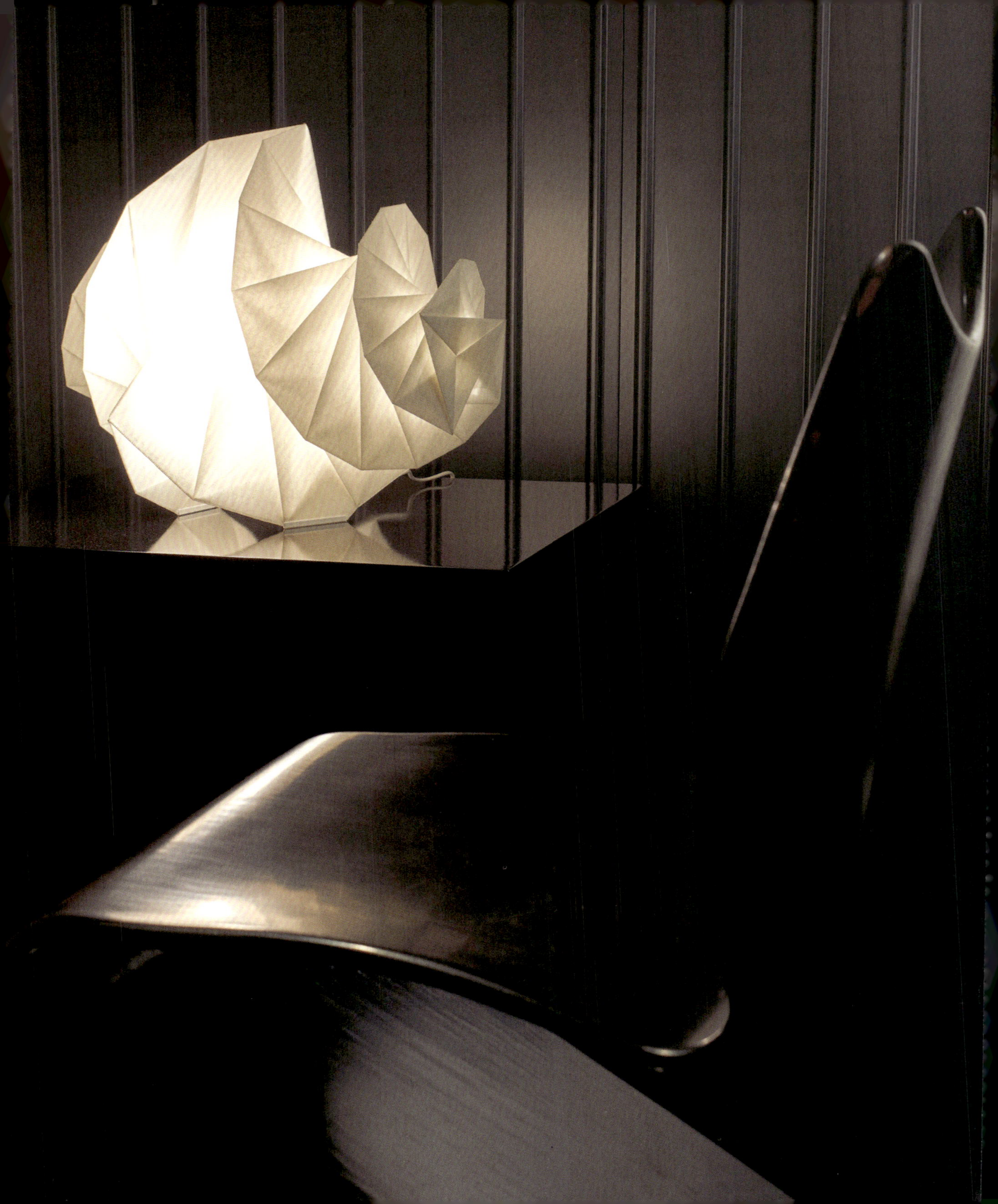

Lilli Hollein
Generaldirektorin, MAK

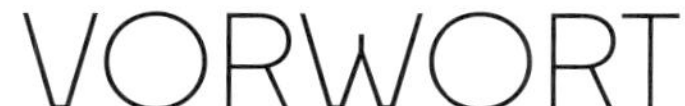

VORWORT

Falten bieten einen breiteren Querschnitt durch die Kunst- und Kultur-, aber auch durch die Menschheitsgeschichte, als man im ersten Moment vermuten würde. Ihre Vielschichtigkeit und ästhetische Vielfalt erstrecken sich über verschiedenste Materialien und Jahrtausende. Das MAK hat dies zum Anlass genommen, eine Ausstellung zu diesem Thema zu gestalten und nun im Nachgang dankenswerterweise diese Publikation herauszugeben.

Die bewusst hergestellte Falte ist eine kunstvolle Transformation des Materials. Allein in der Sammlung des MAK finden sich herausragende Beispiele für den Einsatz von Falten in unterschiedlichen Epochen und Weltgegenden.

Ob in einem plissierten Stück Stoff, als Detail einer metallenen Rüstung, als in Marmor drapierte steinerne Faltenwürfe, ob in Holz, Papier oder Beton: Falten verleihen und untermauern Rang und Bedeutung, sie haben statische Funktionen und ermöglichen Flexibilität; sie dienen der Repräsentation und sie repräsentieren Weisheit und Überfluss.

Auch Falten in der menschlichen Haut werden oft als Zeichen der Transformation gelesen – von den Falten wohlgenährter Säuglinge bis hin zu den Gesichtsfalten des Alters. Die künstlerische Auseinandersetzung damit – ihre Abbildung oder auch Abformung in Form von Masken – führt vor Augen, wie menschliche Falten an unterschiedlichen Orten der Welt gelesen und bewertet werden.

Unsere Kustodin der Asien-Sammlung, Mio Wakita, hat vom asiatischen Raum ausgehend, aber weit darüber hinaus, einen Streifzug durch das künstlerische Universum der Falten unternommen, und es freut mich sehr, dass diese Publikation lange Zeit Dokument dieser Auseinandersetzung sein wird.

Ich danke Frau Wakita für ihr außerordentliches Engagement und Herrn Maki Hiroyuki, CEO von Buffalo Inc., für seine großzügige Unterstützung, die diesen Katalog überhaupt erst möglich gemacht hat. Da diese Publikation auf der 2023 im MAK gezeigten Ausstellung basiert, möchte ich auch allen Leihgeber*innen meinen besonderen Dank aussprechen.

Der geschärfte Blick für dieses faszinierende Phänomen, diese Kulturtechnik, macht Freude – und die wünsche ich Ihnen im Namen des MAK beim Lesen dieses Bandes.

FOREWORD

Lilli Hollein
General Director, MAK

Folds offer a broader cross-section of the history of art, of culture—not to mention of humanity—than one might at first sight suspect. Their complexity and aesthetic diversity range throughout the centuries over a wide variety of materials. The MAK has taken this circumstance as an occasion to present an exhibition on the subject and now, thankfully, in retrospect to publish this catalog.

A fold deliberately created is an artistic transformation of the material involved. In the MAK Collection alone are many outstanding examples of folds from different epochs and locations around the world.

Whether in pleated fabric, as a detail in a metal suit of armor, or as draped folds carved in marble, whether in wood, paper or concrete, folds impart and emphasize rank and significance. They fulfill structural roles and facilitate flexibility; they serve representative functions and represent wisdom and superfluity.

The folds in human skin are also often read as signs of transformation—from the folds in the skin of a well-fed baby to the facial wrinkles of old age. How these are represented in art—how they are portrayed, or even molded in the form of masks—allows us to see how the folds on the human body are interpreted and evaluated in different parts of the world.

The Curator of our Asia collection, Mio Wakita, has undertaken a journey through the cultural universe of folds—starting out from Asian lands but extending far beyond them. And I am delighted that this publication will for many years to come exist as a document of this journey.

My thanks to Ms Wakita for her extraordinary commitment and to Mr. Maki Hiroyuki, CEO of Buffalo Inc., for his generous support, without which this catalog's publication would not have been possible. Since the catalog is based on the 2023 exhibition presented in the MAK, I would also like to extend a heartfelt thanks to all those who loaned works for that exhibition.

Training the eye to appreciate this fascinating phenomenon, this cultural technique, is a source of joy—and such joy I wish you, on behalf of the MAK, in perusing this publication.

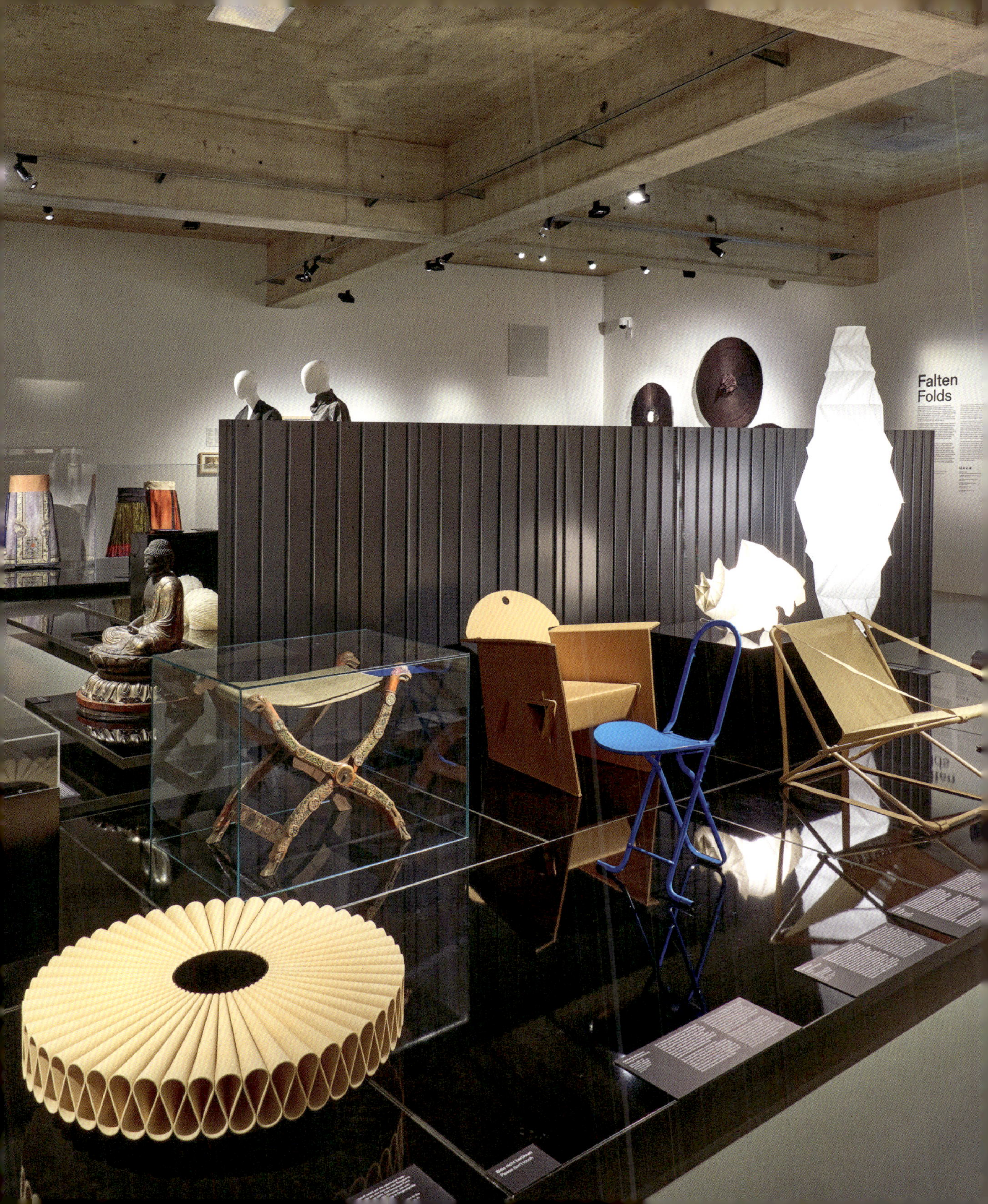

Falten
Folds

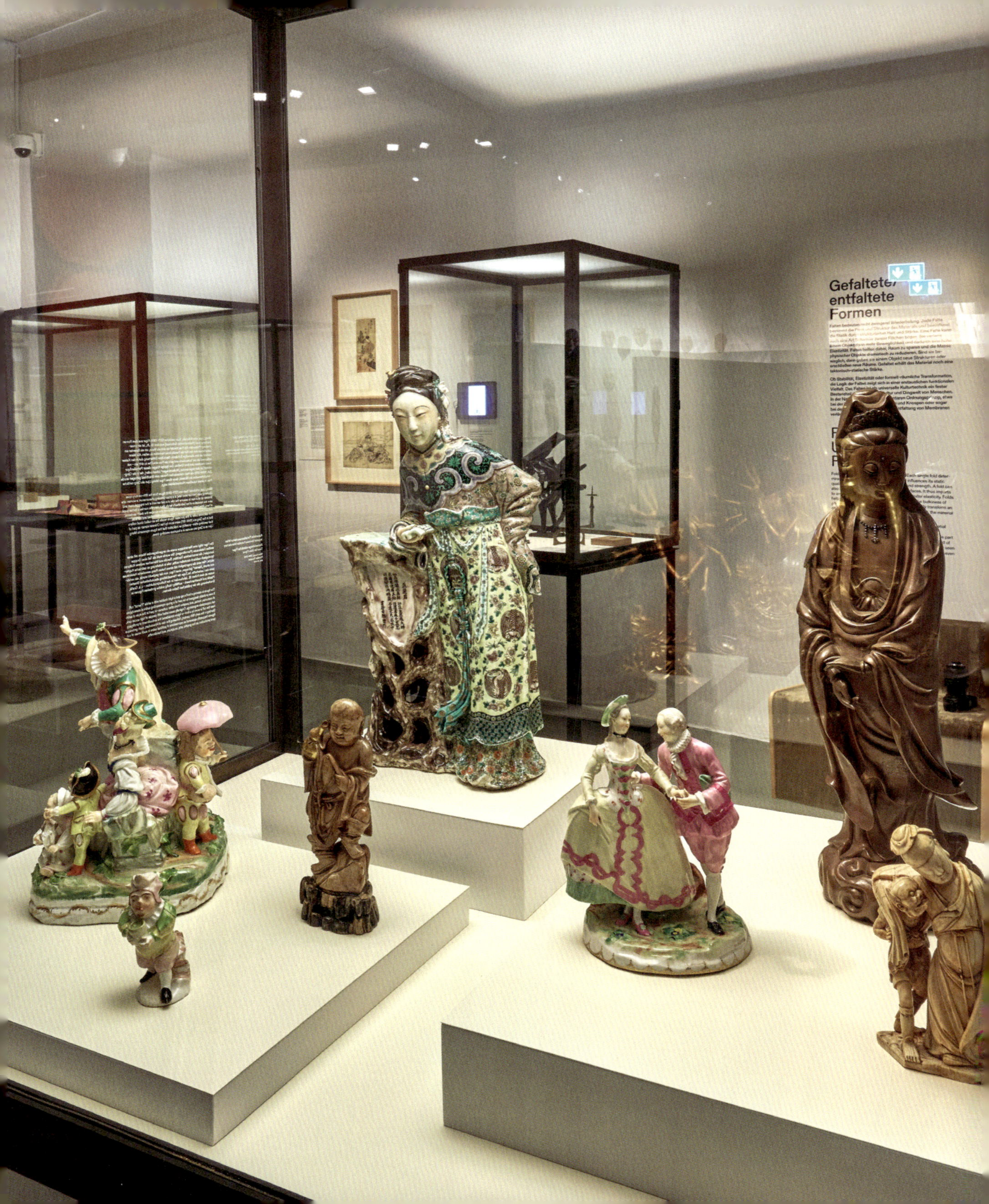

Mio Wakita

FALTEN, VIELFÄLTIG

Falten sind allgegenwärtig: Sie finden sich in geologischen Erdschichten, in Kleidung, in Spielzeug im Kinderzimmer, am Airbag im Auto, an Blüten und zarten Käferflügeln, an unserem eigenen Körper oder in der Architektur. Seit Jahrtausenden werden sie auch als Gestaltungsmittel eingesetzt und spielen eine wichtige Rolle in der angewandten und bildenden Kunst. Als natürliche Erscheinung begleiten uns Falten unser ganzes Leben lang, unser Verhältnis zu ihnen variiert aber stark je nach kultureller Zugehörigkeit, Geschlechtsidentität oder aktuellen Trends.

Das Wort „Falten" hat mehrere Bedeutungen: Es bezeichnet die materielle Manifestation einer zufälligen oder künstlich erzeugten Krafteinwirkung, aber auch die Spuren biologischer Veränderungen oder eine Kulturtechnik. Dieses Buch beleuchtet die Vielschichtigkeit dieses Phänomens aus Sicht der Design-, Kultur-, Kunst- und Ideengeschichte sowie der Kulturanthropologie und widmet sich zwei gegensätzlichen Themenschwerpunkten: gewollten, künstlich erzeugten Falten im Sinne einer gestalterischen Strategie (etwa raffiniert gefaltete chinesische „Nadel-Faden-Taschen" aus Papier oder die nach den 1980er Jahren entstandenen Kollektionen des Modedesigners Issey Miyake) und Falten in Bezug auf den Körper, die physische Welt und die menschliche Wahrnehmung (wie Mizuno Nanbokus physiognomische Studien oder Judith Huemers Faltenstudien).

Die vorliegende Publikation geht aus der gleichnamigen Ausstellung hervor, die 2023 im MAK – Museum für angewandte Kunst in Wien stattgefunden hat. Zahlreiche Beispiele aus Ost und West – von Textilien und Papierarbeiten über Möbel und Malereien bis hin zu Fanartikeln und 3D-gedruckten Masken – offenbaren nicht nur die regionalen und kulturellen Unterschiede der Konzepte, Formen und Praktiken in Bezug auf Falten, sie zeigen auch unerwartete Gemeinsamkeiten und machen u. a. transkulturelle Prozesse sichtbar. Ein erweiterter Blick auf kulturelle und ästhetische Praktiken aus Ostasien bildet dabei den Schwerpunkt.

Unter starker Einbeziehung der historischen MAK Sammlungsbestände treten weitere Themenfelder exemplarisch zutage: Mit ihrer überraschend vielschichtigen Objektbiografie und der Unbeständigkeit ihrer Bedeutungszuschreibung bezeugen einige Objekttypen einen kritischen epistemologischen Wandel in der Kunst- und Kulturgeschichte. Die hier ausgewählten Beispiele offenbaren „Falten" als spannende Schnittstelle, die diverse Felder und Konzepte miteinander verbindet: zwischen Ethnografie und Mode, zwischen Sabotage/Dekonstruktion und ästhetisch-sozialer Demokratisierung der Welt oder zwischen funktionaler Nützlichkeit und Manifestation kosmologischer Gesetzmäßigkeiten. Durch die große zeitliche Bandbreite sowie die mediale Vielfalt der ausgewählten Beispiele wird das breite kultur-, kunst- und design- sowie rezeptionshistorische Spektrum von Falten bzw. gefalteten Objekten erlebbar.

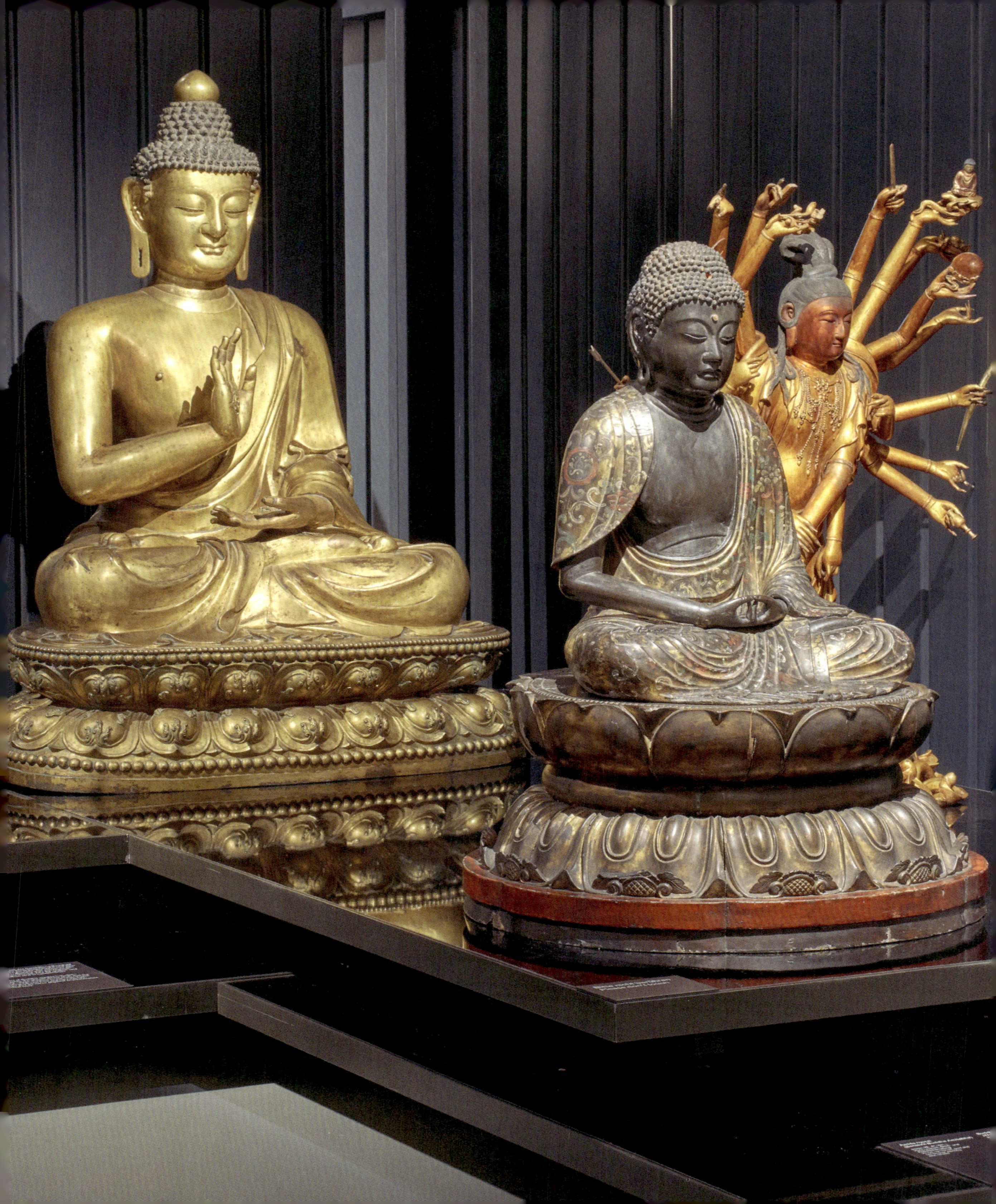

Mio Wakita

FOLDS, MANIFOLD

We are surrounded by folds literally everywhere: in geological strata, in clothing, on toys in the nursery, on airbags, on flower petals and delicate beetles' wings, on our own bodies, and in architecture. For thousands of years, they have also been an indispensable design tool in the applied and visual arts. As a natural phenomenon, folds accompany us our whole life long. Our relationship to them varies greatly, however, according to our cultural affiliation, gender identity, or devotion to the latest fashion trends.

The term "folds" has several meanings. It can refer to material manifestations of deliberate or accidental physical force, to traces of biological transformations, or to folding/pleating as a cultural technique. This book is designed to illuminate this complex phenomenon from the perspective of cultural anthropology and the history of design, culture, art, and ideas. It focuses on two diametrically opposed aspects: artificial folds, deliberately created as a design strategy (e.g. ingeniously folded Chinese "needle-and-thread wallets" made of paper, or the post-1980s collections of fashion designer Issey Miyake) and folds, or wrinkles, in their relationship to the human body, the physical world, and our perception thereof (Mizuno Nanboku's physiognomic studies, or Judith Huemer's study of the relationship between the human body and folds).

This publication documents the special exhibition of the same name presented at the MAK – Museum of Applied Arts in Vienna in 2023. Numerous examples from East and West—ranging from textiles and works made of paper, to furniture and paintings, to fan articles and 3D-printed masks—not only present regional and cultural variations on conceptual, formal, and practical approaches to the art of folding. They also reveal some surprising commonalities, for instance by tracing transcultural processes. A special focus on cultural and aesthetic practices in East Asia form a special feature of this book.

Through a strong focus on the historical MAK Collection, further exemplary themes come to light: the surprisingly complex biographies and volatile identities of some objects bear witness to critical epistemological change in art and cultural history. The examples selected here reveal "folds" as an exciting interface between diverse fields and concepts: between ethnography and fashion, between sabotage/deconstruction and the aesthetic-social democratization of the world, and between utilitarian values and the manifestation of cosmological laws. The immense chronological spectrum and medial heterogeneity of the objects presented here thus bring to life the wide-ranging history of the art, culture, design, and reception of folds and folded objects.

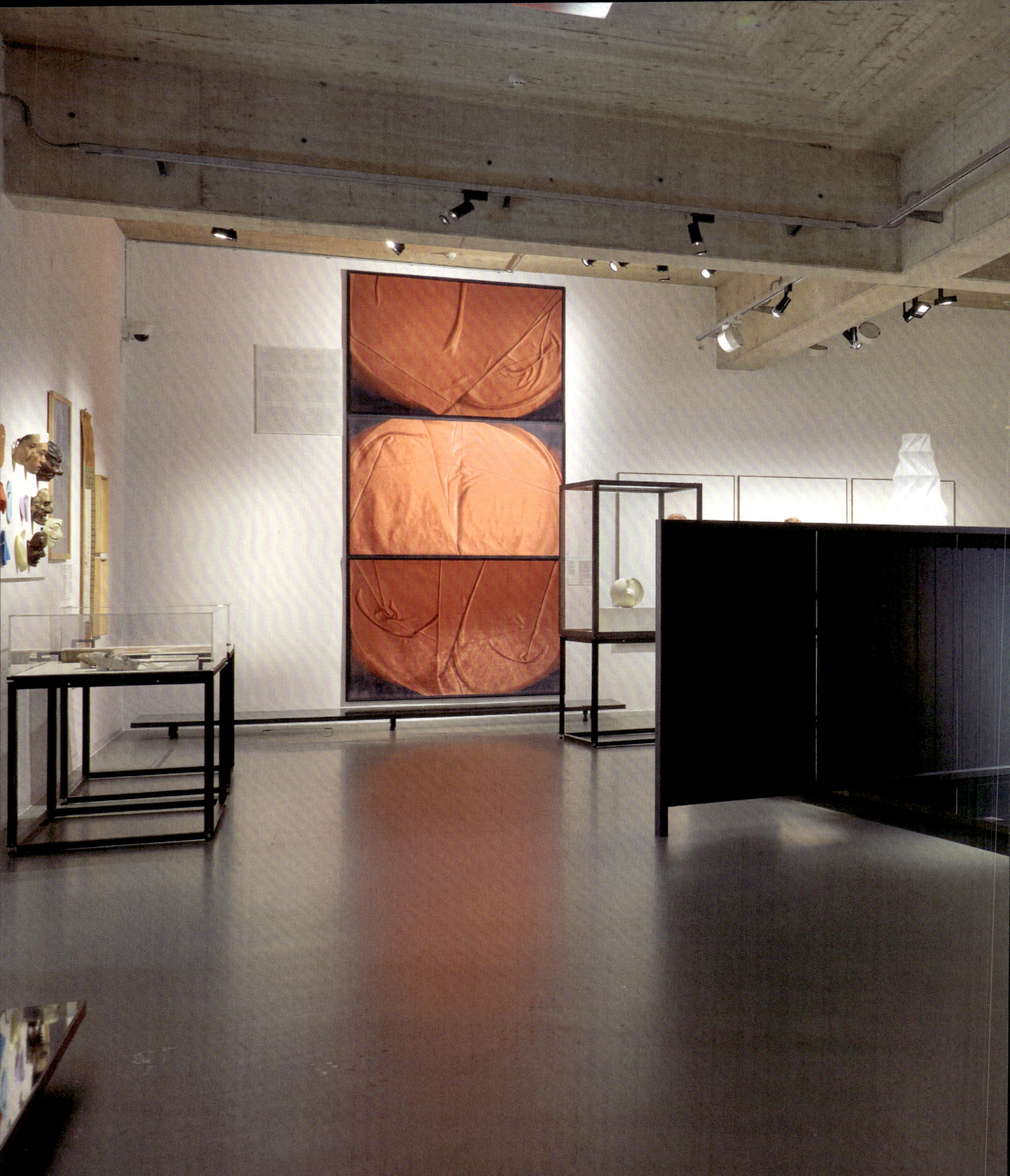

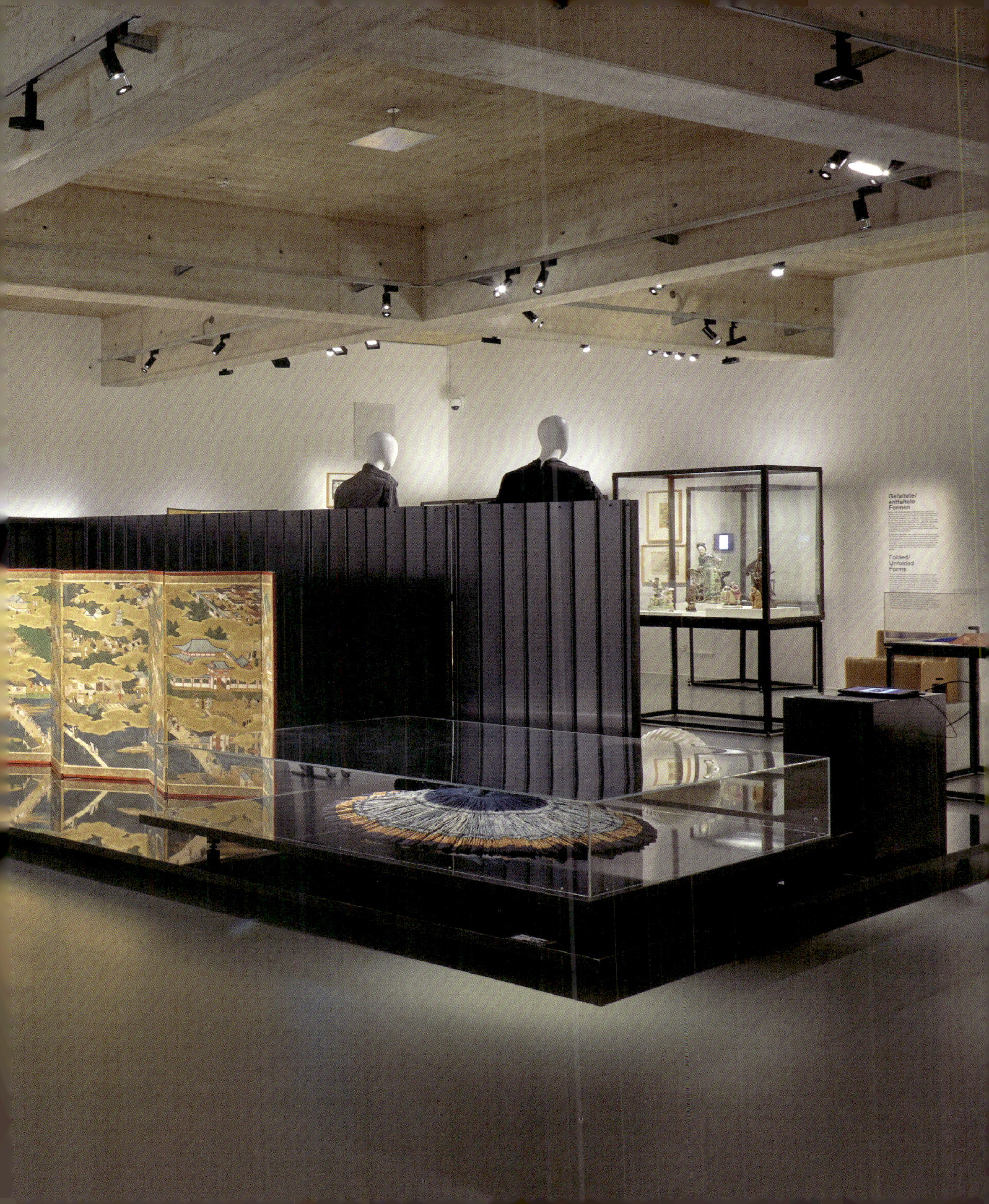

Gefaltete/
entfaltete
Formen

Folded/
Unfolded
Forms

FALTEN ALS ORNAMENT

Falten als formgebende Gestaltungselemente verwandeln sich in einer größeren Anordnung in grandiose Ornamente.

Textilfalten können gewollt/künstlich entstehen oder als Zufallsprodukte, wenn Materie und Schwerkraft zusammenspielen. Das Ornamentale der Falten hat als Element in der Geschichte der Textilgestaltung ein festes technisch-ästhetisches Repertoire. Die Methoden zur Herstellung künstlich gebildeter Falten eines Textils spiegeln die kulturelle Vielfalt wider. Insbesondere Plissiertechniken weisen eine große Bandbreite an Möglichkeiten auf: Sie reichen vom Wechsel zweier unterschiedlicher Maschen über die manuelle, akribische Raffung bis hin zu chemischen Verfahren unter Zuhilfenahme von Plissee-Schablonen.

Ornamentale Falttextilien sind auch visuell erkennbare Zeichen soziokultureller Kleiderordnungen. Ein Gewand mit üppigen, aufwendigen Faltungen ist geradezu prädestiniert dafür, als stoffliches Zeichen für den Reichtum und sozialen Rang seiner Träger*innen zu dienen. Der ornamental gefaltete Stoff wird, wenn man ihn von einem auf ein anderes kulturelles Umfeld überträgt, mit einer neuen Identität überschrieben. Ein neues Kapitel seiner „Objektbiografie" wird aufgeschlagen.

FOLDS AS ORNAMENT

Folds as a formative design element are transformed in larger compositions into magnificent ornamentation.

Folds in textiles may be fashioned deliberately/artificially, or they may be randomly created by the interplay of material and gravity. In the history of textile design, the ornamental quality of folds possesses a fixed technical and aesthetic repertoire. The techniques used to create artificial folds in textiles are as varied as the world's cultures. Pleating methods in particular manifest a broad range of approaches, from using an alternating two-stitch technique, to painstakingly crimping the material by hand, to employing chemical processes complemented by pleating templates.

Ornamentally folded textiles are also a visible indicator of sociocultural dress codes. A garment with elaborate costly folds is almost certainly a material indication of its wearer's wealth and social status. When transferred from one cultural context to another, ornamentally folded textiles assume a new identity, opening up new chapters in their biographies.

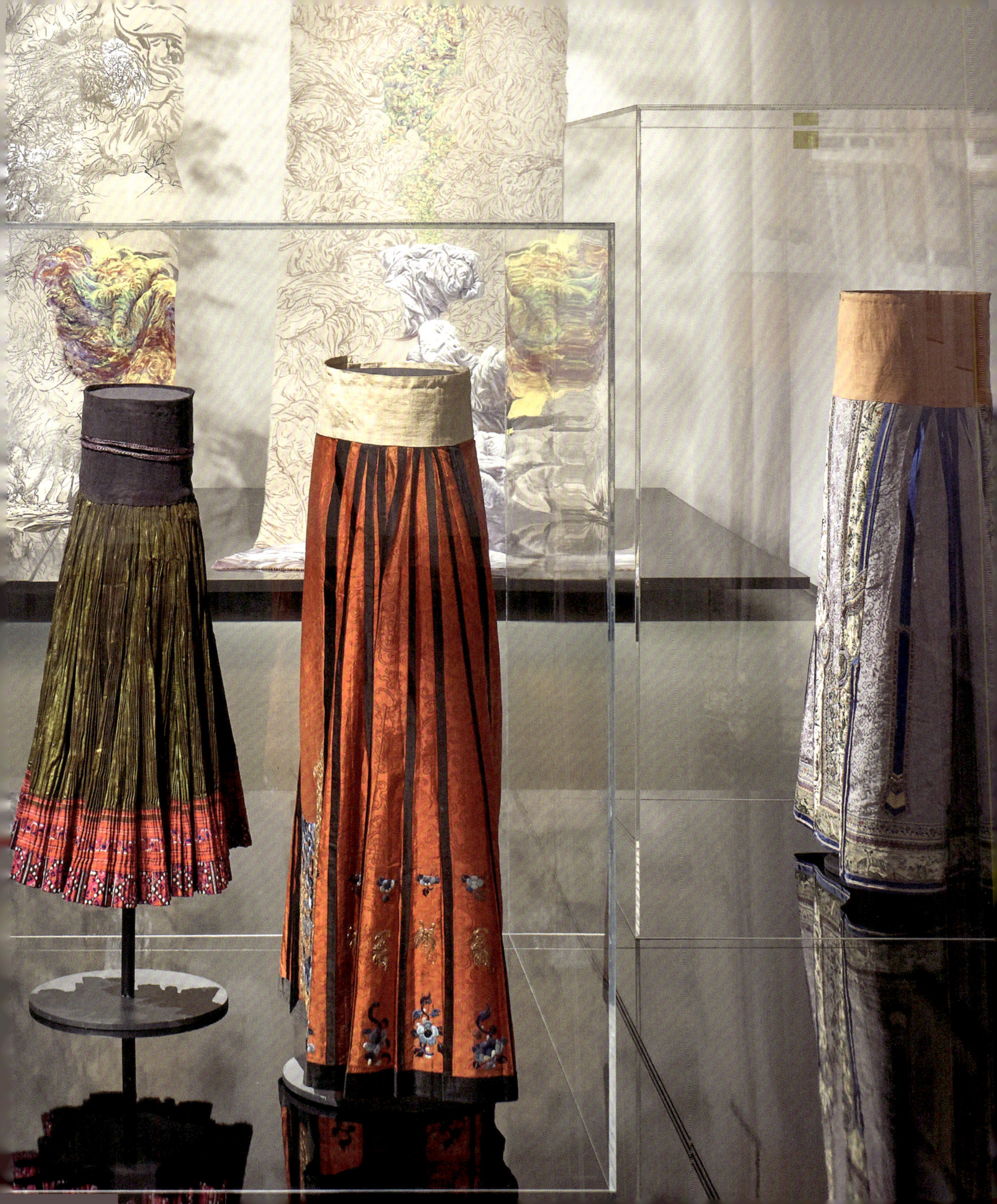

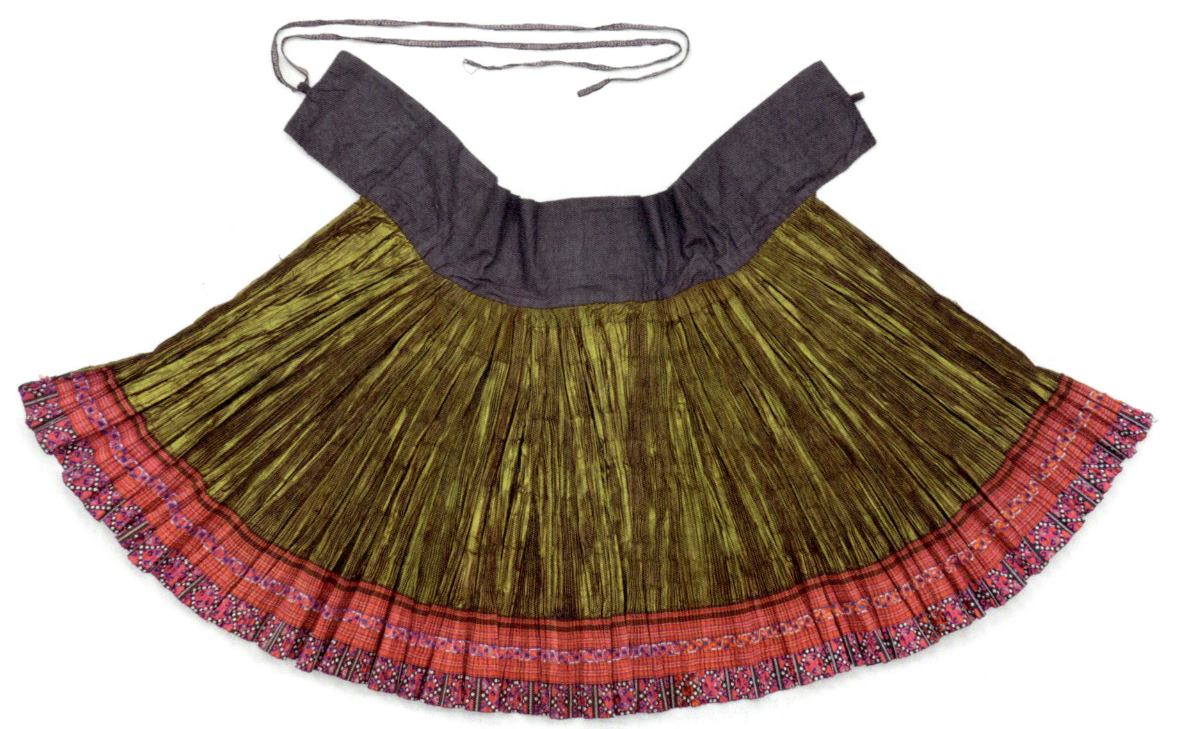

Faltenrock der Miao-Minderheit
Pleated skirt of the Miao people
China, östliche Guizhou-Provinz eastern Guizhou Province,
19./20. Jahrhundert 19th/20th c.
Baumwolle, Indigo-gefärbt, plissiert, genäht und handbestickt
Cotton, indigo dye, pleated, sewn, and hand embroidered
ø 160, H 74
Weltmuseum Wien, 178.763

Faltenrock der Miao-Minderheit (Geija-Stil?)
Pleated skirt of the Miao people (Geija style?)
China, südliche Guizhou-Provinz southern Guizhou Province,
1907
Baumwolle, Indigo-Wachsfärbung, plissiert, genäht und
handbestickt
Cotton, indigo wax dye, pleated, sewn, and hand embroidered
61 × 43 (Bund waistband)
Weltmuseum Wien, 81.130

Sorgfältig von Hand plissierte Faltenröcke aus Indigo-gefärbten und mit Pflanzenextrakten, Tierleim, Eiweiß und manchmal Schweineblut bearbeiteten Stoffen werden von Frauen der sogenannten Miao-Minderheit aus dem gebirgigen Südwesten Chinas sowohl für den alltäglichen Gebrauch als auch für festliche Anlässe hergestellt. Durch das Klopfen der Stoffe entsteht eine stärkere Farbtiefe und vor allem der charakteristische kupferrot-schimmernde Glanz. Je nach Ortschaft gibt es unterschiedliche Plissiertechniken. So wird etwa der fertig verarbeitete Stoff um einen Bottich herum gelegt, befeuchtet und mit einer langen Nadel minutiös gerafft. Anschließend werden Seile um den Bottich gewickelt, um die Falten zu fixieren. Nach dem tagelangen Trockenvorgang wird ein Taillenband angebracht, sodass die Raffung hält. In manchen Gebieten werden die Röcke zusätzlich mit der Wachsreservetechnik dekoriert. Der metallisch-braune Farbton, der für eine ganz bestimmte Region der Provinz Ost-Guizhou typisch ist, geht sehr wahrscheinlich darauf zurück, dass dem Färbemittel der chemische Farbstoff Kristallviolett beigemischt wird.

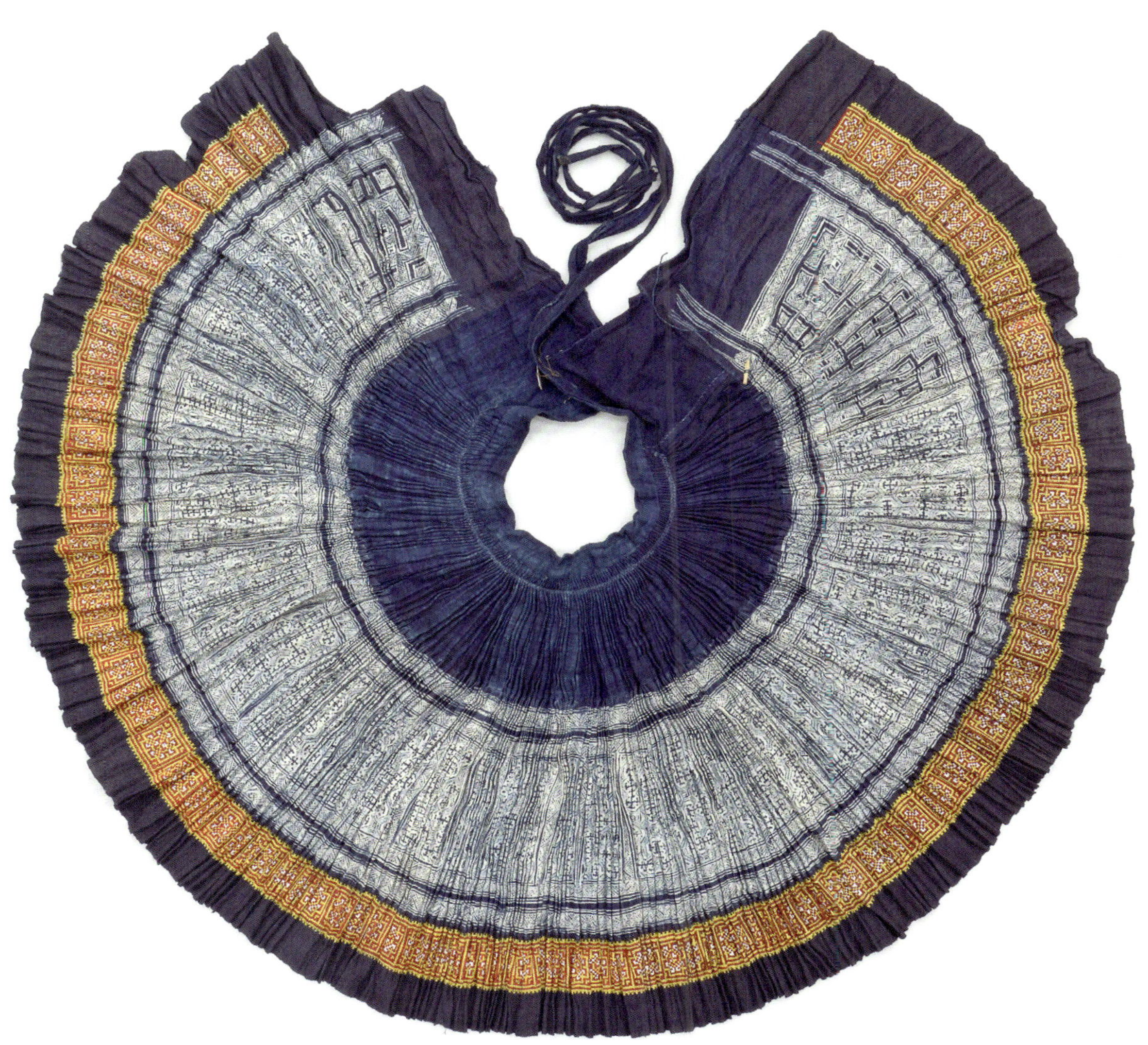

Skirts pleated painstakingly by hand—made from material dyed with indigo and treated with vegetable extracts, animal glue, egg white, and sometimes pig's blood—are made by women of the Miao people from China's mountainous South-west, both for daily use and for festive occasions. Beating the cloth creates a stronger depth of color, and above all a characteristic copper-colored luster. Each location has its own different pleating technique. For instance, the finished cloth might be stretched around a tub, soaked with water, and minutely folded using a long needle. Afterwards ropes are wound around the tub to fix the folds. After a drying process lasting many days, a waistband is attached so that the pleats stay in place. In many places, the skirts are additionally decorated using the wax reserve technique. The metallic brown coloring, typical of a specific region in the east of Guizhou Province, is very probably the result of mixing the chemical colorant crystal violet into the dye.

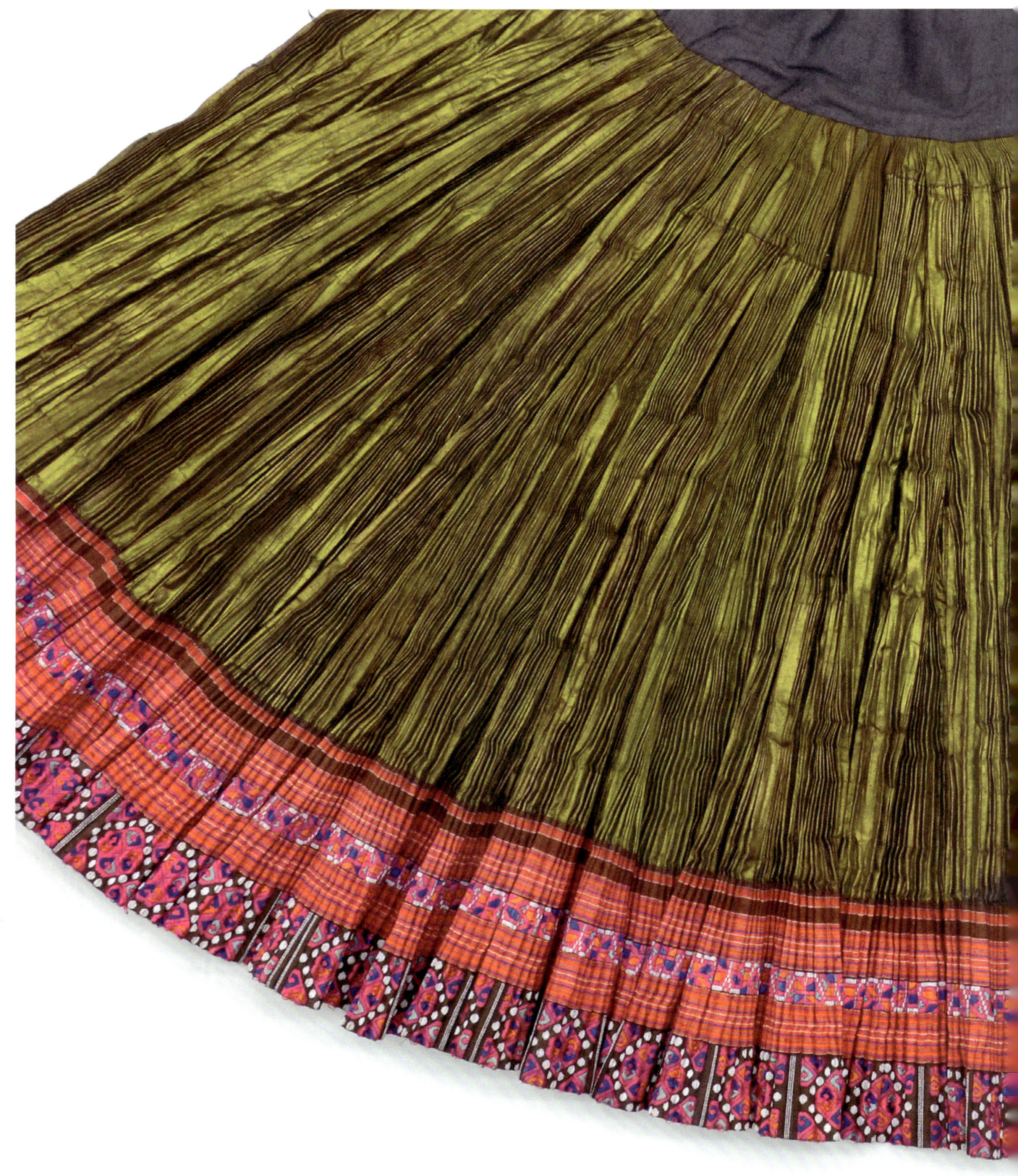

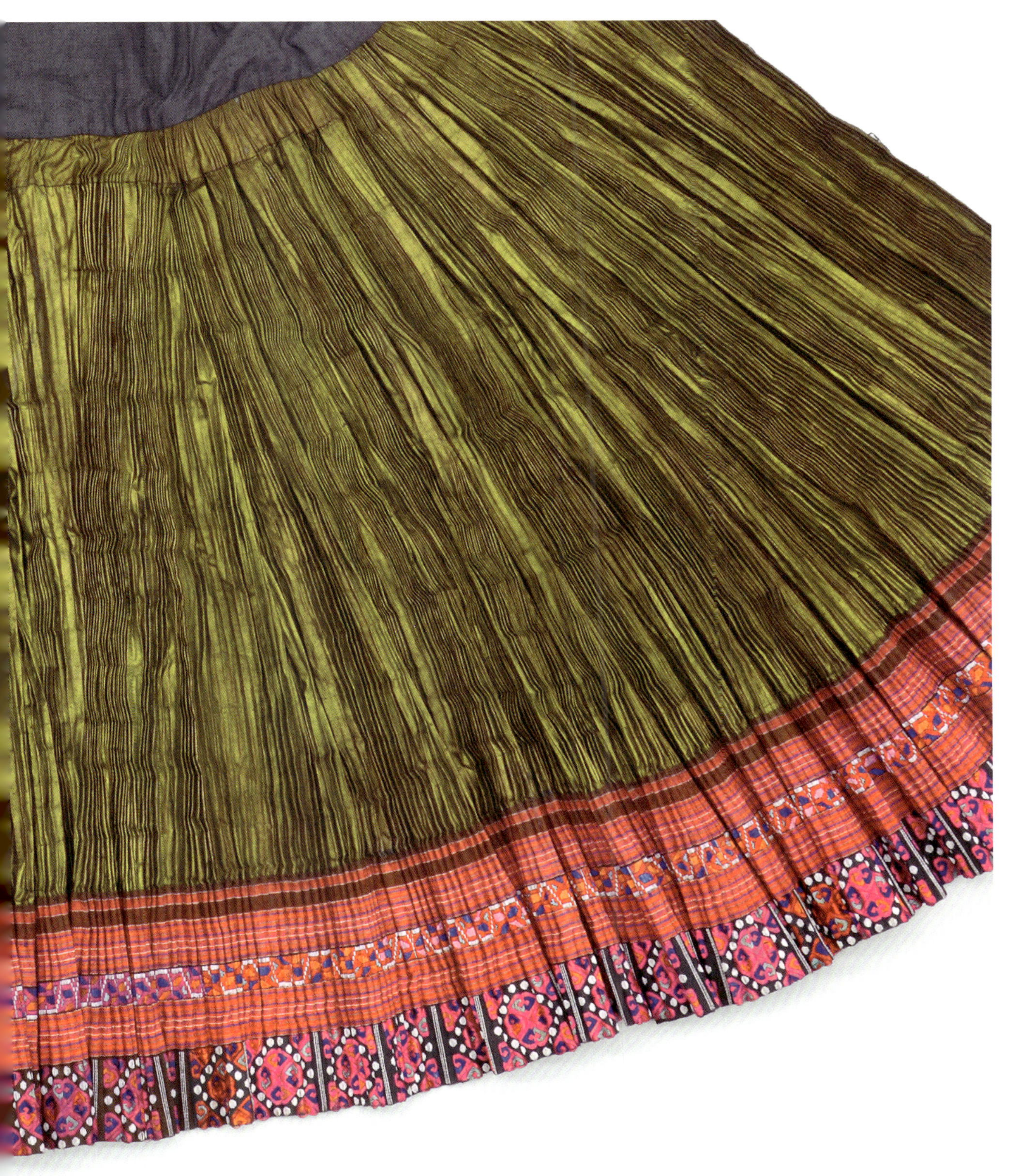

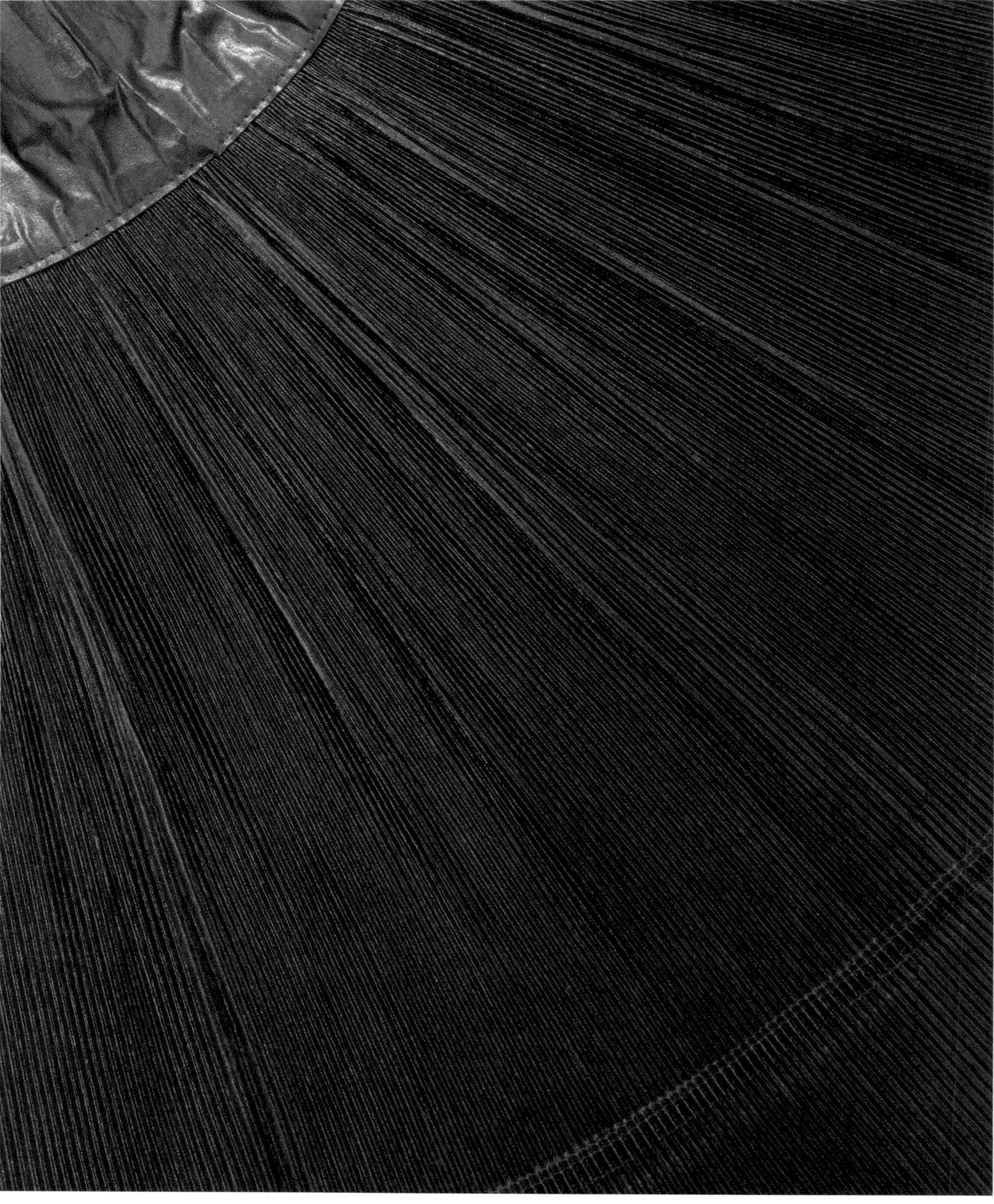

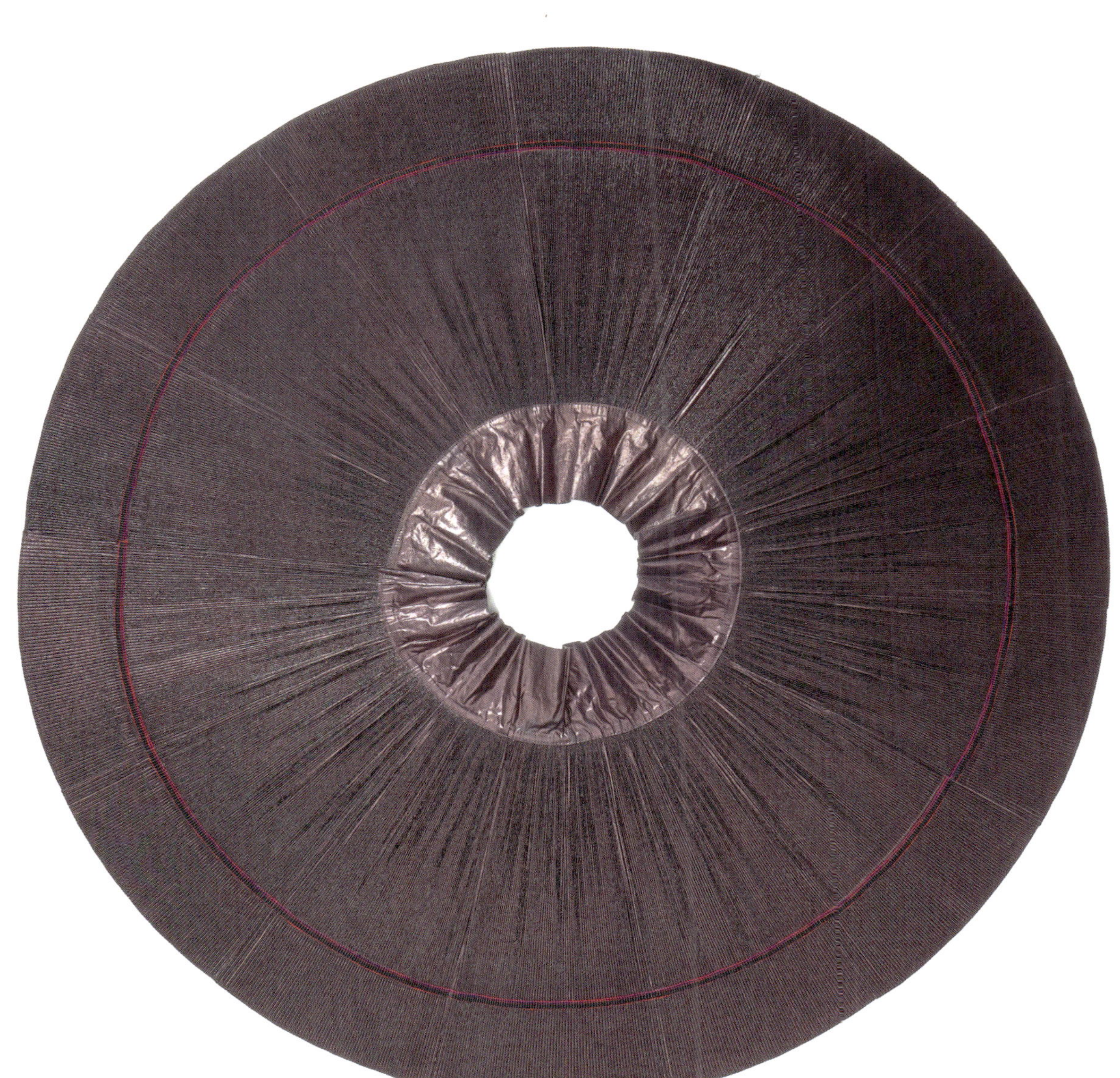

Langrock der Miao aus Tamlong (bei Shidong)
Long skirt of the Miao people from Tamlong (near Shidong)
China, 1980er Jahre 1980s
Baumwolle, Indigo-gefärbt, plissiert, genäht
Cotton, indigo dye, pleated, sewn
ø 147, H 46,5
MAK, T 14930

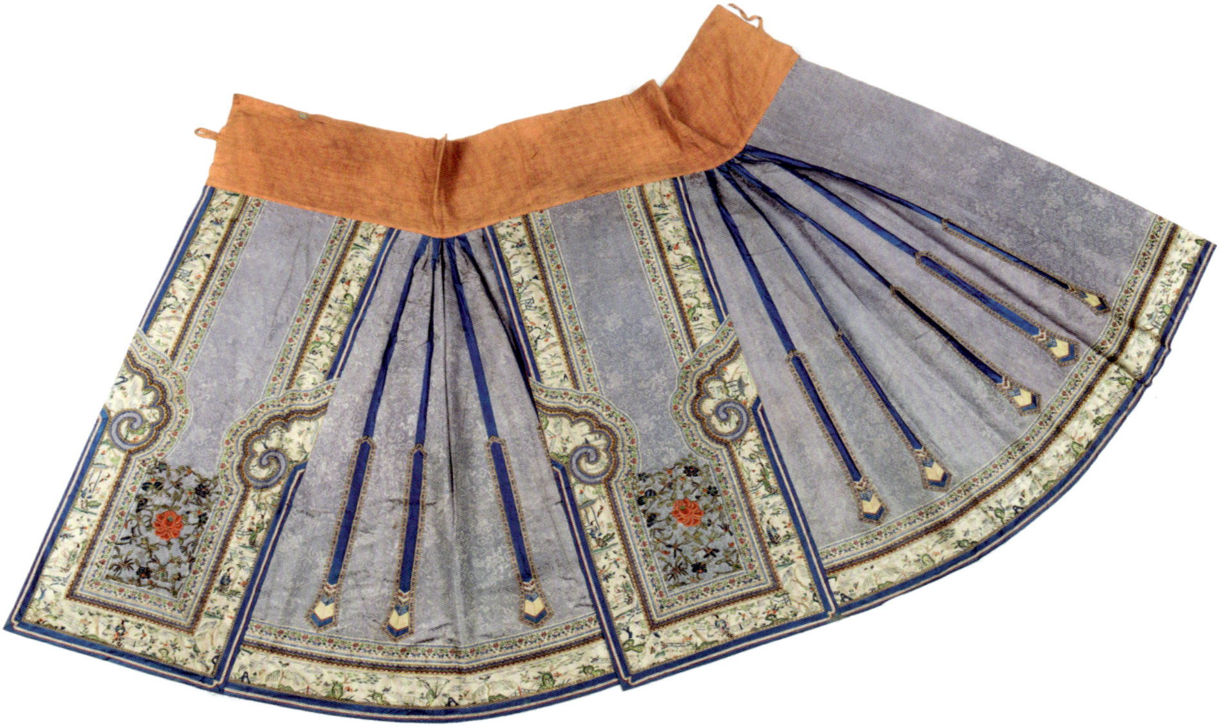

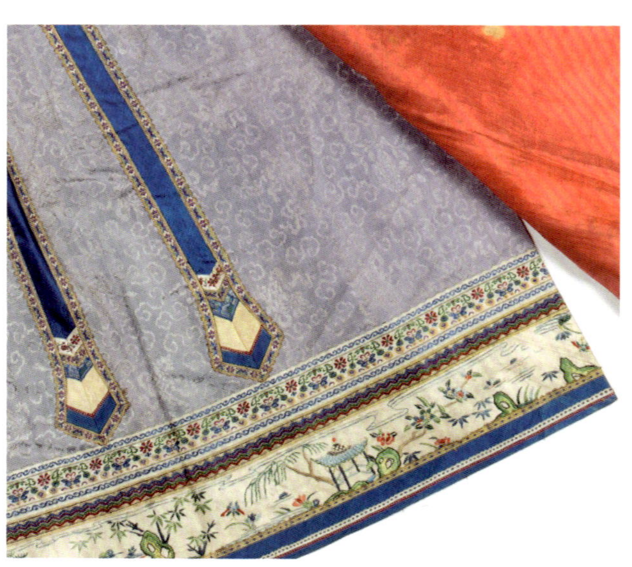

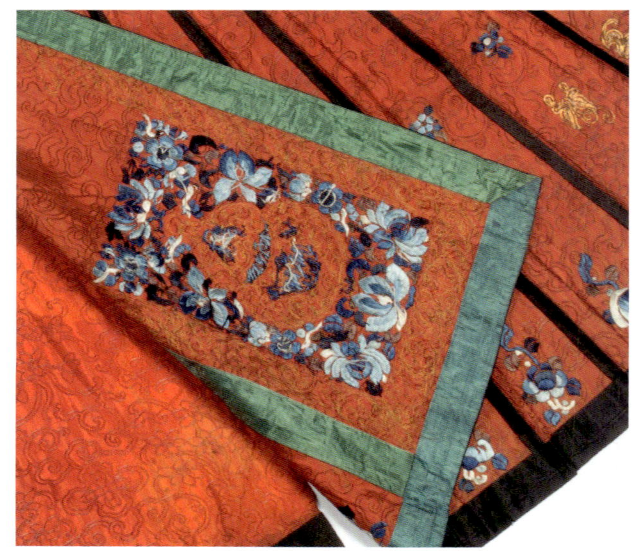

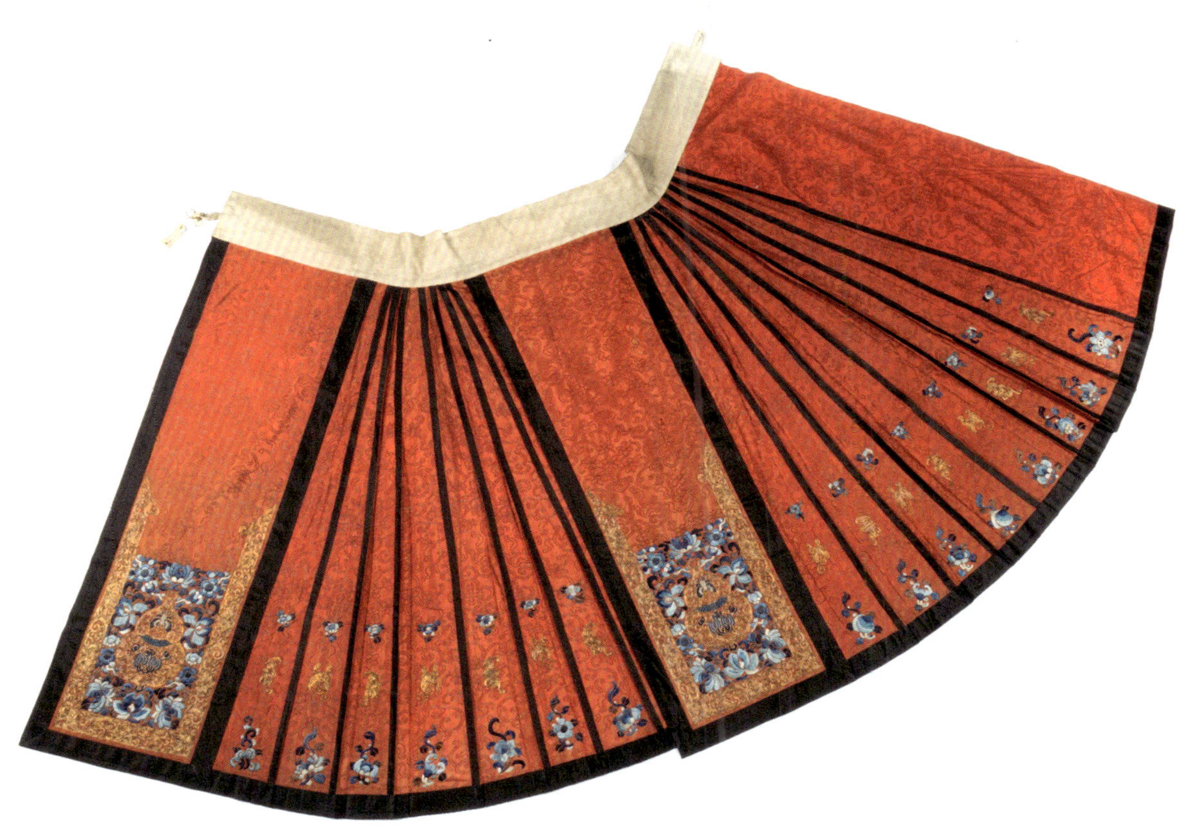

Damenrock
Lady's skirt
China, 19. Jh. 19th c.
Seide, Baumwolle, Metallfaden
Silk, cotton, metal threads
107 × 129
MAK, OR 115

Damenrock
Lady's skirt
China, 19. Jh. 19th c.
Seide, Baumwolle, Metallfaden
Silk, cotton, metal threads
97 × 113
MAK, T 7043

Das multiethnische Qing-zeitliche China (1644–1911) wurde von einer der ethnischen Minderheiten, den Mandschuren, regiert. Trotz Unterdrückung, Vermischung und Assimilation herrschte eine gewisse kulturelle Vielfalt.
Diese beiden knöchellangen Faltenröcke aus dem 19. Jahrhundert wurden von Frauen getragen, die der ethnischen Mehrheit der Han-Chines*innen angehörten.

The multiethnic China of the Qing period (1644–1911) was ruled over by one of its ethnic minorities, the Manchu. Cultural diversity prevailed to a certain extent despite oppression, miscegenation, and assimilation.
These two 19th-century ankle-length pleated skirts were worn by women belonging to the ethnic majority of the Han Chinese.

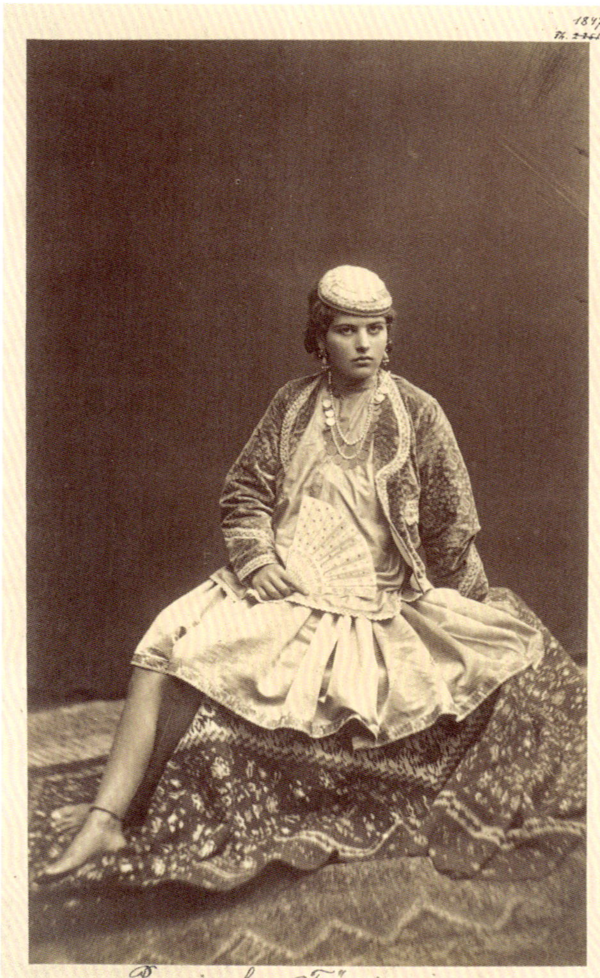

Antoin Sevruguin

Persische Tänzerin
Persian dancing woman
Iran, vor 1887 pre-1887
Fotografie, Albuminabzug auf Karton
Photograph, albumen print on cardboard
20,7 × 12,2
Weltmuseum Wien, VF 1847

Perserin im Haus
Persian lady in the house
Iran, vor 1887 pre-1887
Fotografie, Albuminabzug auf Karton
Photograph, albumen print on cardboard
21 × 12,8
Weltmuseum Wien, VF 1829

Vornehme Perserin im Haus
Noble Persian lady in the house
Iran, vor 1887 pre-1887
Fotografie, Albuminabzug auf Karton
Photograph, albumen print on cardboard
16,9 × 11,7
Weltmuseum Wien, VF 1834

W. Ordèn
Perserin im Ballettkostüm
Persian lady in ballet costume
Iran, vor 1887 pre-1887
Fotografie, Albuminabzug auf Karton
Photograph, albumen print on cardboard
16,5 × 21,7
Weltmuseum Wien, VF 4952

Vor dem Besuch der Wiener Weltausstellung 1873 begab sich der persische Schah Nāser ad-Din (1831–1896) auf eine große Tour durch europäische Metropolen, über die in zeitgenössischen europäischen Zeitungen viel berichtet wurde. Von dieser Reise brachte er seine Begeisterung für Röcke – speziell für Tutus – mit nach Hause, die wohl durch eine Ballettaufführung entfacht worden war. An seinem Hof ließ er nach seiner Rückkehr alle seine Frauen in europäischer Mode kleiden. Knielange Tutus und Tutu-ähnliche Faltenröcke wurden bald auch für Perserinnen außerhalb des höfischen Kontexts zum neuesten Schrei.
Die hier gezeigten historischen Fotografien aus dem Ende des 19. Jahrhunderts bezeugen die transkulturelle Dimension des Faltenrocks.

Before visiting the Vienna World's Fair in 1873, the Shah of Persia, Nāser ad-Din (1831–1896) went on a grand tour of European cities—a journey widely followed in the contemporary European press. From this journey he returned home an enthusiastic fan of skirts, in particular of tutus—probably inspired by a ballet performance. Back in his court, he had all his wives dressed in European fashion. Knee-length tutus as well as tutu-like pleated skirts soon became *de rigueur* for Persian women, even outside the court.
The historical photographs shown here from the end of the 19th century bear witness to the transcultural dimension of the pleated skirt.

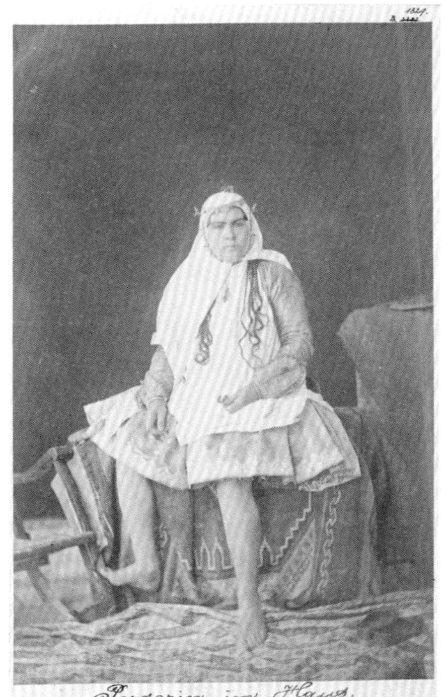

Perserin im Haus.

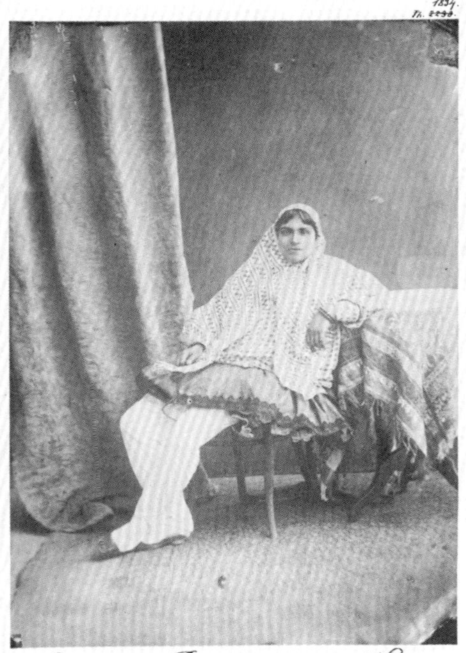

Vornehme Perserin im Hause.

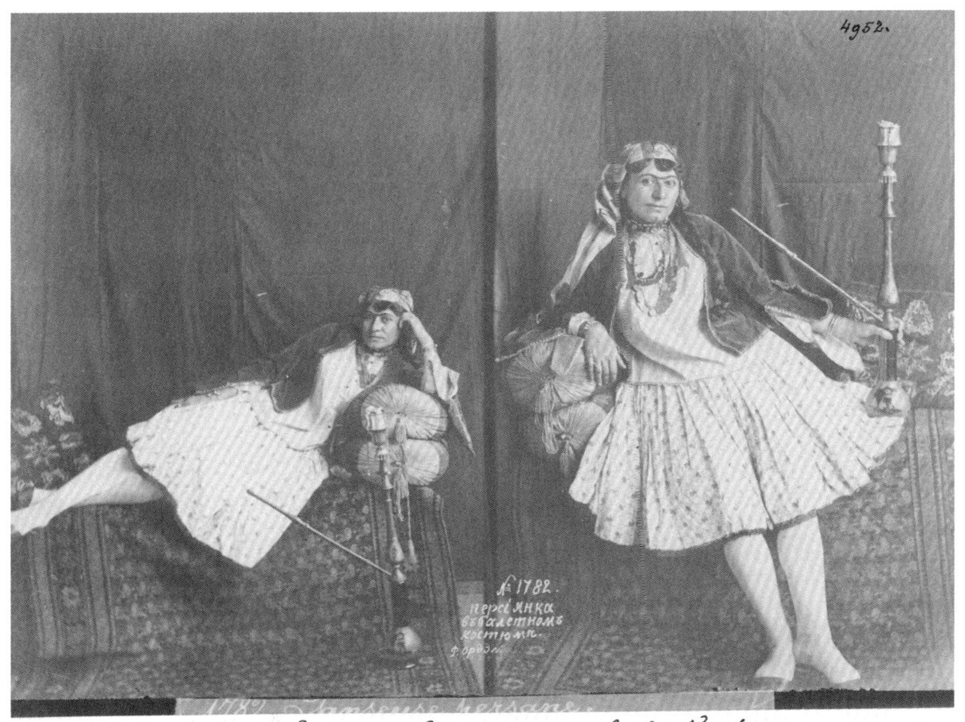

Perserin im Ballet = Costüm.   (Coll. Ordén).

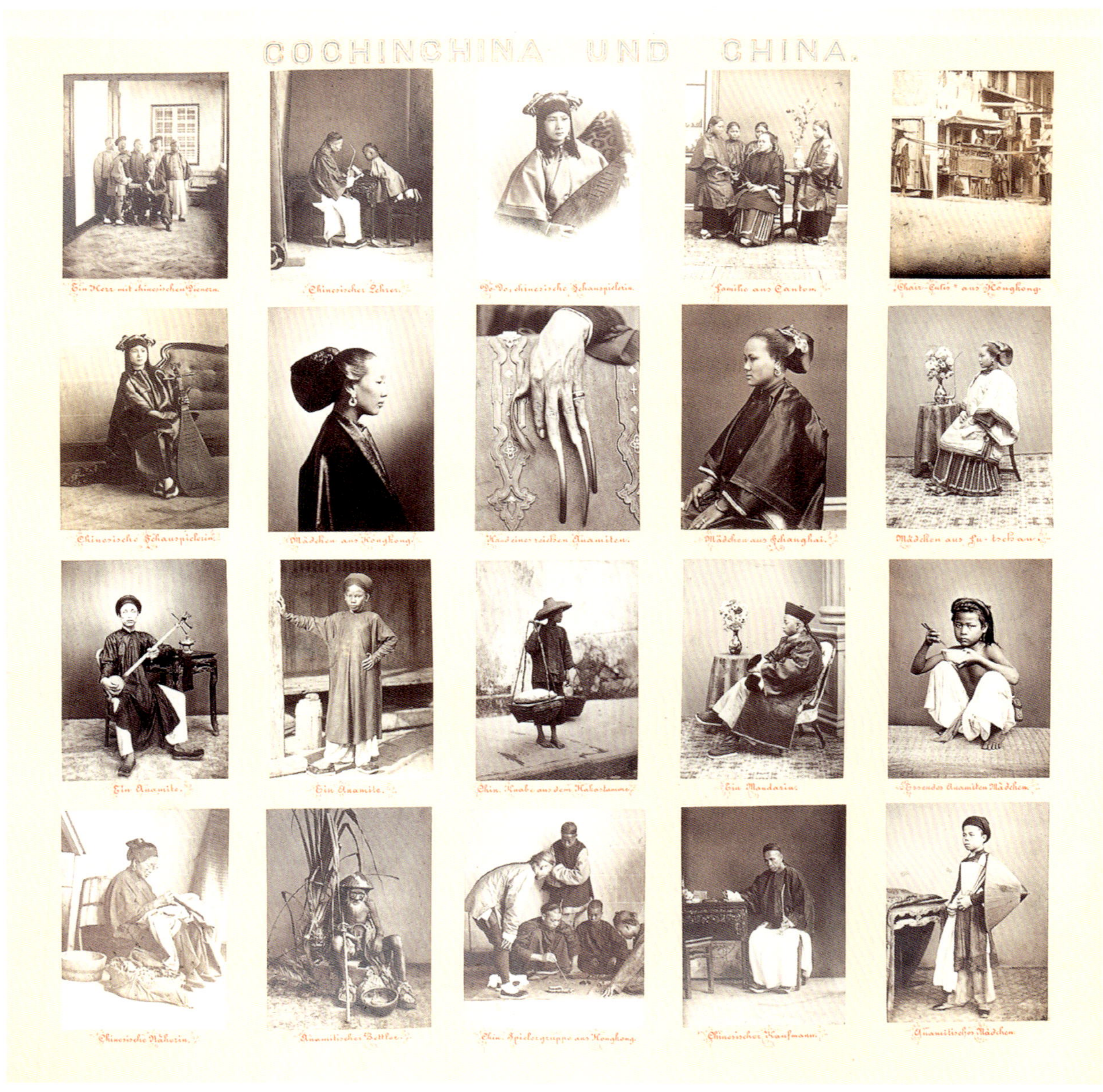

Cochinchina und China, aus dem Album mit Fotografien aus Siam, China und Japan von Wilhelm Burger, entstanden auf der „k. k. Mission nach Ostasien und Südamerika"
Cochin-China and China, from the album with photographs of Siam, China, and Japan by Wilhelm Burger, taken during the "Imperial Royal Expedition to Eastern Asia and Southern America"
1868–1871
Fotografie, Albuminabzug auf Karton Photograph, albumen print on cardboard; 8,1 × 6,4
MAK, KI 13660-7

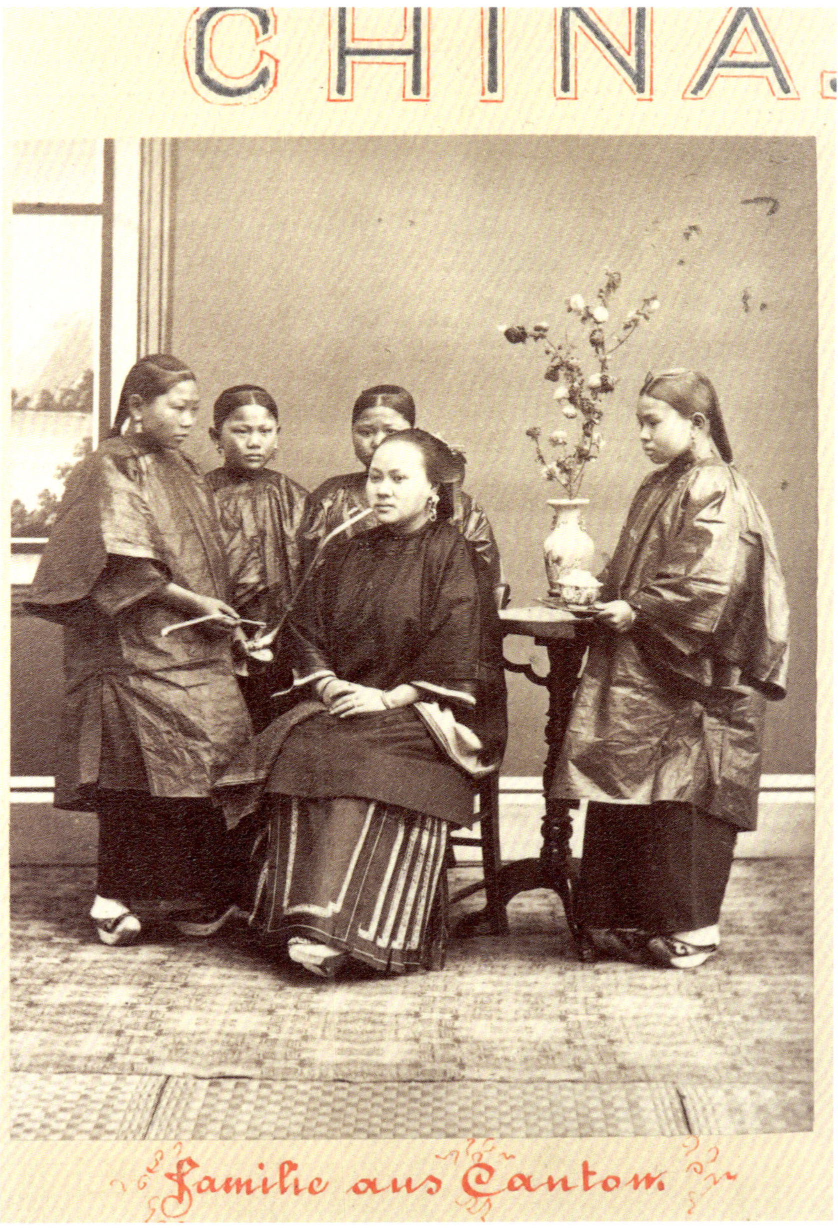

Familie aus Canton.

Die Aufnahmen aus Cochinchina (Gebiet im Süden des heutigen Vietnam) und China stammen aus einem Prachtband mit über 200 Fotografien, die während der k. k. Mission nach Ostasien und Südamerika zwischen 1868 und 1871 teils von lokalen Fotostudios in Asien erworben wurden. Die Auswahl der Motive spiegelt das damalige ethnografische Interesse an fremden Kulturen aus Asien wider: Die in der zweiten Hälfte des 19. Jahrhunderts von der europäischen Kundschaft am meisten nachgefragten Themen der außereuropäischen Fotografie waren neben Landschaftsaufnahmen Berufe, Alltagskultur, Trachten (wie die Faltenröcke der Han-Chinesinnen) und Kuriositäten.

The photographs from Cochin-China (the south of today's Vietnam) and China originate from a splendid volume of over 200 photographs acquired during the Imperial Royal Expedition to Eastern Asia and Southern America between 1868 and 1871, in part from local photographic studios in Asia. The selection of motifs mirrors the ethnographic interest of that time in Asian cultures: in the second half of the 19th century, non-European photographic motifs most in demand by European clients included, in addition to landscape photographs, trades and professions, everyday culture, folk costumes (for instance pleated skirts worn by Han-Chinese women), and curios.

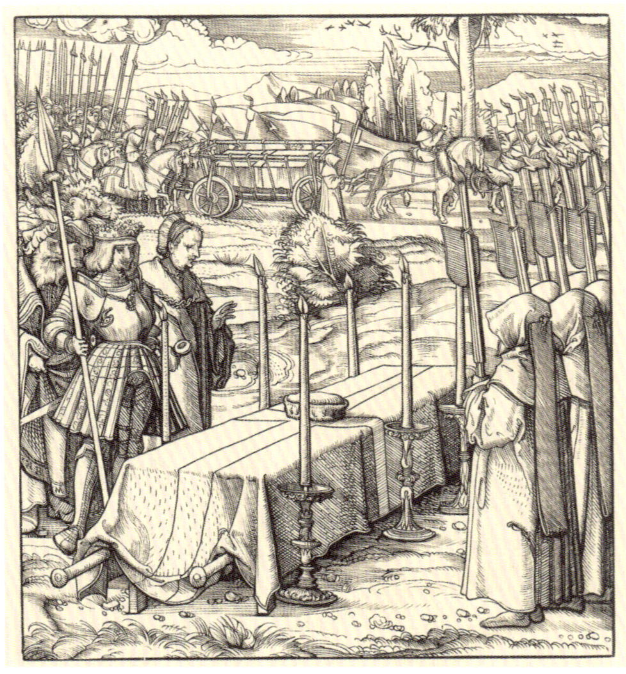

„Begräbnis des berühmten Fürsten", aus dem
*Jahrbuch der Kunsthistorischen Sammlungen des
Allerhöchsten Kaiserhauses: Der Weißkunig*, Bd. VI
"Burial of the famous prince," from the *Yearbook
of the Art-historical Collection of the Most High
Imperial House: The White King*, vol. VI
Wien Vienna, 1888
Universitätsbibliothek Heidelberg
University Library Heidelberg

„Wie der junge Weißkunig mit seinen Haupt-
leuten Rat hält", aus dem *Jahrbuch der Kunst-
historischen Sammlungen des Allerhöchsten
Kaiserhauses: Der Weißkunig*, Bd. VI
"How the young White King holds council with
his Captains," from the *Yearbook of the Art-
historical Collection of the Most High Imperial
House: The White King*, vol. VI
Wien Vienna, 1888
Universitätsbibliothek Heidelberg
University Library Heidelberg

Die Holzschnittillustration „Begräbnis des berühmten Fürsten" aus dem *Weißkunig*, einer autobiografischen Veröffent-
lichung Kaiser Maximilians I., zeigt einen Harnisch mit Fal-
tenrock aus Stahl. Als Vorbild für diese Art von Harnisch
dienten Faltenröcke aus Stoff, die in der Renaissance Teil
des Männerkostüms waren – zu sehen in der zweiten Illustration: „Wie der junge Weißkunig mit seinen Hauptleuten
Rat hält". Faltenrockharnische sind äußerst selten, es gibt
weltweit lediglich fünf Stück dieses Typus, zwei davon in
der Sammlung des Kunsthistorischen Museums in Wien.

The woodcut "Burial of the famous prince" from the *White
King*, an autobiographical publication by the Emperor
Maximilian I, shows a suit of armor with steel pleated skirt.
This type of armor was modeled on pleated skirts made of
cloth that were a part of a man's costume in the Renaissance—as may be seen in the second illustration: "How
the young White King holds council with his Captains."
Pleated skirt armor is extremely rare; there are only five
such examples in the world, of which two are in the Kunst-
historisches Museum Vienna.

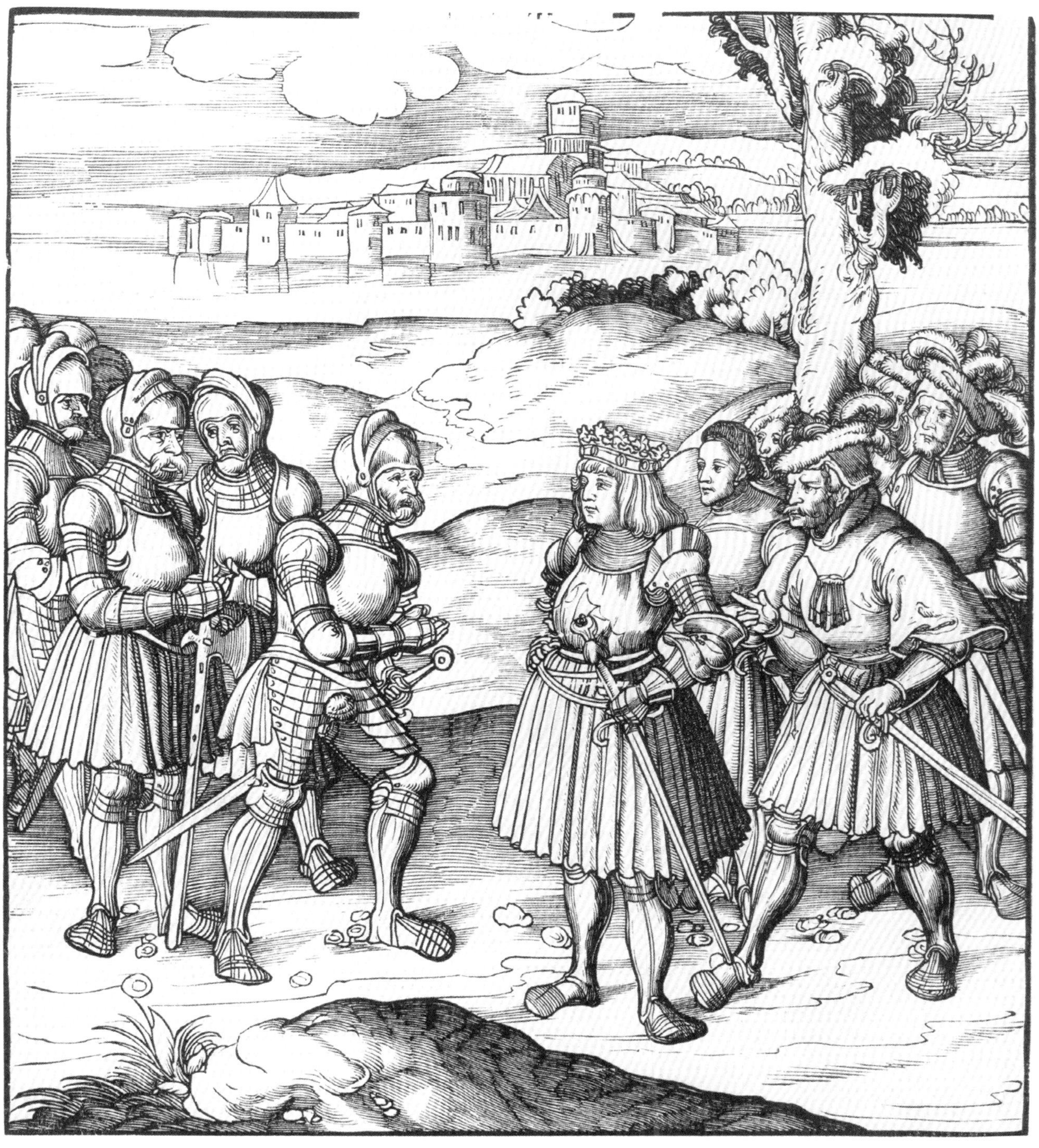

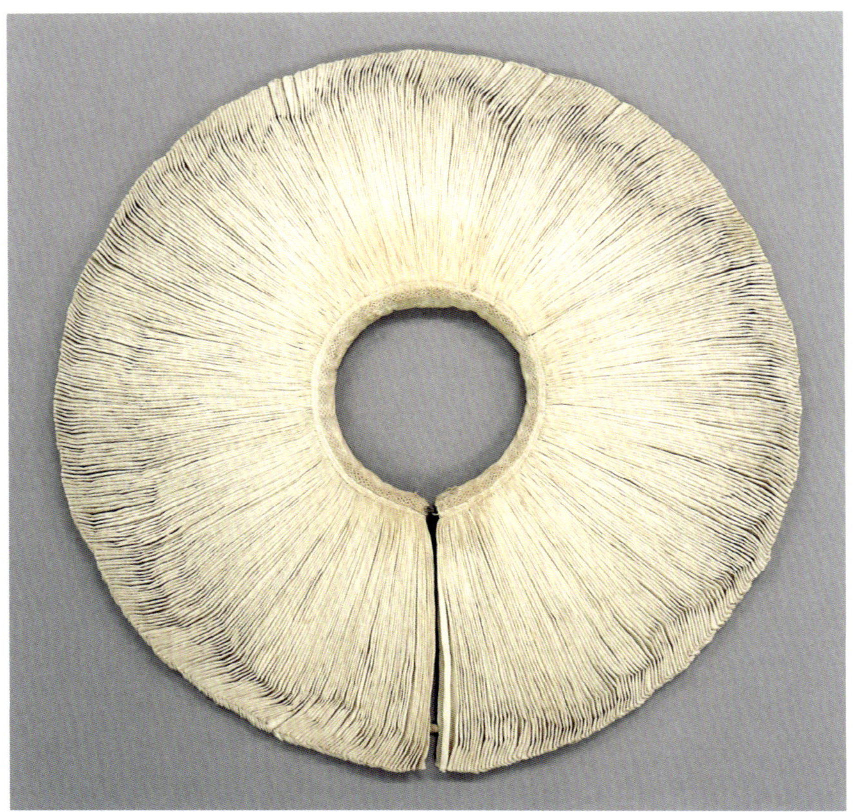

Mühlsteinkragen
Millstone collar
1. Hälfte 17. Jh. 1st half 17th c.
Leinen, Metall
Linen, metal
ø 50, H 2,5
MAK, F 44

Die Halskrause besteht in der Regel aus weißem Leinenstoff und ist mit Draht unterzogen sowie steif gestärkt. Sie entwickelte sich im 16. Jahrhundert aus dem Saum des Hemdes zu einem selbstständigen Kleidungsstück für Frauen und Männer. Während sie in Frankreich bereits ab den 1580er Jahren durch einen flach aufliegenden Kragen oder Spitze ersetzt wurde, galt sie in Spanien noch bis Anfang des 17. Jahrhunderts als modisches Charakteristikum, und in den Niederlanden wurde die Halskrause von älteren Frauen noch bis in die 2. Hälfte des 17. Jahrhunderts getragen. Bis heute hat sie sich im Kontext von Amts- und Volkstrachten erhalten.
Diese Halskrause besteht aus einem ca. 18 Meter langen Stoff, der aus insgesamt 21 Bahnen zusammengesetzt und dann in 588 Falten gelegt wurde. Sie ist das Ergebnis feinster Handarbeit: Die einzelnen Falten wurden paarweise eng aneinandergepresst und an eine Halsleiste genäht; der Außenumfang ist mit einem 0,9 mm breiten Saum mit unsichtbaren Stichen versäubert.

Ruffs are usually made of white linen, strengthened by wires, and stiffly starched. They developed in the 16th century out of shirt collars into separate pieces of clothing for both men and women. Whereas in France, starting in the 1580s, ruffs were already being replaced by flat collars or lace, in Spain they were still being worn as fashionable accessories at the beginning of the 17th century. In the Netherlands, ruffs were worn by elderly women well into the second half of that century. Ruffs still exist today as appurtenances to official uniforms and folk costumes.
This particular ruff consists of a piece of material some 18 meters long, made up of 21 strips and folded 588 times. It is a piece of exquisite needlework: the individual folds were pressed in pairs closely together and sewn to a neck band, and the outer circumference was trimmed with a 0.9 mm ribbon attached with invisible stiches.

Wilhelm Gmeiner
Fotografie einer
Halskrause
Photograph of a ruff
Wien Vienna, 1905/06
Fotografie, Albuminabzug
auf Karton
Photograph, albumen
print on
cardboard
21 × 23,7
MAK, KI 7717-250

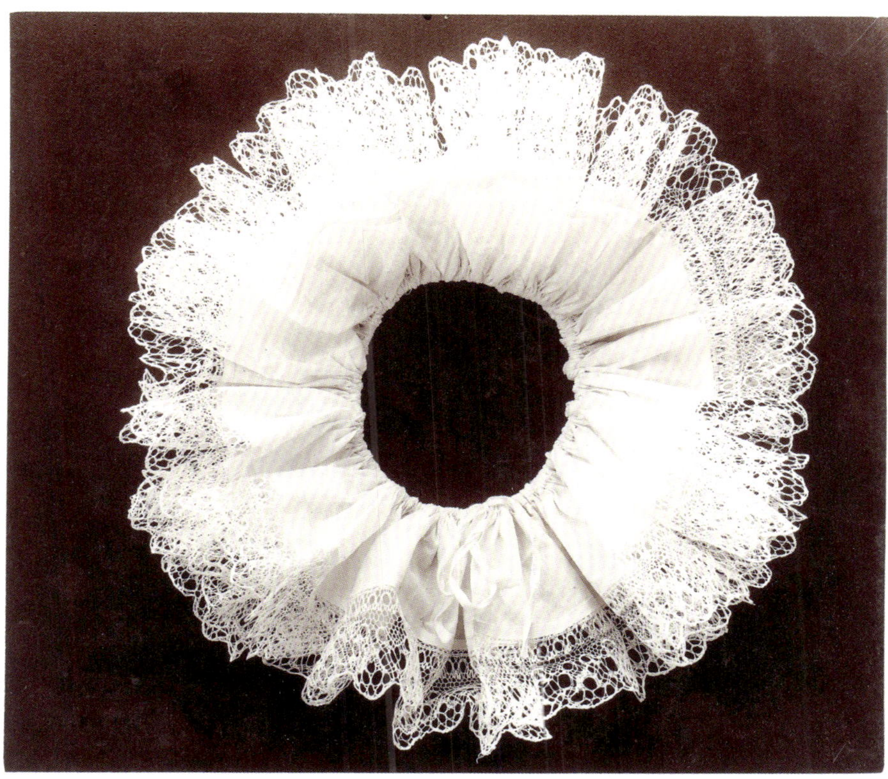

Diese Fotografie wurde 1905/06 zusammen mit 480 weiteren in der Ausstellung österreichischer Hausindustrie und Volkskunst im Österreichischen Museum für Kunst und Industrie (heute MAK) aufgenommen. Es könnte sich dabei um eine Halskrause aus Mähren, dem östlichen Drittel des heutigen Tschechien, handeln. Wie im Begleitkatalog von damals erwähnt, galt die weiße bestickte Halskrause ab den 1820er Jahren als fester Bestandteil der mährischen Volkstrachten. Auch weitere handwerkliche Objekte wie Stickereien, Tongefäße oder Körbe wurden präsentiert. Im Ausstellungsprogramm spiegelt sich das damalige Interesse wider sowie die Gründungsagenda des Museums, einheimisches Kunstgewerbe zu fördern. Hier sollte der Öffentlichkeit erstmals die positive Wirkung der regionalen kunstgewerblichen Fachschulen auf die ländliche Hausindustrie präsentiert werden. Die Schau war ein großer Erfolg, vor allem Künstler*innen, Entwerfer*innen und Kritiker*innen zeigten sich begeistert von der Kreativität und Vielfalt der lebendigen Volkskunst und den kunsthandwerklichen Traditionen.

This photograph was taken in 1905/06, together with 480 others, at the Exhibition of Austrian House Industry and Folk Art in the Austrian Museum for Art and Industry (today's MAK). The ruff may originate from Moravia, the eastern third of what is today the Czech Republic. As is mentioned in the accompanying catalog from that time, white embroidered ruffs such as this one had been part of traditional Moravian dress since the 1820s. Other handcrafted objects such as embroidery, earthenware and baskets were also on show. The exhibition program reflected the interest of that time—as well as the museum's founding agenda—in promoting indigenous arts and crafts. For the first time the positive effect of regional arts and crafts schools on rural house industries was here presented to a broader public. The exhibition was a great success; above all, artists, designers, and critics were impressed by the creativity and diversity of living folk art and handicraft traditions.

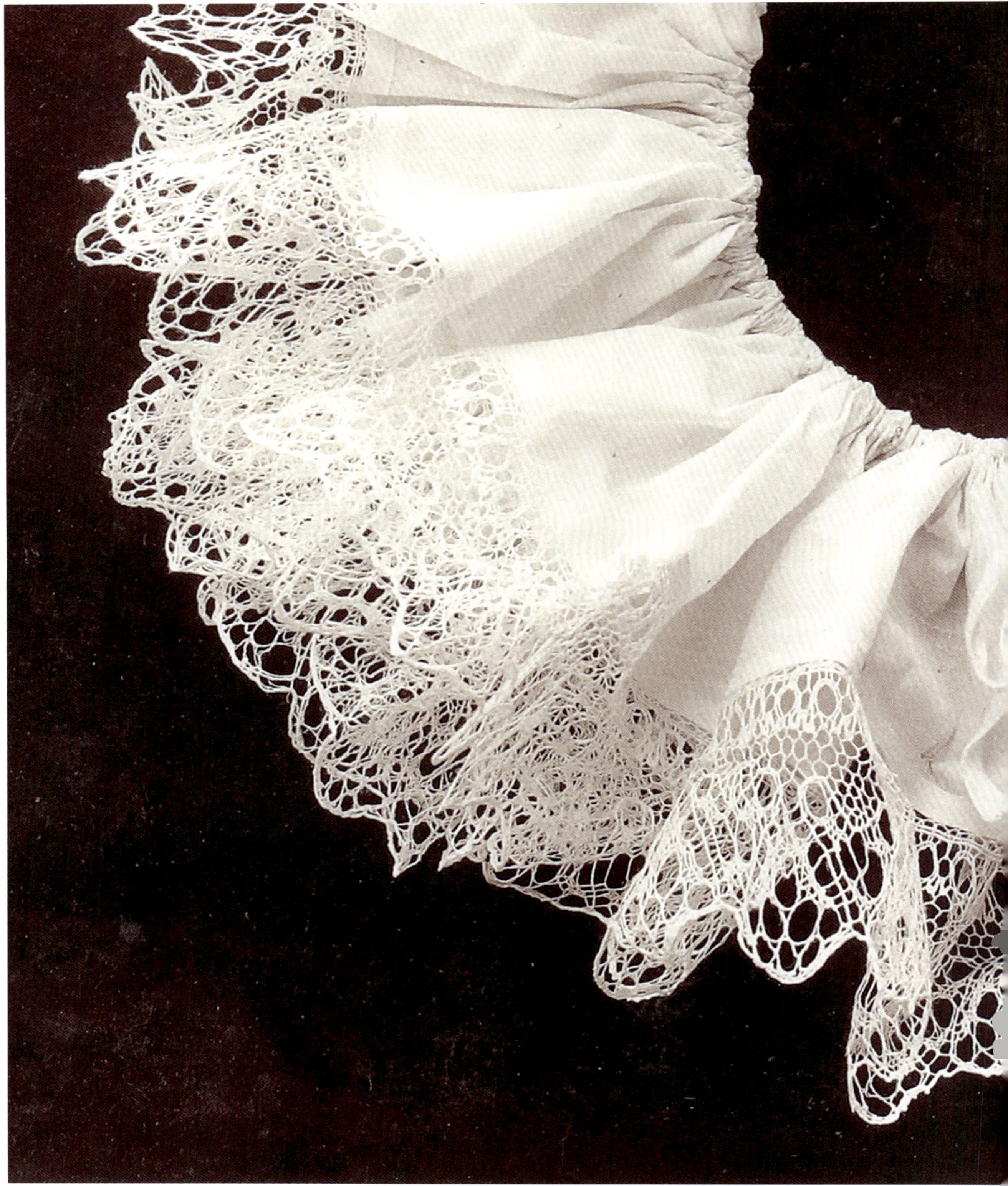

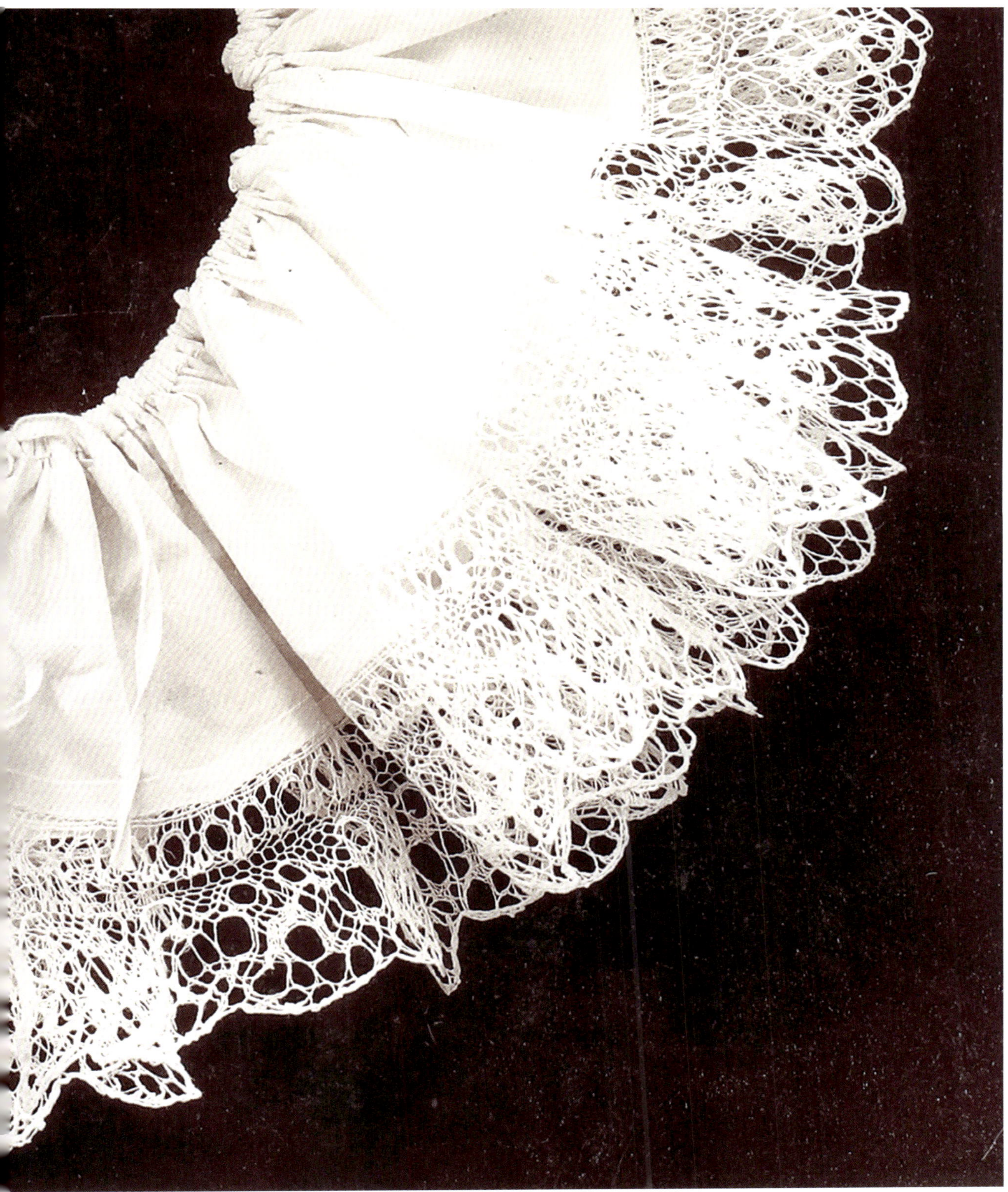

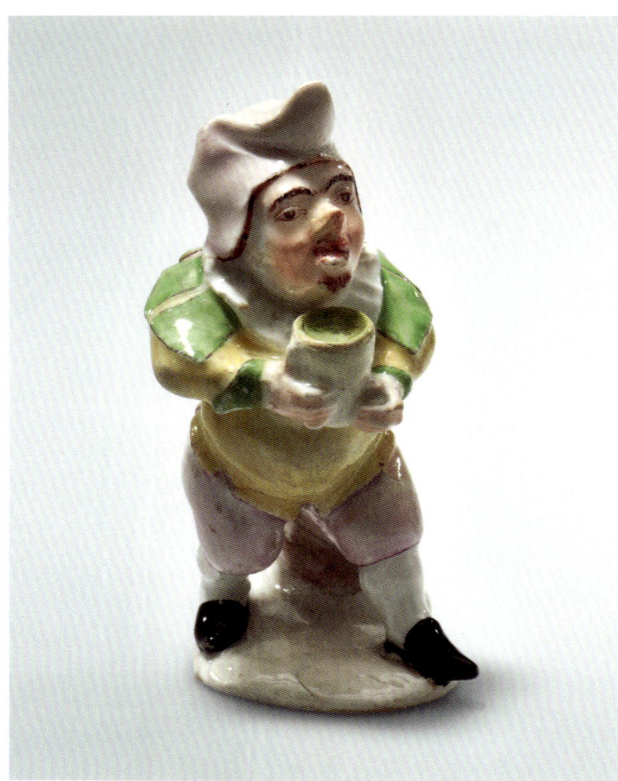

Kaiserliche Porzellanmanufaktur Wien   >
Imperial Vienna Porcelain Manufactory

Kavalier und Dame
Cavalier and lady
Wien Vienna, 1760–1765
Porzellan Porcelain
ø 16,1, H 21,7
MAK, KE 7294

Dame mit Kavalier, zwei Kindern
und Zwerg
Lady with cavalier, two children,
and dwarf
Wien Vienna, ca. 1780
Porzellan Porcelain
28,5 × 20,2 × 20,1
MAK, KE 7950

Kaiserliche Porzellanmanufaktur Wien
Imperial Vienna Porcelain Manufactory
Kleinwüchsige männliche Figur Dwarfish male figure
Wien Vienna, 1744–1749
Porzellan Porcelain; ø 6, H 11,1
MAK, KE 4633

Die Figur trägt eine Narrenkappe sowie ein enganliegendes Wams mit einer weißen Halskrause (Pierrotkragen). Sie wurde wohl als Teil einer Gruppe konzipiert, die verschiedene Trachten, Berufe und Menschen anderer Kulturen typologisch-satirisch darstellen sollte, teils in Anlehnung an satirische Kupferstiche. Hier wird die ursprünglich mit einem hohen Rang assoziierte Halskrause von einem „Narren" getragen, einer Figur, von der geglaubt wurde, sie würde das Lasterhafte verkörpern. Im Zuge der Herausbildung absolutistischer Staaten traten ab dem frühen 18. Jahrhundert in der Kulturproduktion – u. a. Grafik, Plastik und Kunsthandwerk – auffällig häufig solche grotesken Figuren in Erscheinung, die der politischen Satire dienten.

The figure is wearing a fool's cap and a tight doublet with a white "Pierrot" ruff. It was probably designed to be part of a group representing satirical stereotypes of costumes, trades, and peoples from other cultures—in part in the style of satirical copper plate engravings. Originally associated with people of high social rank, here the ruff is worn by a fool—a figure considered the embodiment of profligacy. Starting in the early 18th century, following the rise of Absolutism, such grotesque figures frequently appeared as expressions of political satire in such areas of cultural production as the graphic arts, sculpture, and handicrafts.

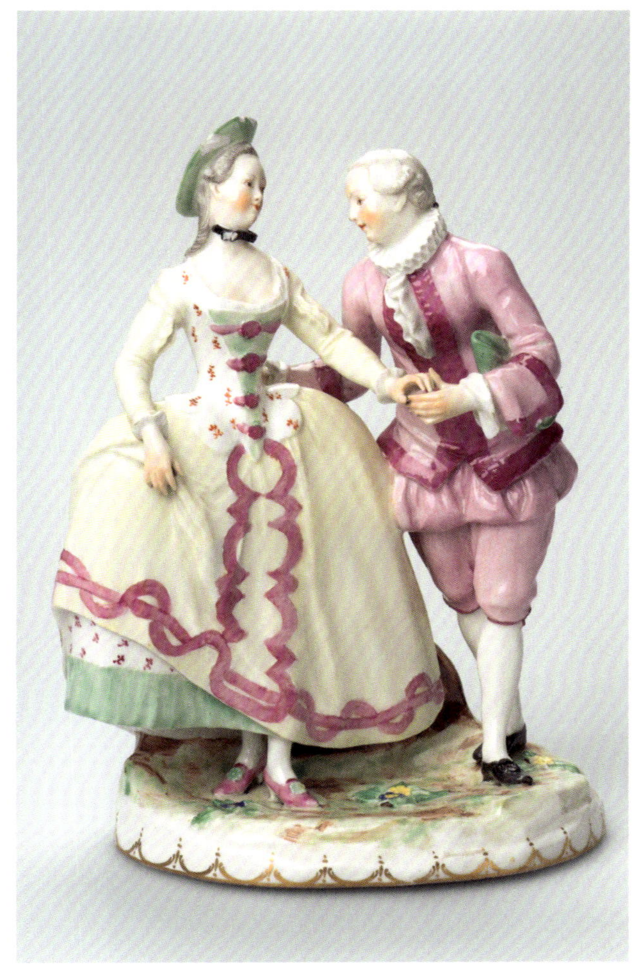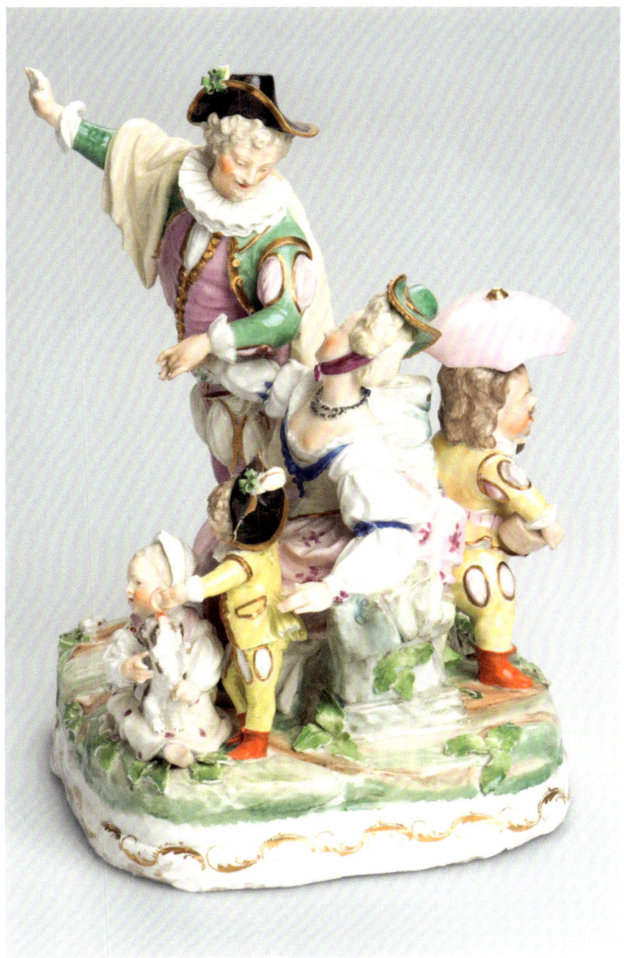

Die Figuren der Wiener Porzellanmanufaktur spiegeln die Praktiken, Lebensformen und Vorstellungswelten ihrer Entstehungszeit dreidimensional wider. Das Besondere an den beiden Tafelaufsätzen ist, dass sie zwar aus dem Rokoko stammen, die Figuren jedoch historische Bauernkleidung aus dem Frühbarock tragen. Erkennen lässt sich dieser modische Anachronismus an den Halskrausen und den gebauschten Kniehosen der Kavaliere sowie bei den Damen an den engen langen Ärmeln, die an den Schultern gerafft sind.

Die altertümliche Darstellung soll als Anspielung auf den mythischen Ort Arkadien verstanden werden, der für das idyllische, naturverbundene Leben im Goldenen Zeitalter steht – ein unwiederbringlicher Sehnsuchtsort, der in der damaligen Literatur häufig beschworen wurde.

The figures of the Vienna Porcelain Manufactory are three-dimensional reflections of the customs, life forms, and imaginary worlds of the age in which they were created. What is noteworthy about the two centerpieces is that, although they were created in the Rococo era, the figures are wearing historical peasants' clothing from the early Baroque. This anachronistic style is recognizable from the cavaliers' ruffs and baggy knee breeches, as well as from the ladies' long, tight sleeves gathered at the shoulders.

The archaic style is an allusion to the mythological realm of Arcadia, where in the Golden Age humankind lived an idyllic existence in harmony with nature—a realm whose irredeemable loss is frequently and nostalgically lamented in the literature of the era.

Clemens Auer
Coffee Table
2013/16
Tischplatte: Polymethylmethacrylat, epoxidbeschichtet;
Tischfuß: Stahlblech, pulverbeschichtet, 3D-Druck
Tabletop: polymethylmethacrylate, epoxy-coated;
table foot: sheet steel, powder-coated, 3D print
ø 80, H 22
MAK, H 4019

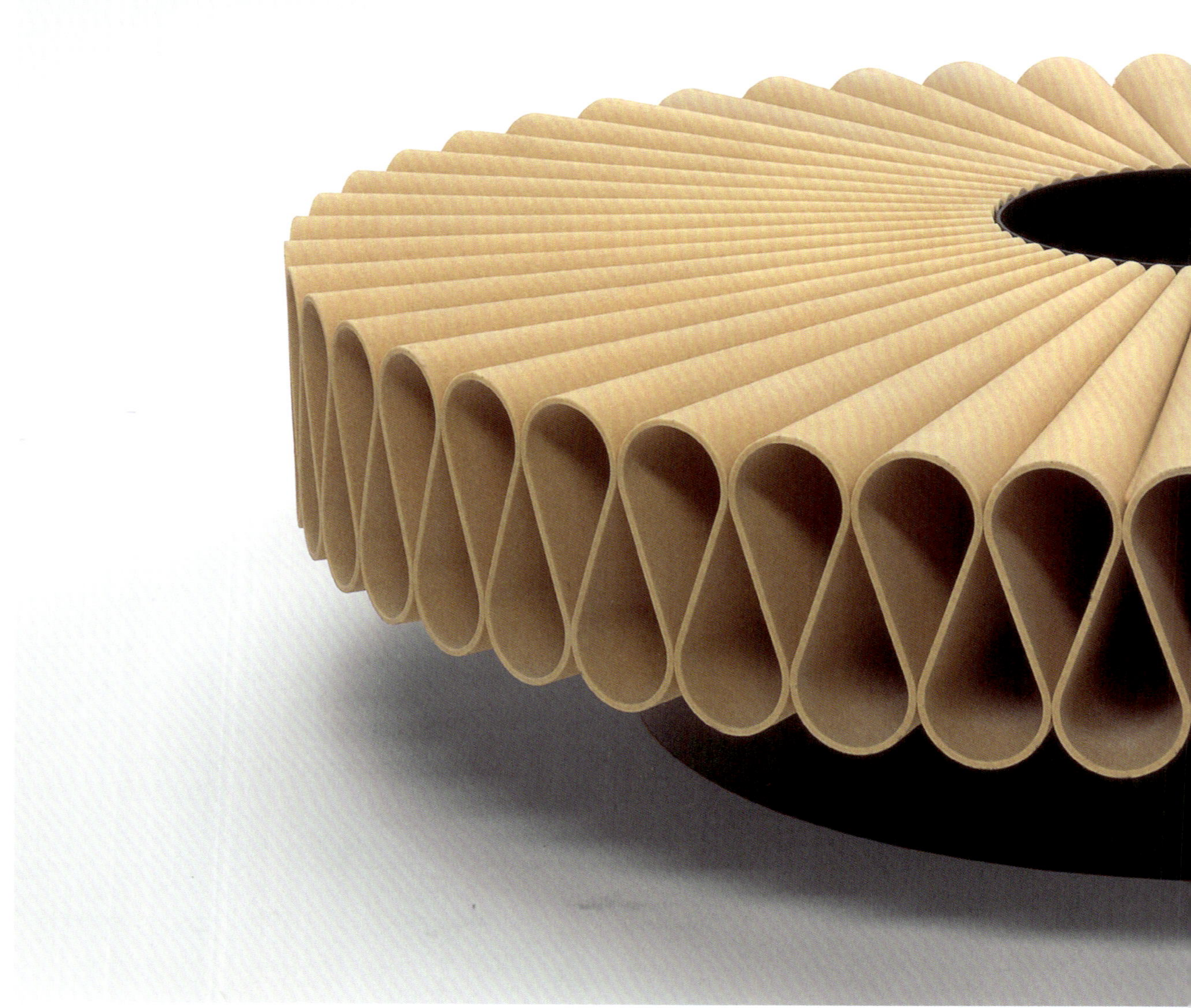

Dieser Tisch aus Kunststoff spielt auf die spanische Halskrause des 16. Jahrhunderts an, wie man sie zum Beispiel in Gemälden von Diego Velázquez sieht. Die komplexe Form der Tischplatte stammt aus einem 3D-Drucker, der Stücke in Originalgröße produziert.

This table made of synthetic materials is an allusion to the 16th-century Spanish ruff that one sees, for instance, in paintings by Diego Velázquez. The complex form of the tabletop is created by a 3D printer that produces full-sized pieces of furniture.

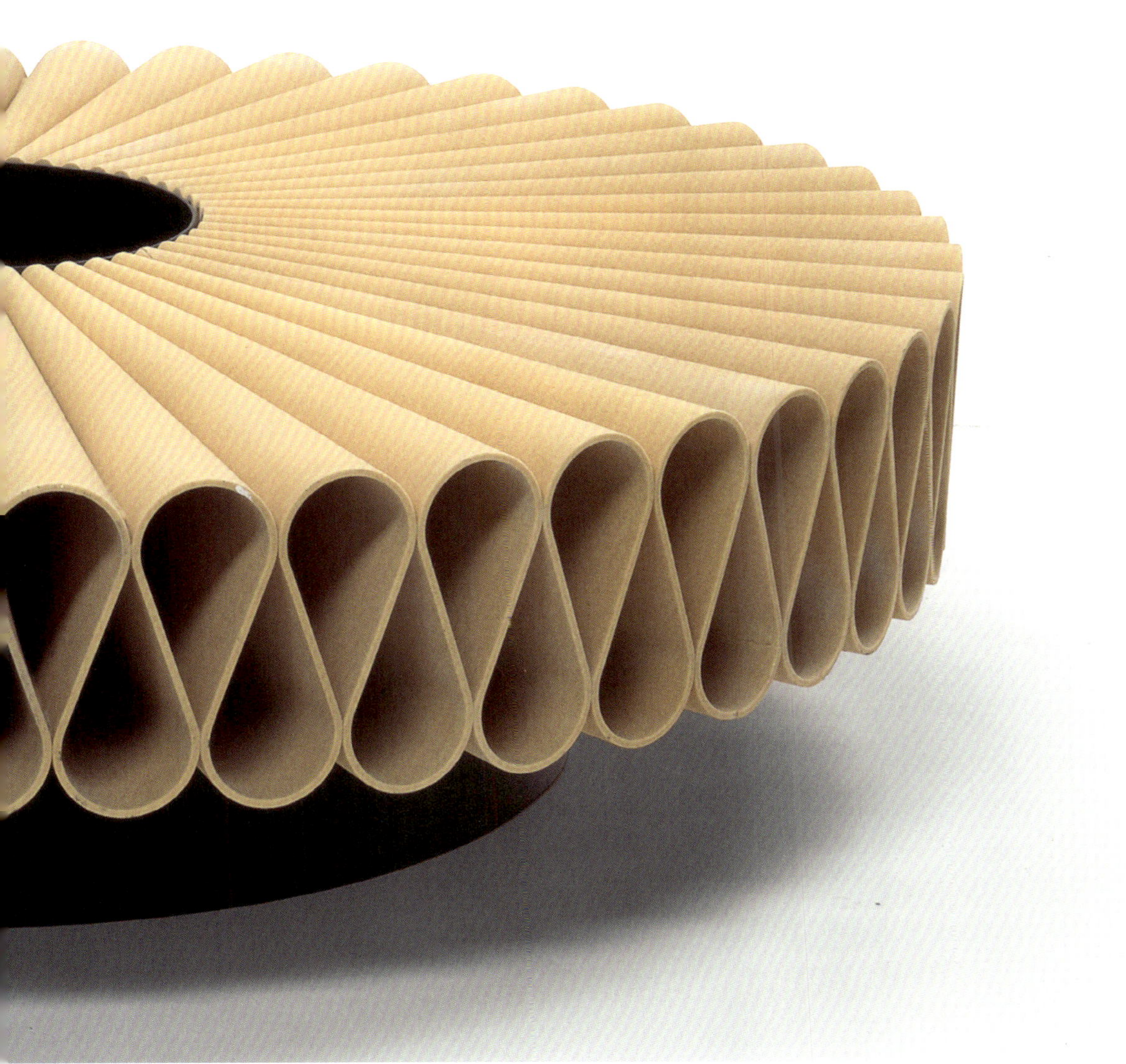

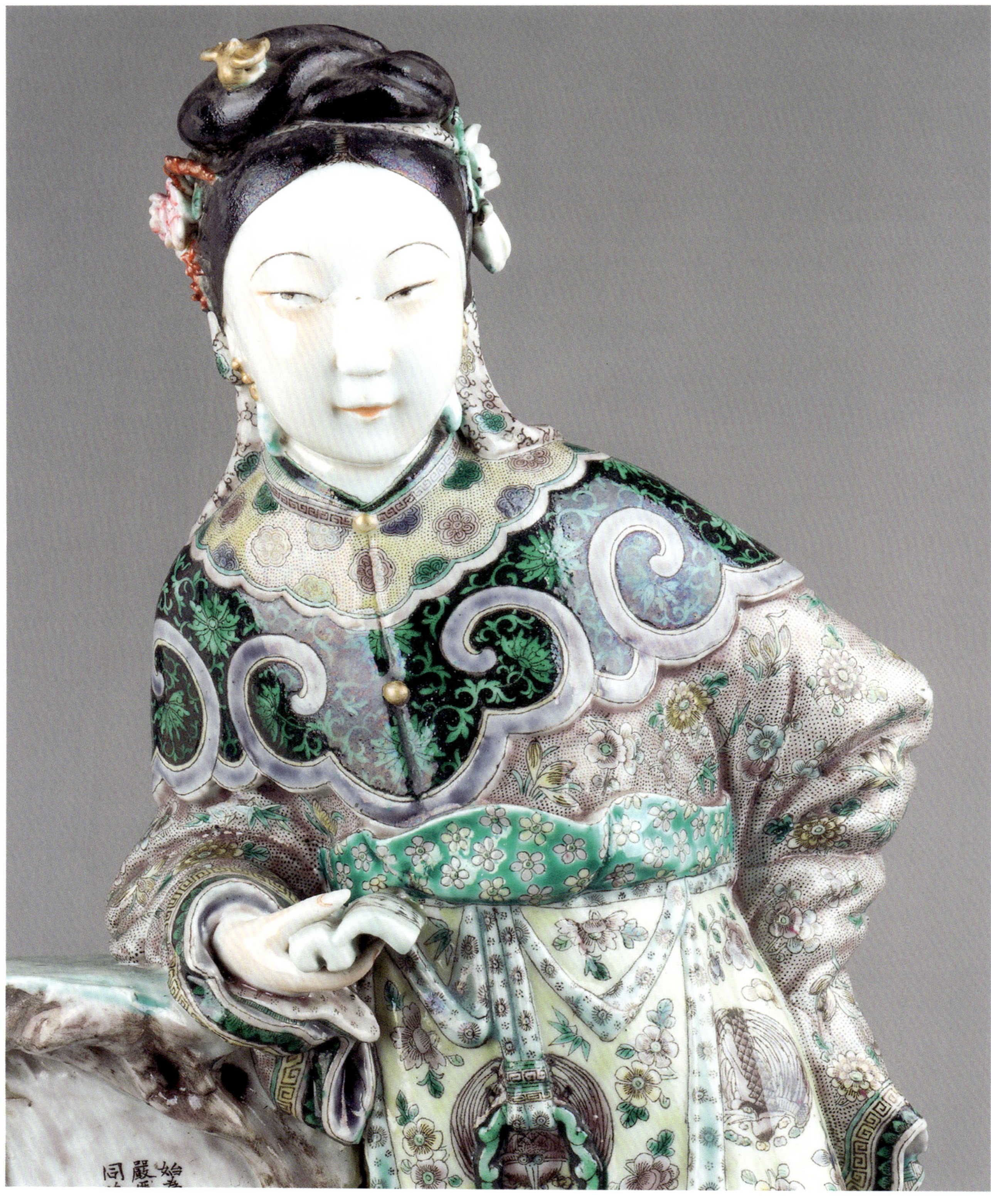

始
嚴
同

Weibliche Figur (Meng Lijun)
Female figure (Meng Lijun)

China, 18. Jh. 18th c.
Porzellan mit *famille verte*-Überglasurmalerei
Porcelain with *famille verte* overglaze painting
51,2 × 25,3 × 17,5
MAK, KE 10209

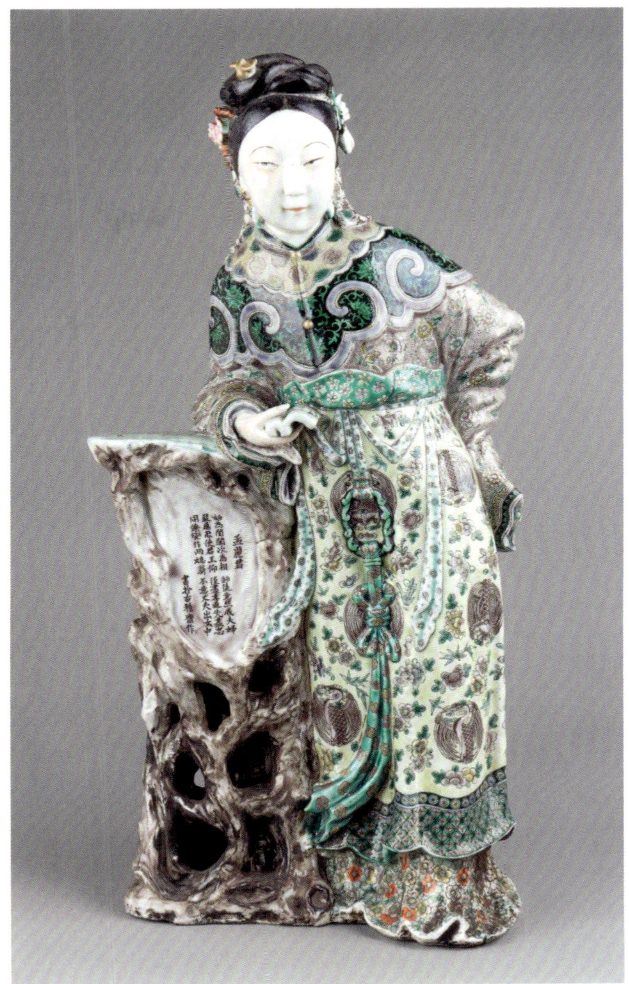

Meng Lijun, eine fiktionale Yuan-zeitliche (1271–1368) Figur aus dem Roman *Zaisheng yuan* [Reinkarniertes Schicksal] aus dem 18. Jahrhundert, ist ein *cross-dressing*-Phänomen: Als Frau kleidet sie sich als Mann, um als Beamter am kaiserlichen Hof den Ruf der Familie ihres Verlobten zu retten. Als Mann heiratet sie ihre ehemalige Schülerin. Nach ihrer Enttarnung durch den Kaiser entkommt sie der Todesstrafe und geht schließlich als Frau eine Ehe zu dritt ein – mit ihrem Verlobten und ihrer Ehefrau.

Der üppige Kragen dieser Porzellanfigur erinnert an den sogenannten „Wolkenkragen" (*cloud collar*), der in der Qing-Zeit (1644–1911) von Han-chinesischen Frauen zum Brautkleid getragen wurde – möglicherweise ist diese Figur von Meng Lijung in einem zeitgenössischen luxuriösen Hochzeitskleid ein Hinweis auf das aufregende Ende des Romans.

Meng Lijun, a fictional Yuan-era (1271–1368) figure from the 18th-century novel *Zaisneng yuan* [Reincarnated Fate] is a cross-dressing phenomenon: a woman, she dresses up as a man to assume the role of a civil servant at the imperial court and save the reputation of her betrothed's family. As a man, she marries a former pupil of hers. After being unmasked by the emperor, she escapes the death sentence, and as a woman enters a *mariage à trois*—with her betrothed and her wife.

The elaborate collar of this porcelain figure recalls the so-called cloud collars that in the Qing era (1644–1911) were worn by Han Chinese women as part of their wedding attire—possibly an indication that this figure of Meng Lijun as a Qing-era woman in a luxurious wedding dress alludes to the story's gripping finale.

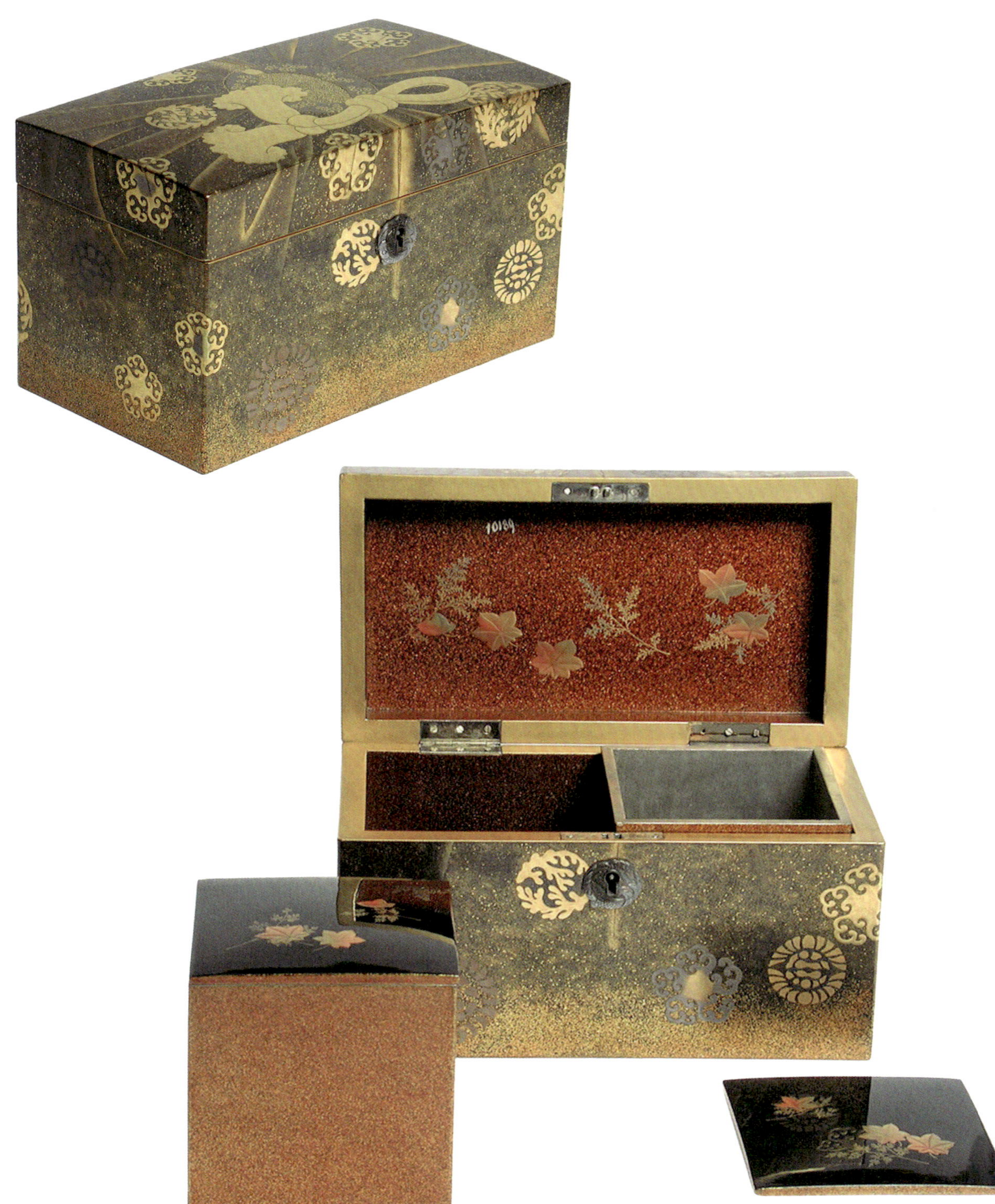

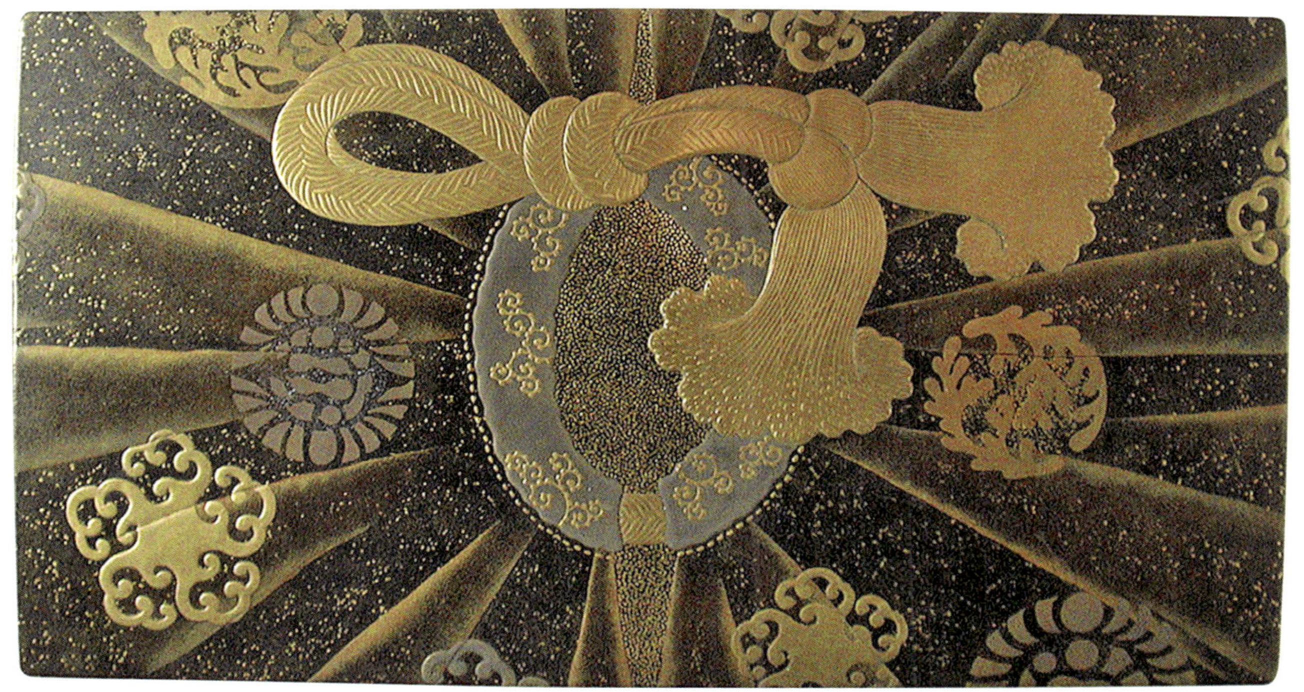

Teekästchen mit zwei Deckeldosen
Casket for tea utensils with two lidded boxes

Japan, 1868–1872
Schwarzlack, Streudekor in Gold und Silber auf Holz, *hiramakie* (flaches „Streubild")
und *takamakie* (Relief „Streubild") auf *nashiji* (Birnenhaut)-Grund
Lacquer on wood with gold and silver *hiramaki-e* (flat "sprinkled picture"),
and *takamaki-e* (raised "sprinkled picture") on *nashiji* ("pear-skin") ground
12 × 21,5 × 11
MAK, OR 3830

Das Verpacken oder Einpacken eines wertvollen Gegenstandes mit einem besonderen Stoff oder in ein speziell dafür angefertigtes Behältnis ist eine symbolische Geste, die darauf hinweist, dass ein Objekt wertvoll ist. Eine fehlende Verpackung würde im kulturellen Kontext Japans den Gegenstand sogar als wertlos markieren bzw. entwerten. Kleine, kostbare Utensilien für die *chanoyu*-Teezeremonie und besondere Gegenstände erhalten in Japan daher ganz selbstverständlich eine besondere Hülle. Lack- oder Keramikobjekte werden gern mit Beutelchen aus Brokatstoff mit Kordelverschluss verkleidet. Der ornamental gefaltete Textilüberzug wird als Teil des Gesamtensembles verstanden und macht somit einen Teil des Wertgehalts aus, sodass sein Erscheinungsbild sogar als Materialimitation zur Dekoration wird.

Packing or wrapping a valuable object in a distinctive material or container specially constructed for the purpose is a symbolic gesture indicative of the object's worth. In Japanese culture, an object lacking packaging might even be considered worthless or debased.
In Japan, small utensils for the *chanoyu* tea ceremony and other valuable objects are thus as a matter of course wrapped in special packaging. Lacquer wares or ceramic objects are typically encased in brocade fabric sachets closed with a drawstring. The ornamentally folded textile envelope is considered part of the ensemble and thus of its value content, so that the envelope's appearance, even as material imitation, becomes a decorative pattern.

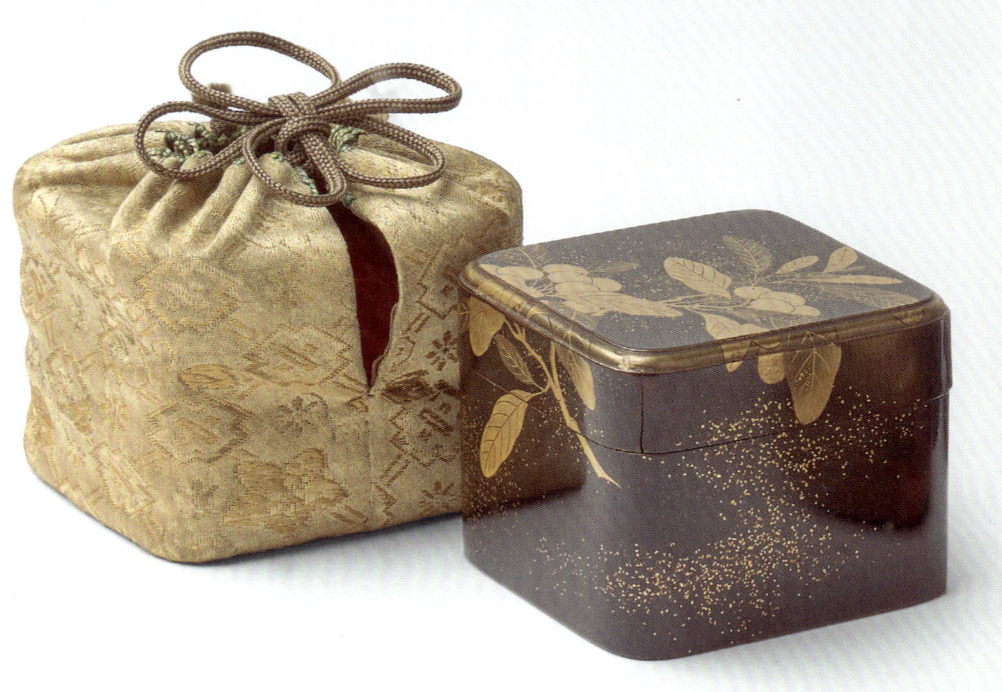

Deckeldose in Seidenbeutel
Lidded box in silk bag
19. Jh. 19th c.
Schwarzlack, Streudekor in Gold auf Holz,
hiramakie (flaches „Streubild")
Lacquer on wood with gold and silver *hiramaki-e*
(flat "sprinkled picture")
5 × 6,1 × 6,1
MAK, OR 3837

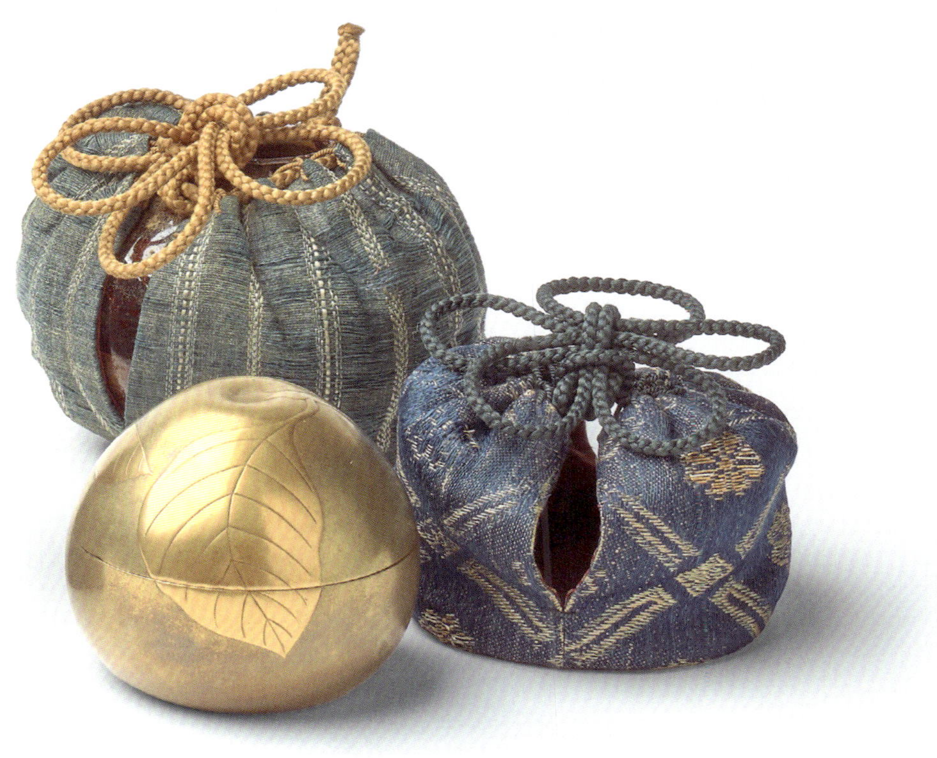

Teebüchse in Seidenbeutel
Tea caddy in silk bag
Japan, Ende 19. Jh./Anfang 20. Jh.
Japan, late 19th c./early 20th c.
Seto-Keramik Seto ceramic
ø 6,8, H 5,2
MAK, KE 11808

Deckeldose in Seidenbeutel
Lidded box in silk bag
vor 1873 pre-1873
Schwarzlack, Streudekor in Gold auf Holz, *hiramakie* (flaches „Streubild")
und *takamakie* (Relief „Streubild")
Lacquer on wood with gold *hiramaki-e* (flat "sprinkled picture"),
and *takamaki-e* (raised "sprinkled picture")
ø 5, H 4,5
MAK, LA 51

GEFALTETE/ ENTFALTETE FORMEN

Falten bedeuten nicht zwingend Wiederholung. Jede Falte bestimmt die Form und Struktur des Materials und beeinflusst die Statik durch strukturierten Halt und Stärke. Eine Falte kann auch eine Art Scharnier zwischen zwei Flächen bilden. Sie verleiht einem Objekt dann mehr Beweglichkeit und dadurch eine hohe Elastizität. Falten helfen dabei, Raum zu sparen und die Masse physischer Objekte dramatisch zu reduzieren. Wenn sie beweglich sind, können sie einem Objekt neue Strukturen geben oder neue Räume erschließen. Gefaltet erhält das Material eine zusätzliche tektonische und statische Kraft.

Ob Stabilität, Elastizität oder formell-räumliche Transformation, die Logik von Falten zeigt sich in einer erstaunlichen funktionalen Vielfalt. Als universelle Kulturtechnik ist das Falten ein fester Bestandteil der materiellen Kultur und Dingwelt der Menschen. Dadurch, dass es sich um ein einfach zu bewältigendes manuelles Verfahren handelt, steht es zudem in direktem Zusammenhang mit der (Gegen-)Kultur des Do-it-yourself und ihren ideologischen und technischen Schwerpunkten.

FOLDED/ UNFOLDED FORMS

Folds do not necessarily imply repetition. Each single fold determines a material's form and structure and influences its static qualities by providing structured support and strength. A fold can also create a kind of hinge between two surfaces. It thus imparts to an object greater mobility and therefore greater elasticity. Folds help to save space and dramatically to reduce the bulkiness of physical objects. If they are flexible, they structurally transform an object or open up new spaces within it. When folded, the material maintains its tectonic and static power.

Whether through their stability, elasticity, or formal and spatial transformability, the logic of folds manifests an astonishing functional variety. As a universal cultural technique, folding is part and parcel of our material world and its artefacts. An easily mastered manual skill, it is also directly related to the ideological and technical principles of do-it-yourself counter-culture.

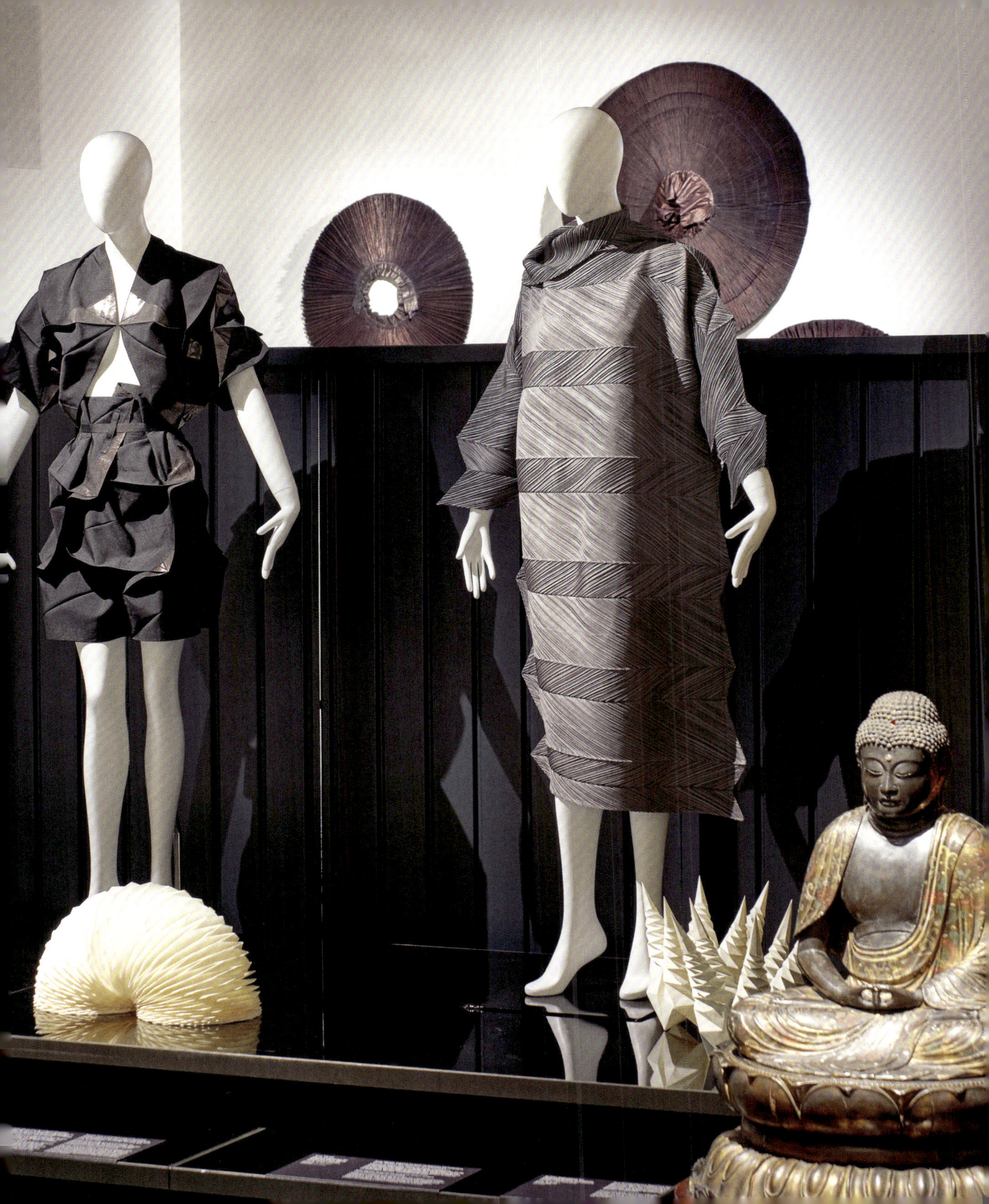

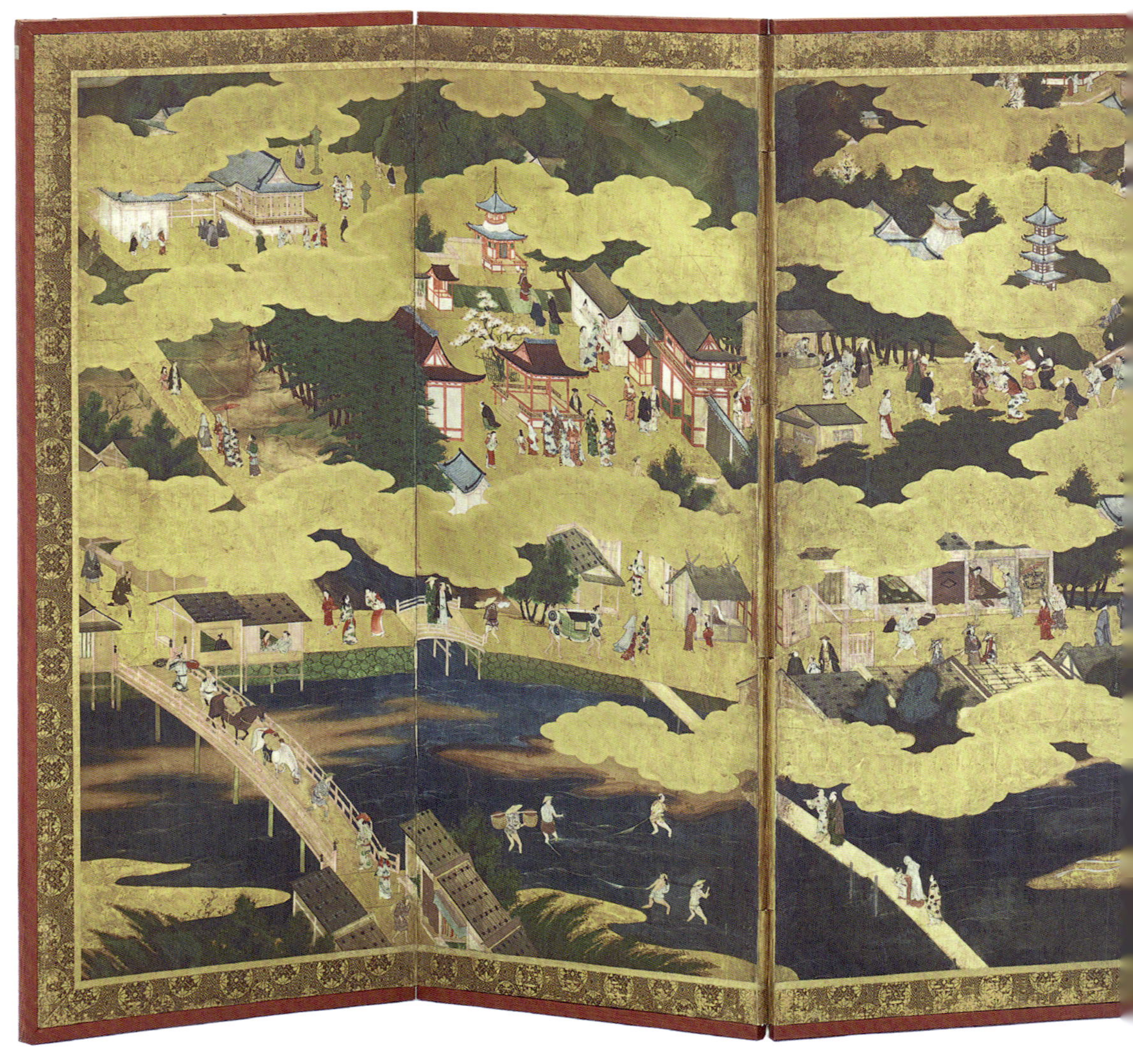

Sechsteiliger Stellschirm (*byōbu*)

Six-panel folding screen (*byōbu*)

Japan, 1591–1600
Tusche, Farbe, Papier und Gold auf Papier
Ink, color, paper, and gold on paper
290 × 116,5
MAK, MAL 165

Ein japanischer Stellschirm besteht aus mehreren Paneelen, die durch ein Scharnier aus reißfesten Papierstreifen miteinander verbunden sind und trotz großen Formats im aufgefächerten Zustand kompakt zusammengefaltet werden können. Als flexibles Multifunktionsmöbel war der Stellschirm in Japan ab der Heian-Zeit (794–1185) Teil der Wohn- und Repräsentationsräume der Elite – er diente etwa als Windschutz, Raumteiler oder visuelle Markierung von Räumlichkeiten je nach Jahreszeit, Anlass und sozialem Status. Als in Ostasien typischer Bildträger bietet ein Stellschirm mit mehreren Paneelen einen Bildraum von monumentaler Größe. Obwohl die japanische Malerei auf Stellschirmen

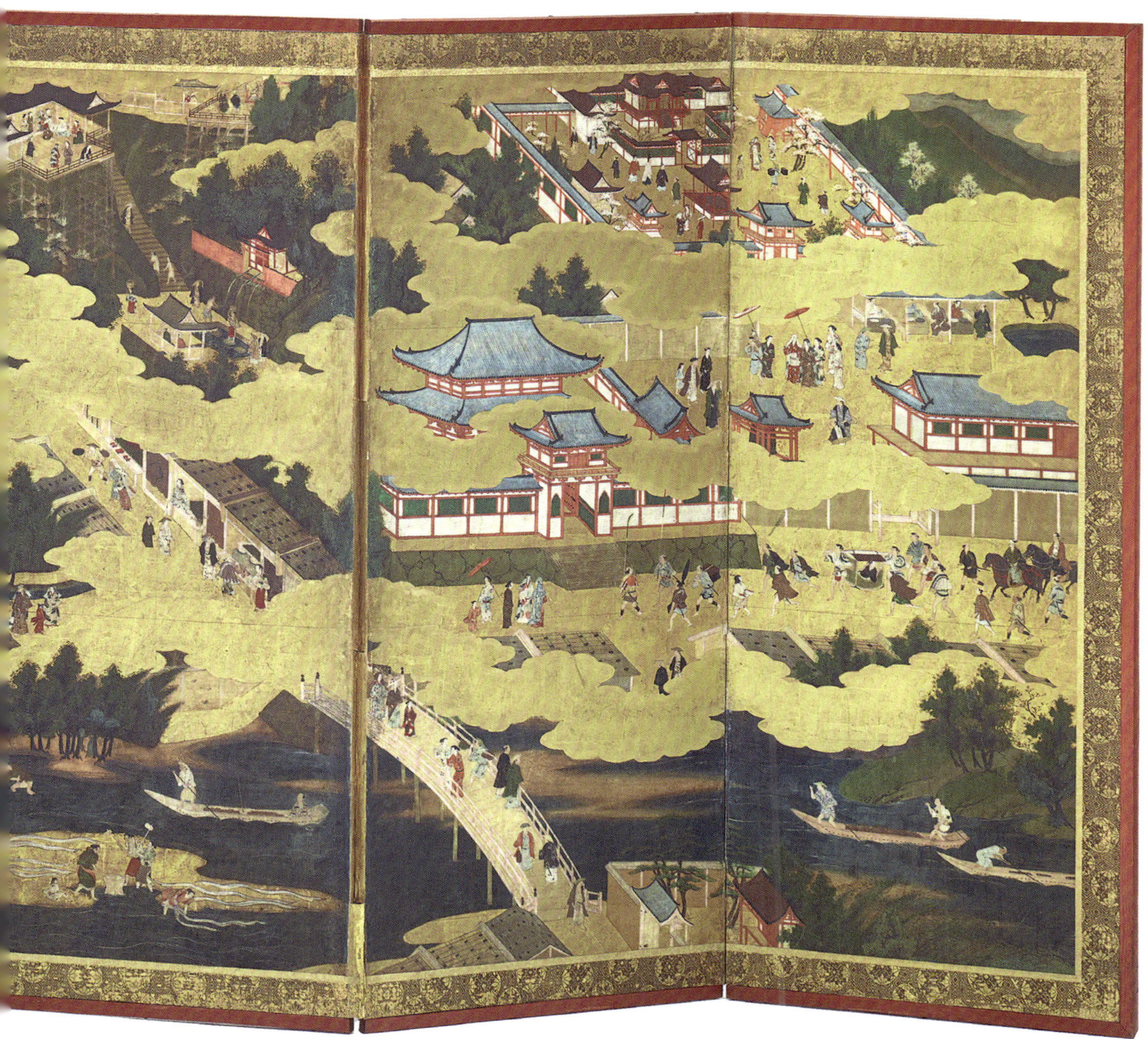

bis ins späte 19. Jahrhundert weitgehend ohne das Prinzip der Zentralperspektive ausgeführt wurde, entsteht durch das leicht gefaltete Aufstellen des Möbels eine nahezu dreidimensionale Wirkung der stark zur Flächigkeit neigenden Darstellung und eine überraschend lebendige, dynamische Bildwirkung.

A Japanese folding screen consists of several panels that are hinged together by tear-resistant paper strips and can be folded compactly from their unfolded state despite their size. As flexible multifunctional pieces of furniture, screens have been part of elite living and representational spaces in Japan since the Heian period (794–1185)—for example as windbreaks, room dividers or visual space markers depending on the season, occasion, and user's social status. A typical East Asian image medium, the multi-paneled screen offers a picture space of monumental scale. While Japanese paintings on folding screens were largely executed without using central perspective until the late 19th century, the erected screen's zigzag shape transforms the strictly two-dimensional image into an almost three-dimensional representation, creating a surprisingly animated, dynamic sense of pictorial space.

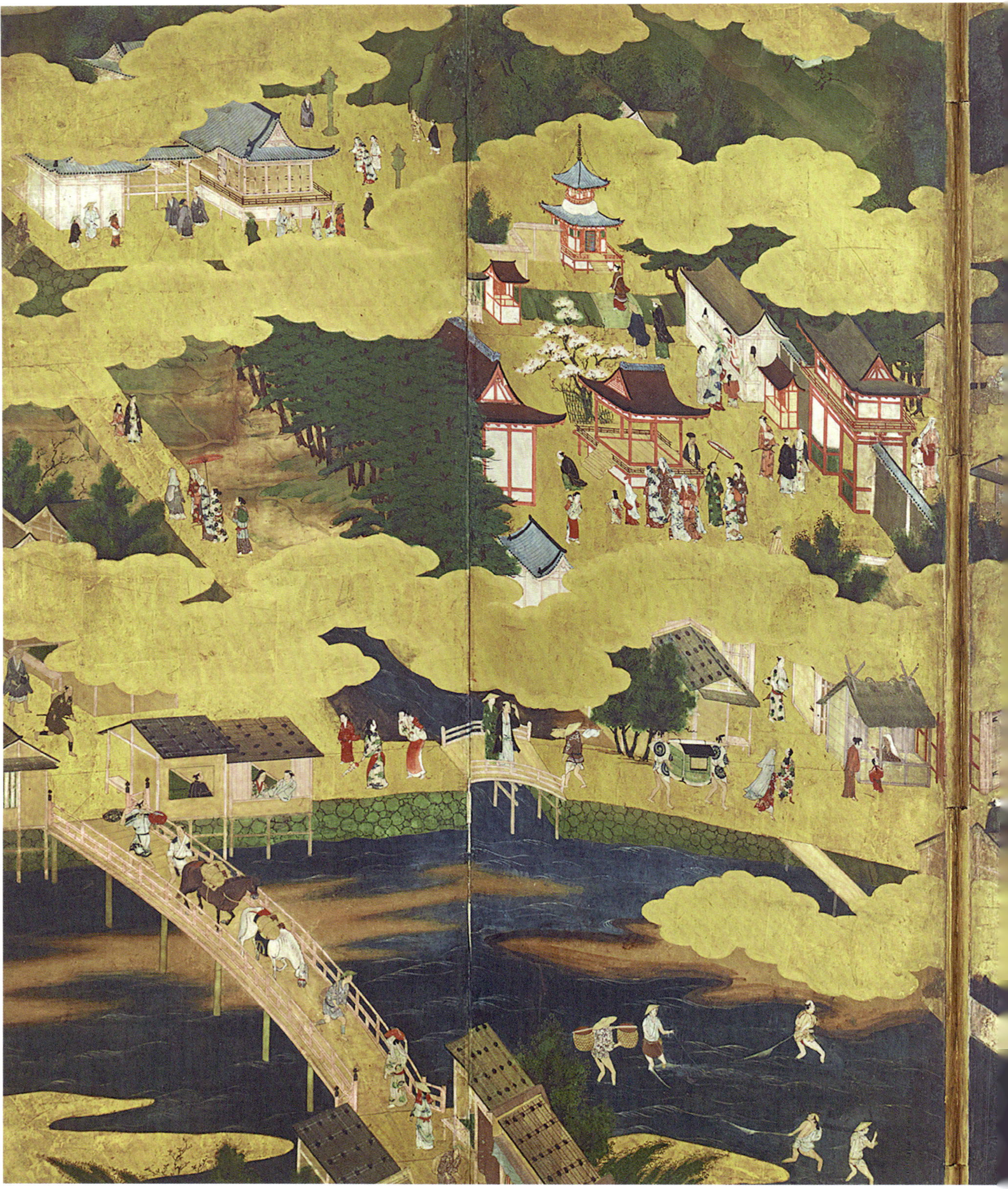

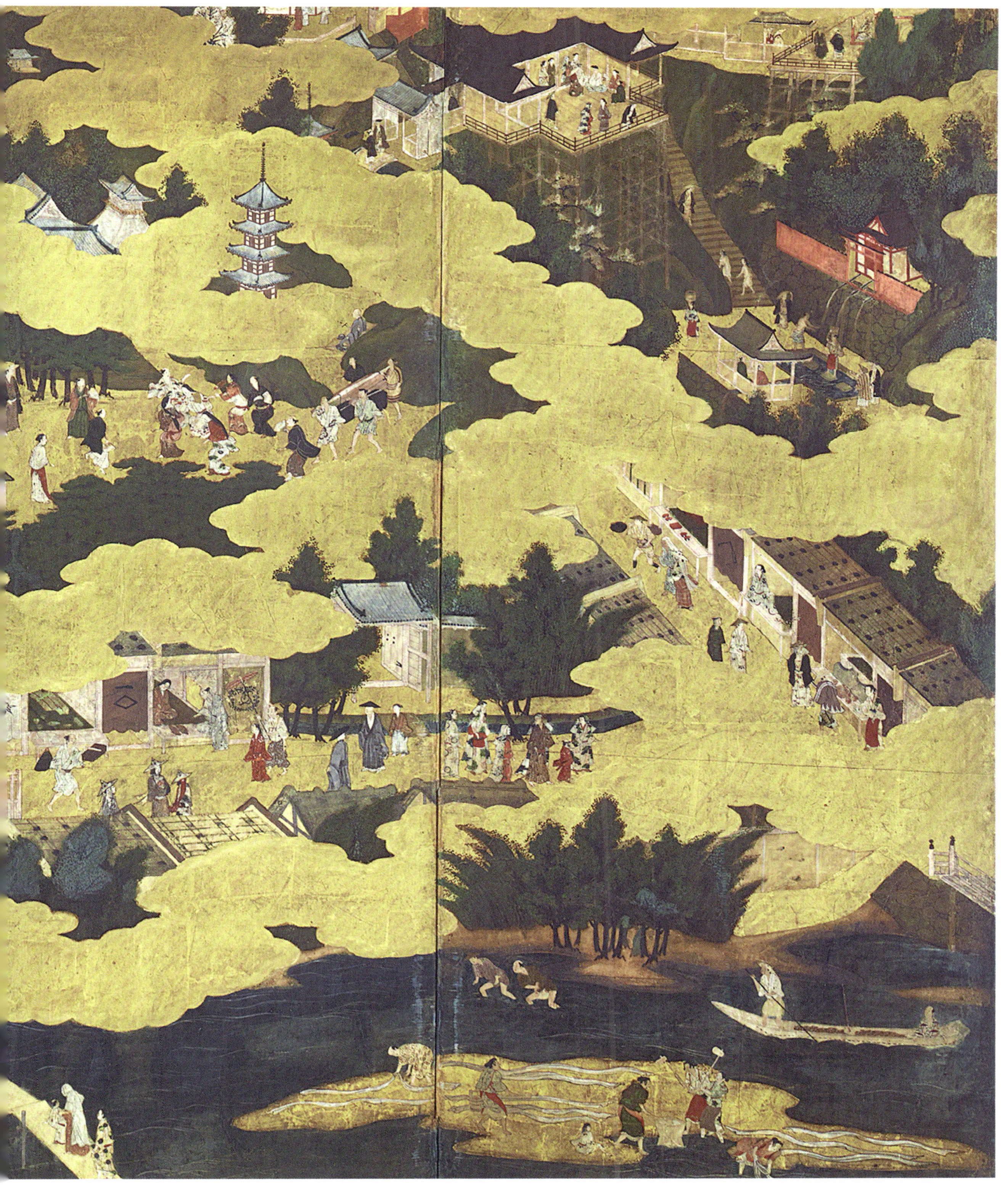

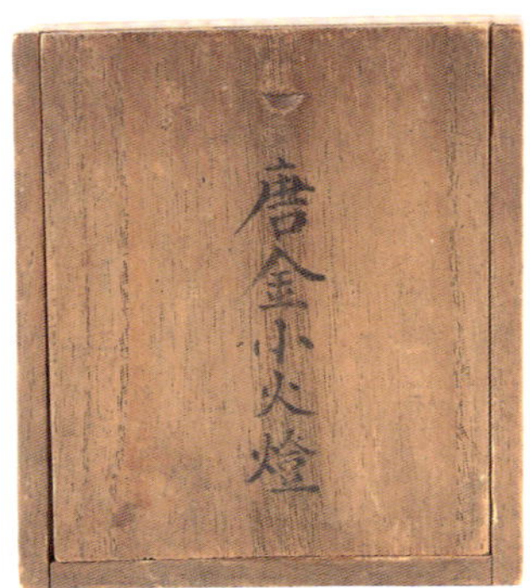
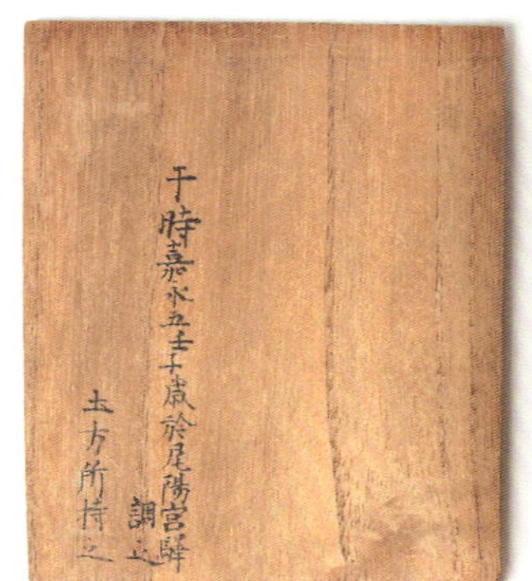
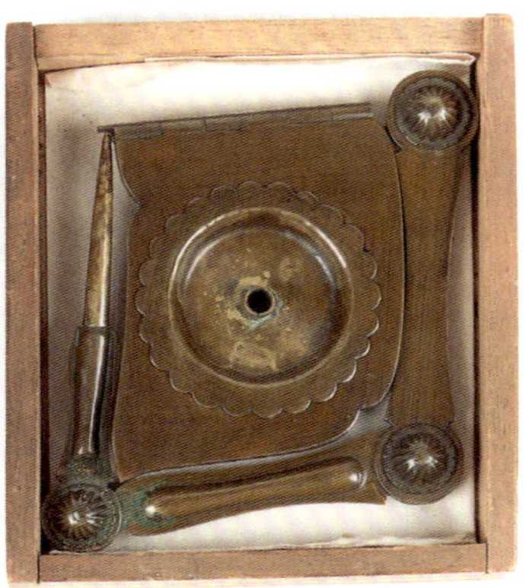

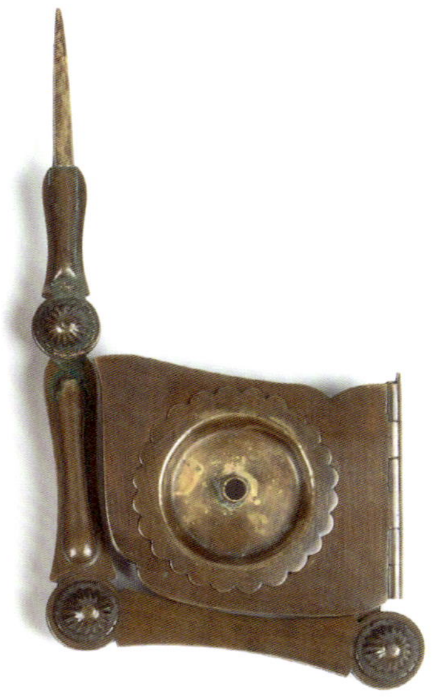

Faltbarer Kerzenständer mit einem
Aufbewahrungskästchen aus *kiri*-Holz
Pocket candlestick with a container
made of *kiri* wood
Japan, Mitte 19. Jh. mid-19th c.
Messing Brass
13,4 × 11,7 × 1,5 (in gefaltetem Zustand in folded condition);
ø 12,9, H 33,3 (ausgeklappt unfolded)

Das Originalmodell für diesen Kerzenständer wurde 1834
von Tanaka Hisashige entworfen, dem Gründer des heutigen
japanischen Elektrokonzerns Toshiba. Das Besondere an
diesem Objekt ist, dass es sich mit ein paar Handgriffen in
eine leicht transportable Scheibe verwandeln lässt: Die kleine runde Stellfläche kann abgenommen werden, wodurch
der Schaft entlang der Scharniere zusammengefaltet und
um den zusammengeklappten dreibeinigen Fuß herumgelegt
werden kann. Der Hohlraum der übereinanderl egenden
Fußscheiben bietet wiederum den passenden Platz für die

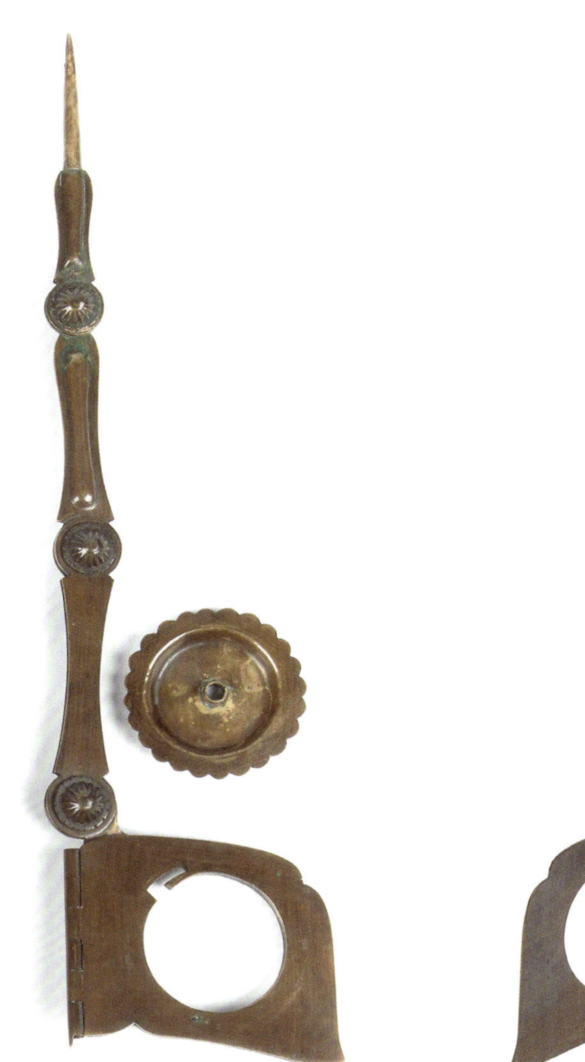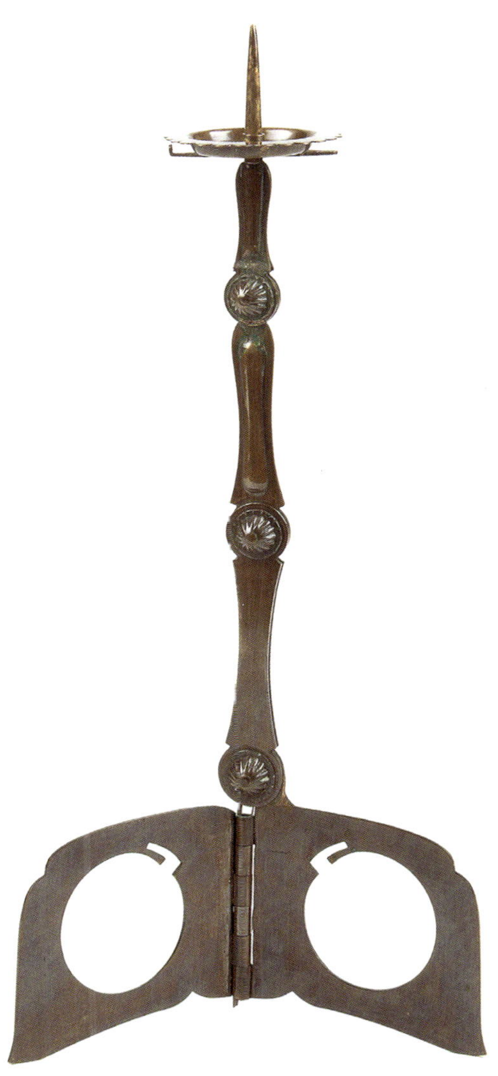

Stellfläche – so wird aus einem ca. 30 cm hohen Kerzen-ständer eine kompakte Scheibe. Ärzte verwendeten solche Kerzenständer gerne für Hausbesuche. Im Deckel des Käst-chens steht u. a. der Name des Besitzers, der dieses Stück 1852 erworben haben soll.

The original of this candlestick was designed in 1834 by Ta-naka Hisashige, the founder of what is today the Toshiba electronic corporation. In just a few steps it can be trans-formed into an easily transportable disk: the small round platform can be removed, allowing the candlestick shaft to be folded at its hinges and laid around the collapsed tripod foot. The candle platform then fits into the cavity of the folded feet. A 30 cm high candlestick is thus transformed into a compact flat disk. Doctors often used such candle sticks for house visits. The inscription on the inside of the storage box lid includes the name of the person who ac-quired this object in 1852.

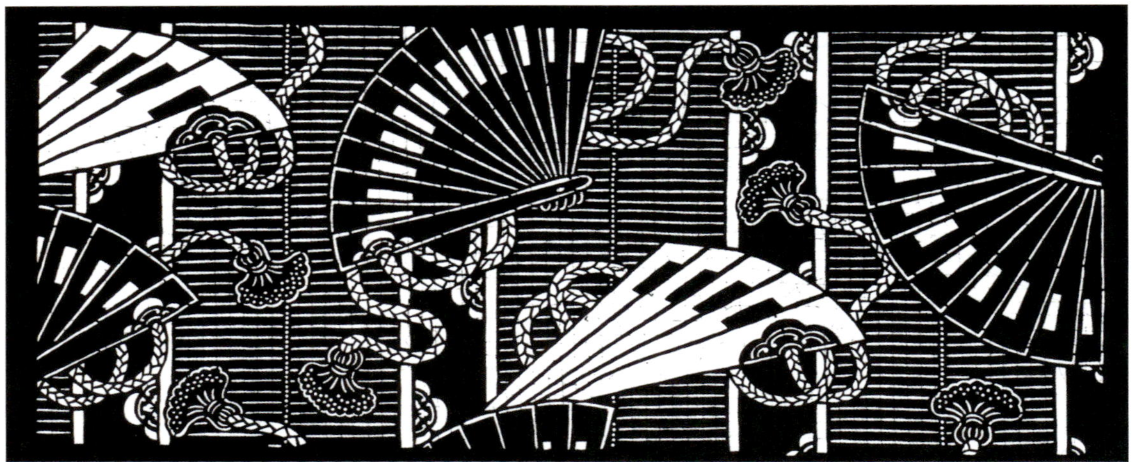

Färbeschablone, Bambus-Jalousie (*misu*)
und Fächer
Stencil, bamboo blind (*misu*), and fan
Japan, 19. Jh. 19th c.
Papier, imprägniert, geschnitten
Treated paper, push carving
22,8 × 41,3
MAK, OR 3925-4974

Färbeschablone, Fächer und aufsteigender
Dampf (*tatewaku*)
Stencil, fans, and rising steam (*tatewaku*)
Japan, 19. Jh. 19th c.
Papier, imprägniert, geschnitten
Treated paper, push carving
25,7 × 41,6
MAK, OR 3925-3341

Färbeschablone, *fundō tsunagi* (Netzmuster in
Form von *fundō* [japanisches Gewicht]) mit
Gittermuster und Fächer(?)formen mit
Holzmaserung (*mokume*)
Stencil, *fundō tsunagi* (net pattern in *fundō*
[Japanese weight]) form with lattice pattern,
and fan (?) shapes with wood grain (*mokume*)
Japan, 19. Jh. 19th c.
Papier, imprägniert, geschnitten
Treated paper, push carving
25,5 × 40,7
MAK, OR 3925-5082

Färbeschablone, *matsukawabishi* („Pinien-Rinde-
Rauten"-Muster), Fächer und Kirschblüten (?) mit
Gittermuster, Ballonblumen und Schmetterlingen
Stencil, *matsukawabishi* ("pine-bark-diamonds"
pattern), fans and cherry blossoms (?) with lattice
pattern, balloon flowers, and butterflies
Japan, 19. Jh. 19th c.
Papier, imprägniert, geschnitten Treated paper, push carving
24,8 × 40
MAK, OR 3925-2392

Faltbare Papierfächer wurden vermutlich bereits im späten
7. Jahrhundert in Japan verwendet, möglicherweise gehen
sie auf frühere faltbare Fächer aus dünnen Holzpaneelen
zurück. Sie gelten als praktisches wie rituelles Accessoire
für ihre Träger*innen. Da sie eine optische Ähnlichkeit mit
Fledermäusen aufweisen, wurden sie in Japan früher auch
„Fledermaus-Fächer" genannt. Papierfächer dienten in Ostasien zudem als Trägermedium für Malerei oder Kalligrafie.
Mit ihrer ornamentalen Form zählen sie zum festen Repertoire an Mustern für Textilien, Lackarbeiten oder Keramik
aus Japan.

Folding fans were probably already in use in late 7th-century
Japan, possibly based on earlier folding fans made of thin
wooden panels. They are both practical and ritual accessories, used by men as well as by women. Since they look
rather like bats, in early Japan they were also called "bat-
fans." In Eastern Asia, paper fans were also a medium for
painting or calligraphy. With their ornamental form, they
were integral to the repertoire of patterns used on textiles,
lacquer work, and ceramics from Japan.

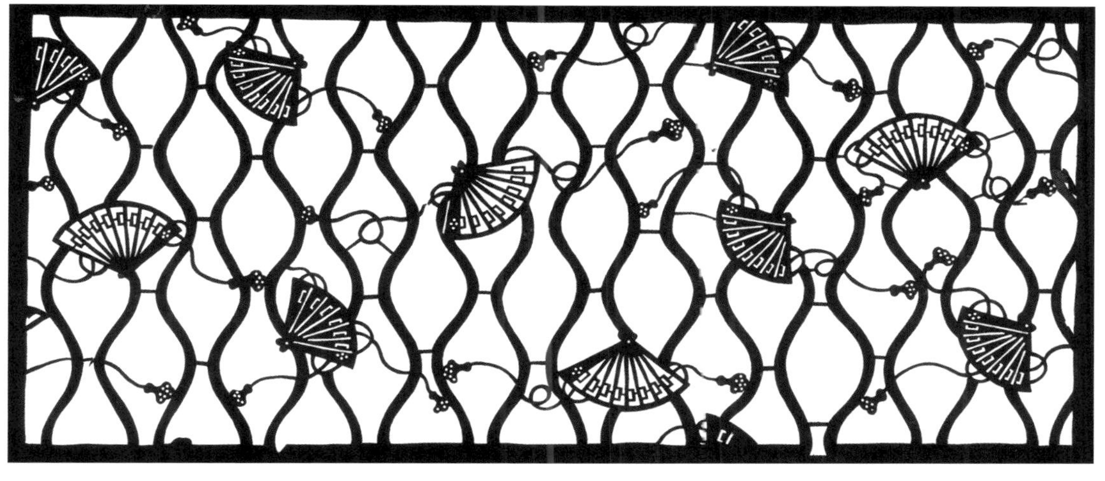

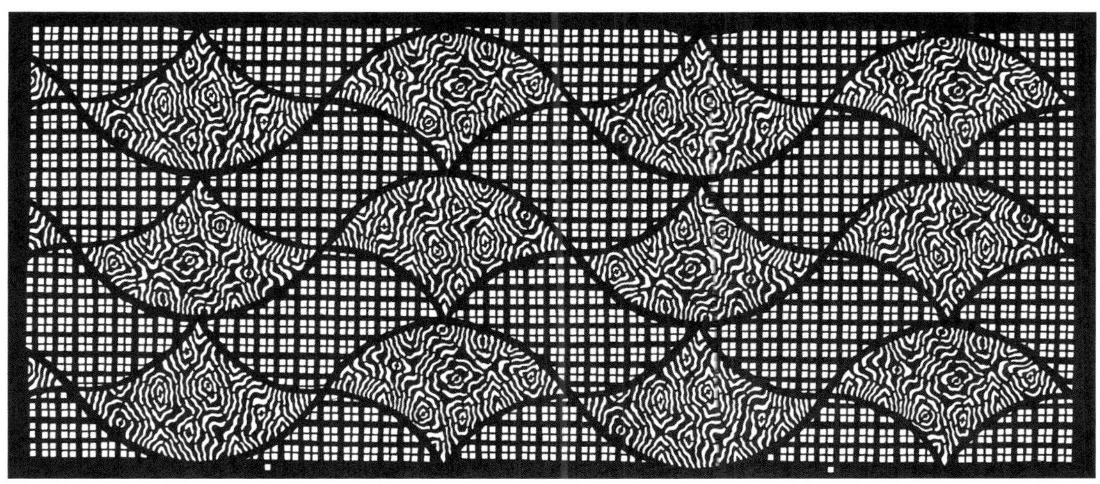

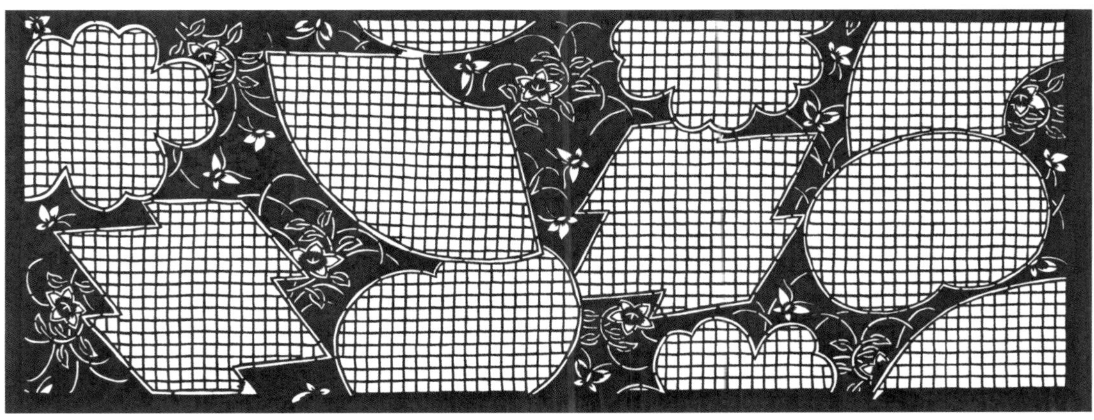

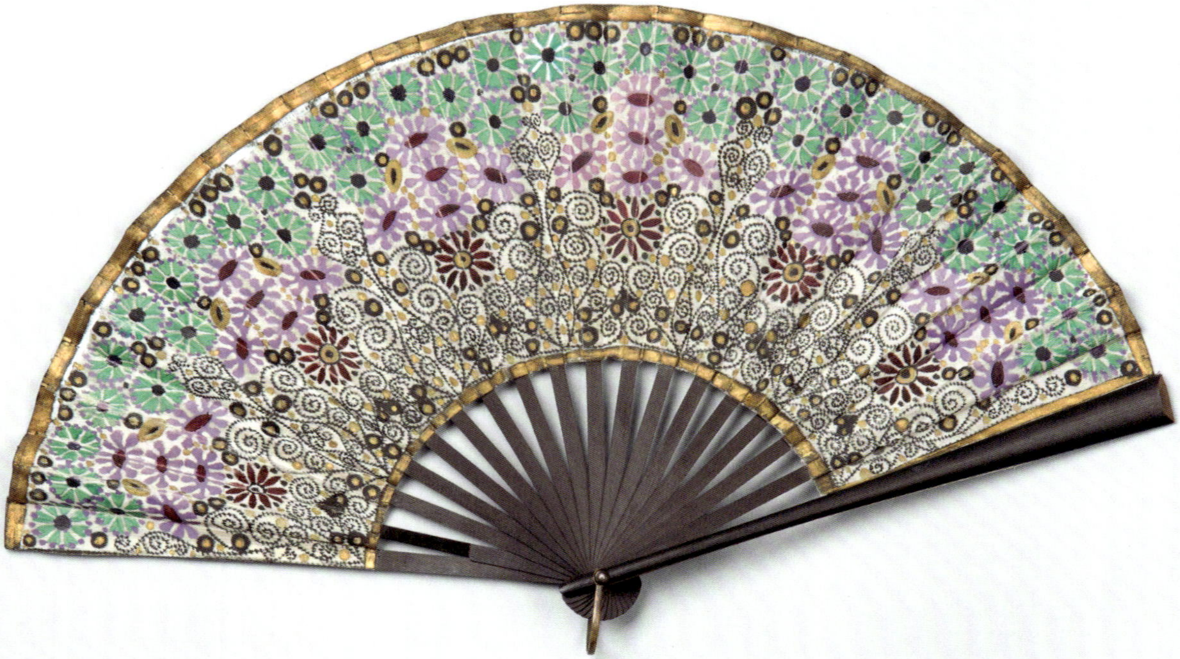

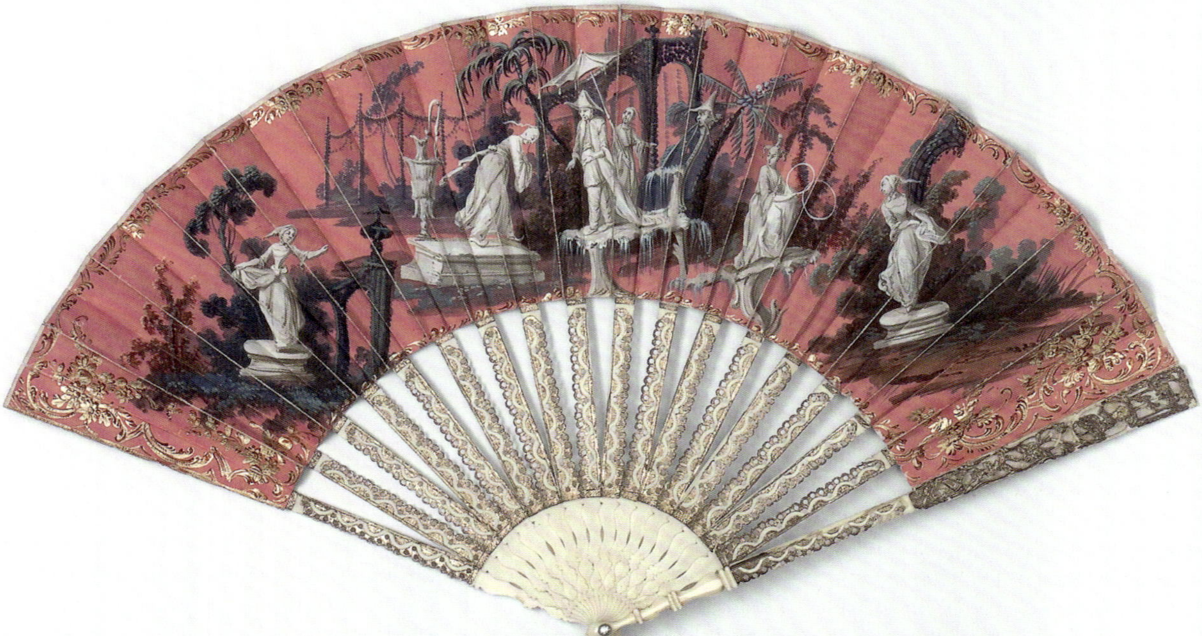

Anna Österreicher
Faltfächer, Spiralmuster
mit Blumen
Folding fan, spiral pattern
with flowers
Wien Vienna, 1901–1912
Seide, Holz, Metall Silk, wood, metal
22 × 40
MAK, WI 1041

Anonym Anonymous
Faltfächer, Chinoiserie-Szenen
Folding fan, Chinoiserie scenes
Frankreich France, 1751–1775
Papier, Goldfarbe, Gouache,
Metall, Strass, Bein
Paper, gold paint, gouache, metal,
rhinestone, bone
27 × 49
MAK, F 228

Anonym Anonymous
Faltfächer, Silberornament mit Federn
Folding fan, silver ornamentation with feathers
Österreich Austria, 1901–1910
Seide, Metallfaden, Elfenbein, Papier
Silk, metal threads, ivory, paper
37,5 × 62
MAK, T 10465

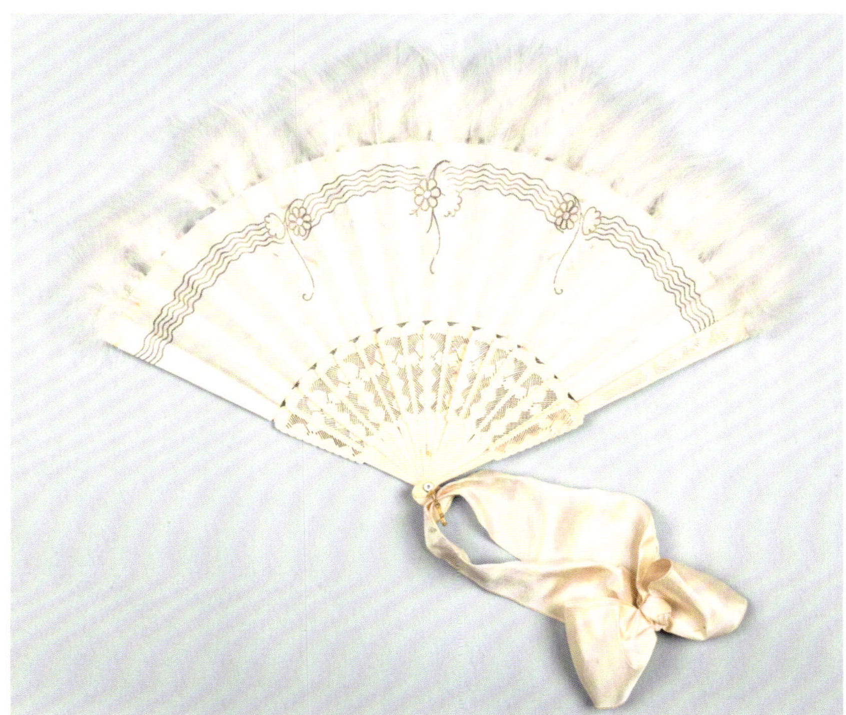

Faltfächer wurden im 12. Jahrhundert von Japan aus nach China und Korea exportiert. In einer beidseitig bespannten Variante fanden sie im 15. Jahrhundert ihren Weg von China nach Korea und wieder zurück an den Ursprungsort, nach Japan. Auch in Europa wurden ostasiatische Faltfächer bald populär: Im 16. Jahrhundert gelangten sie nach Portugal, Spanien und Mitteleuropa, wo sie ab dem 17. Jahrhundert auch selbst hergestellt wurden. In Europa waren sie genderspezifisch konnotiert: Faltfächer galten für Frauen – vor allem aus gesellschaftlich höhergestellten Kreisen – als elegantes Accessoire, das nicht nur kühlen sollte. Als Kommunikationsmittel für die „Fächersprache" war der Faltfächer auch ein bedeutender Bestandteil kultureller Praxis.

Folding fans were exported in the 12th century from Japan to China and Korea. A variant covered on both sides found its way in the 15th century from China to Korea and thence back to Japan, the fan's country of origin. In Europe too folding fans from the Far East soon became popular: in the 16th century they reached Portugal, Spain, and Central Europe, where starting in the 17th century they were also manufactured. In Europe they were gender-connotated: for women—especially those from the upper classes—folding fans were an elegant accessory that served not only to keep the owner cool. A tool for communicating in "fan language," folding fans were an important instrument of cultural practice.

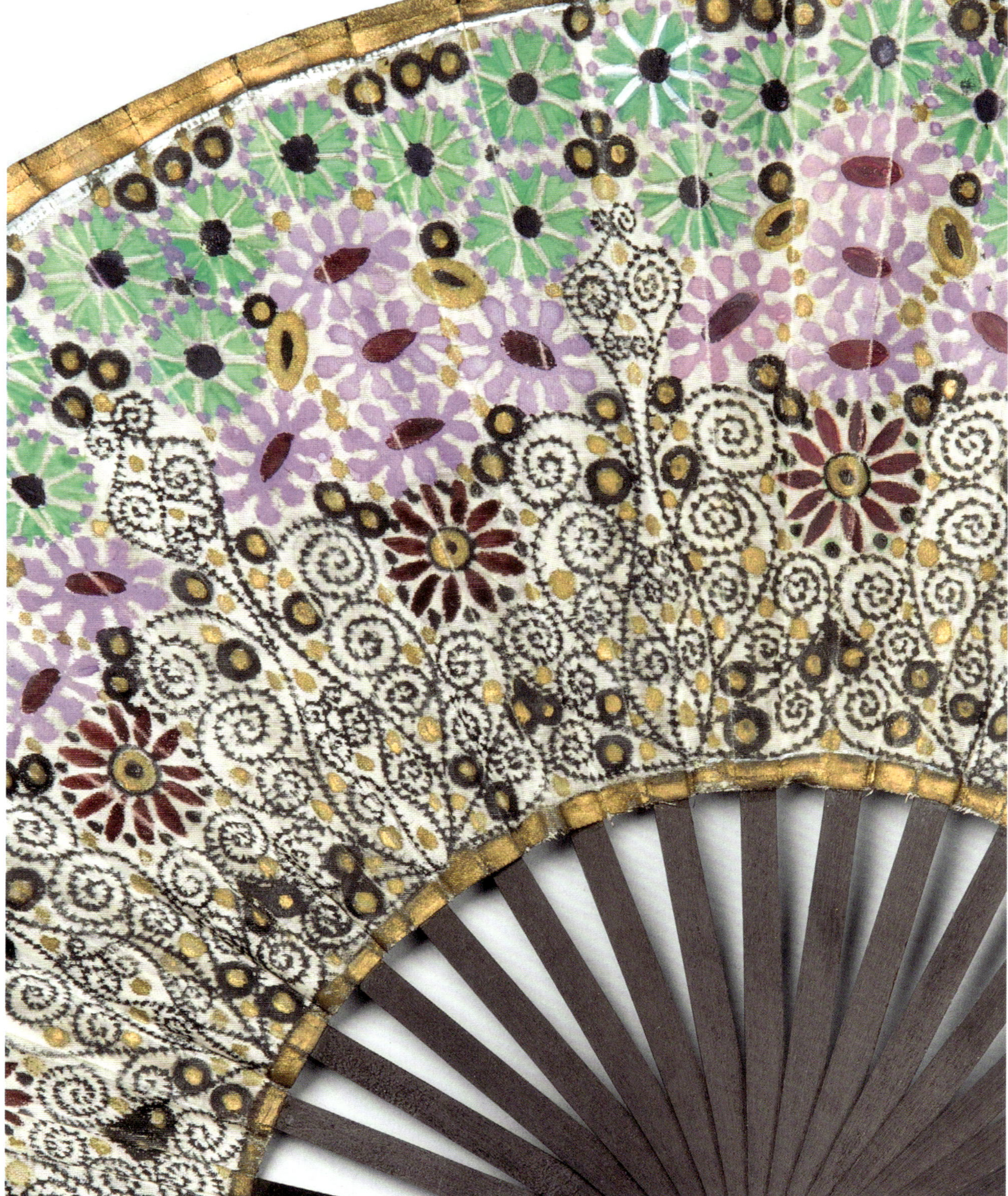

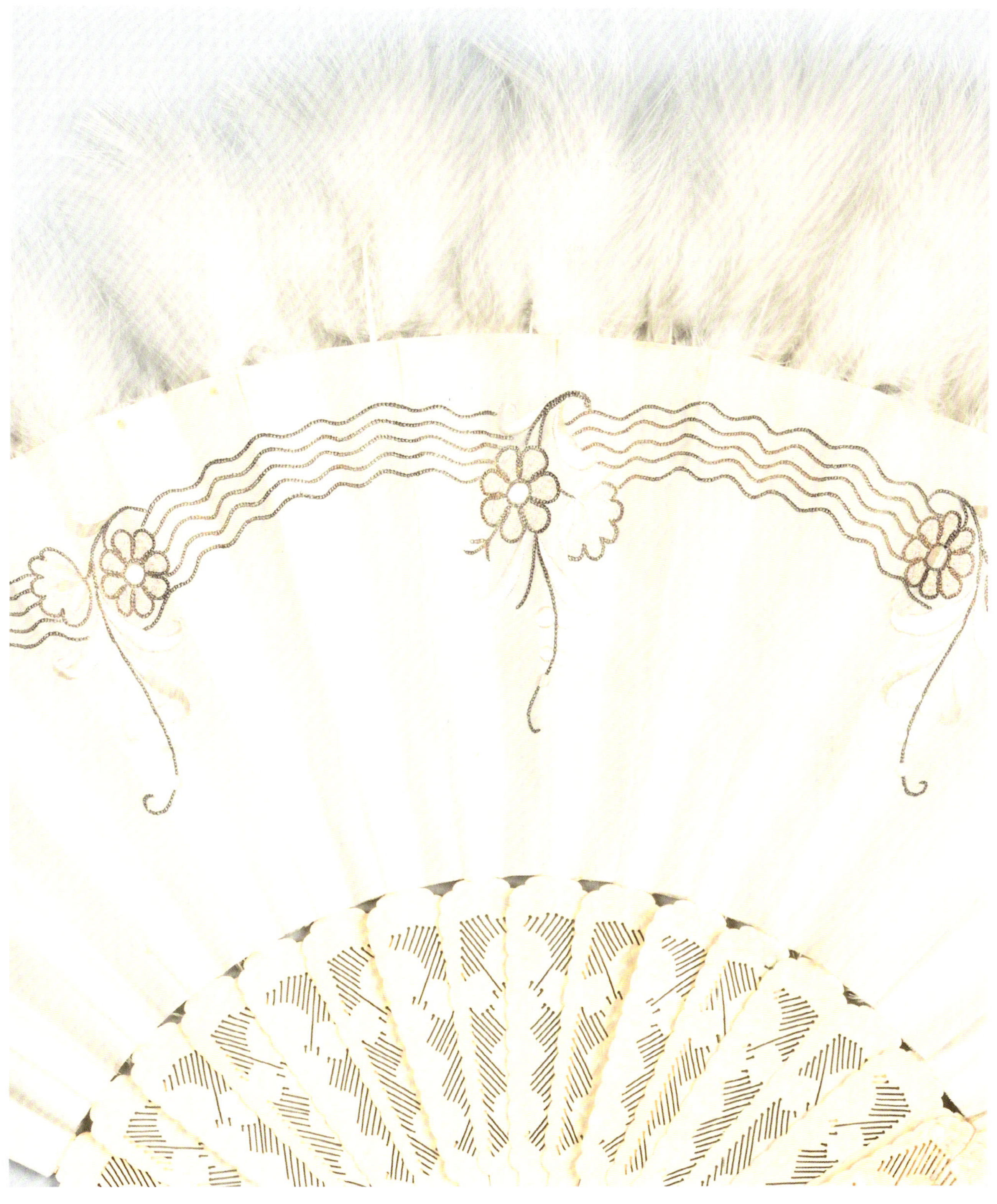

Katsushika Hokusai
„Frau Oiwa" (*Oiwa san*), aus der Serie *Hundert
Geistergeschichten* (*Hyaku monogatari*)
"Mrs. Oiwa" (*Oiwa san*), from the series *One
Hundred Ghost Stories* (*Hyaku monogatari*)
Japan, 1818–1830
Farbholzschnitt, Tusche und Farbe auf Papier
Color woodblock print, ink, and color on paper
24,6 × 18,5
MAK, KI 11038

Dieses Blatt wurde vom berühmten Ukiyoe-Künstler Katsushika Hokusai geschaffen. Es zeigt eine der populärsten
Geisterfiguren aus den Gruselgeschichten Japans, Frau
Oiwa. Von ihrem grausamen Ehemann zuerst betrogen und
dann vergiftet, erscheint Frau Oiwa ihrem Gatten als Geist.
Hokusai bedeckte ihr durch das Gift entstelltes Gesicht
mit einer zerrissenen gefalteten Papierlaterne.

This picture was created by the famous *ukiyoe* artist Katsushika Hokusai. It portrays one of the most popular ghosts
in Japanese horror stories: Mrs. Oiwa. Cheated, then poi-
soned, by her cruel husband, Mrs. Oiwa appears to the husband as a ghost. Hokusai covers her face, disfigured by the
poison, with a torn folded paper lantern.

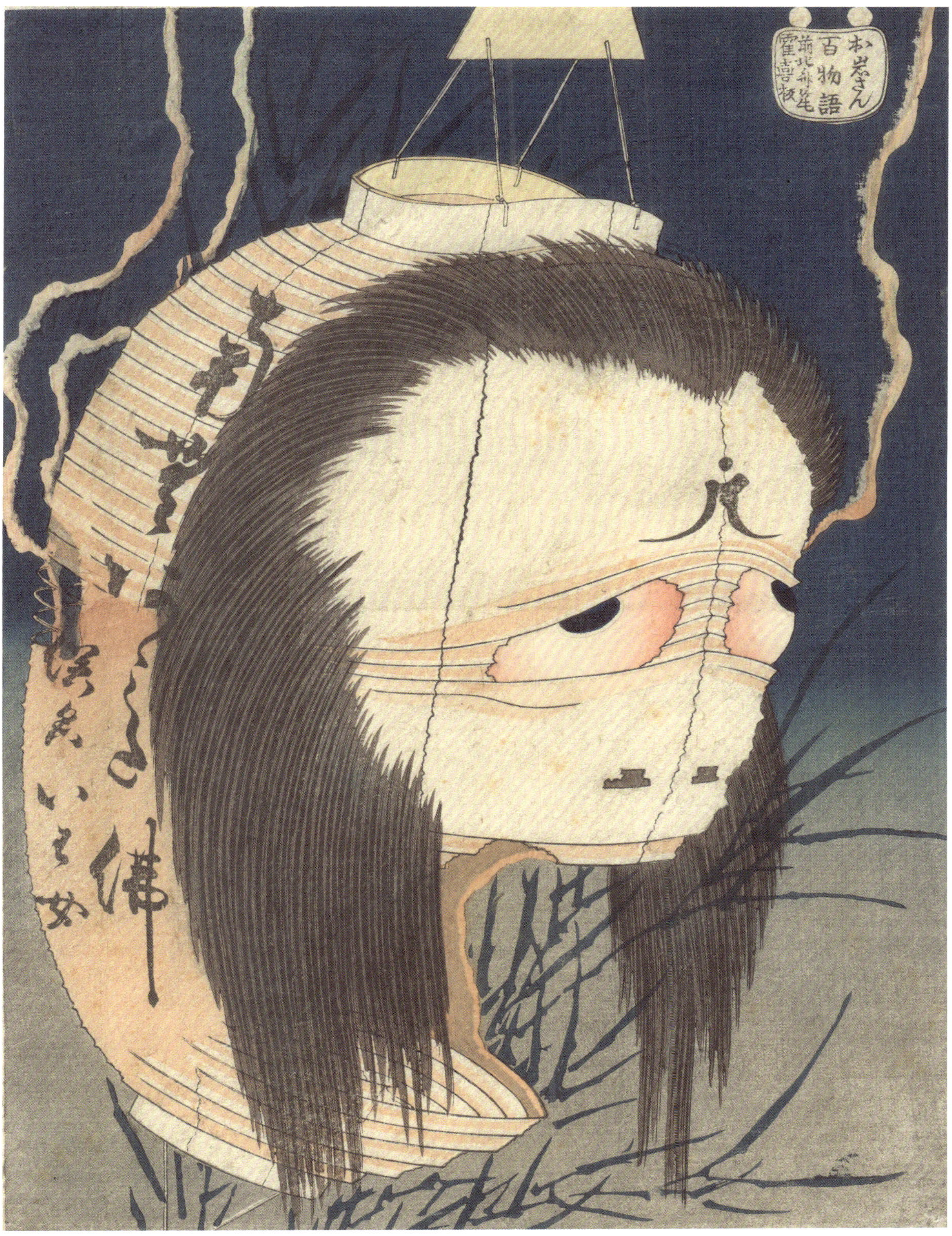

お岩さん
百物語
前北斎筆
雷奮校

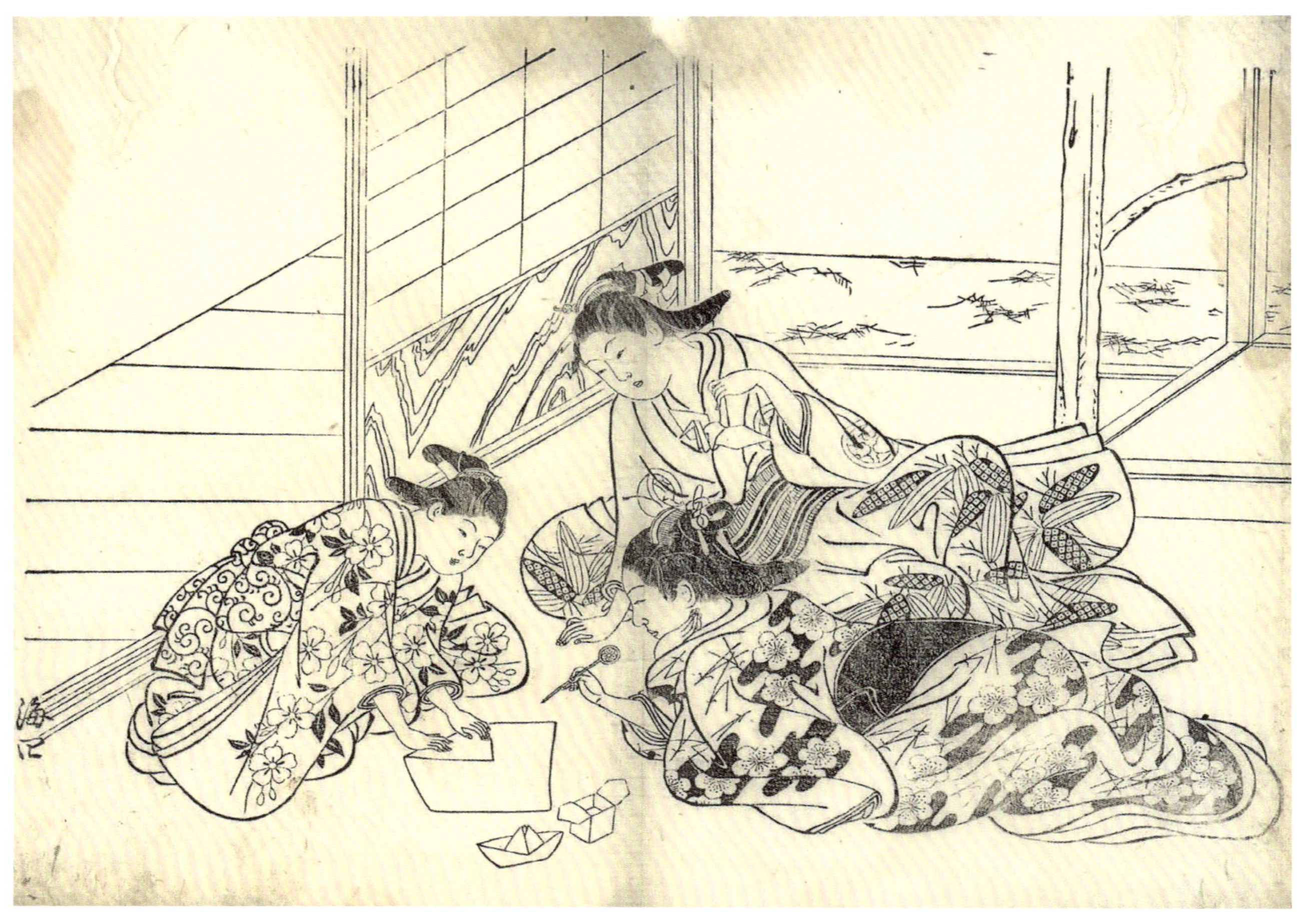

Hishikawa Moronobu (?)
Origami-Falten
Folding origami
Japan, 1. Hälfte 18. Jh. 1st half 18th c.
Holzschnitt, Tusche auf Papier
Woodblock print, ink on paper
26 × 36,9
MAK, KI 10812

Das Falten von Papier ist eine alte, weltweit verbreitete Kulturtechnik, die in Europa wohl seit dem 17. Jahrhundert praktiziert wird. Etwa Mitte des 19. Jahrhunderts wurde es von Friedrich Fröbel (1782–1852) in sein reformpädagogisches Konzept integriert.

In Japan, wo die Technik der Papierherstellung im 7. Jahrhundert aus China eingeführt worden war, war das Papierfalten zunächst nur sozial Höhergestellten als Teil ihrer rituell-zeremoniellen Praxis vorbehalten. Gegen Ende des 17. Jahrhunderts wurde die Technik schließlich auch in breiteren Bevölkerungsschichten und bei Kindern und Erwachsenen populär. Im Bestseller *Kōshoku ichidai otoko* [Das Leben eines verliebten Mannes] (1682) von Ihara Saikaku (1642–1693) kommt das Papierfalten als Topos vor.

Hier sind zwei bekannte Beispiele für japanische Farbholzschnitte zu sehen, die das Falten von Papier zum Thema machen.

Ippitsusai Bunchō
Geisha, einen Kranich faltend
Geisha folding a crane
Japan, ca. 1766
Farbholzschnitt, Farbe und Tusche auf Papier
Color woodblock print, paint, and ink on paper
29,6 × 14
MAK, KI 11230

Paperfolding is a primordial cultural technique that may be found throughout the world and has been practiced in Europe since the 17th century. In the mid-19th century Friedrich Fröbel (1782–1852) integrated paperfolding into his reformist educational program.
In Japan, where the technique of paper manufacturing was introduced from China in the 7th century, paper folding was at first restricted to the upper-classes and was integral to their ceremonial rituals and practices. Around the end of the 17th century, the technique finally became popular among a broader public, including both adults and children. Paperfolding is a theme in the 1682 bestseller *Kōshoku ichidai otoko* [The Life of a Man in Love] by Ihara Saikaku (1642–1693).
Here are two well-known examples of Japanese color woodblock prints on the theme of paperfolding.

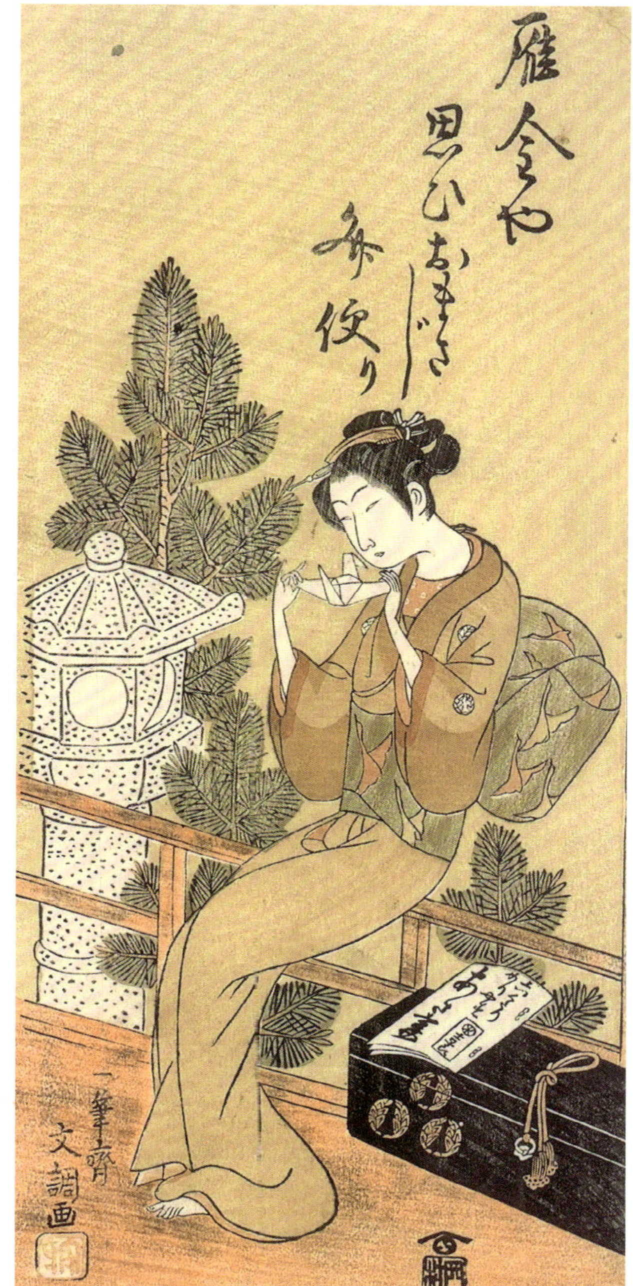

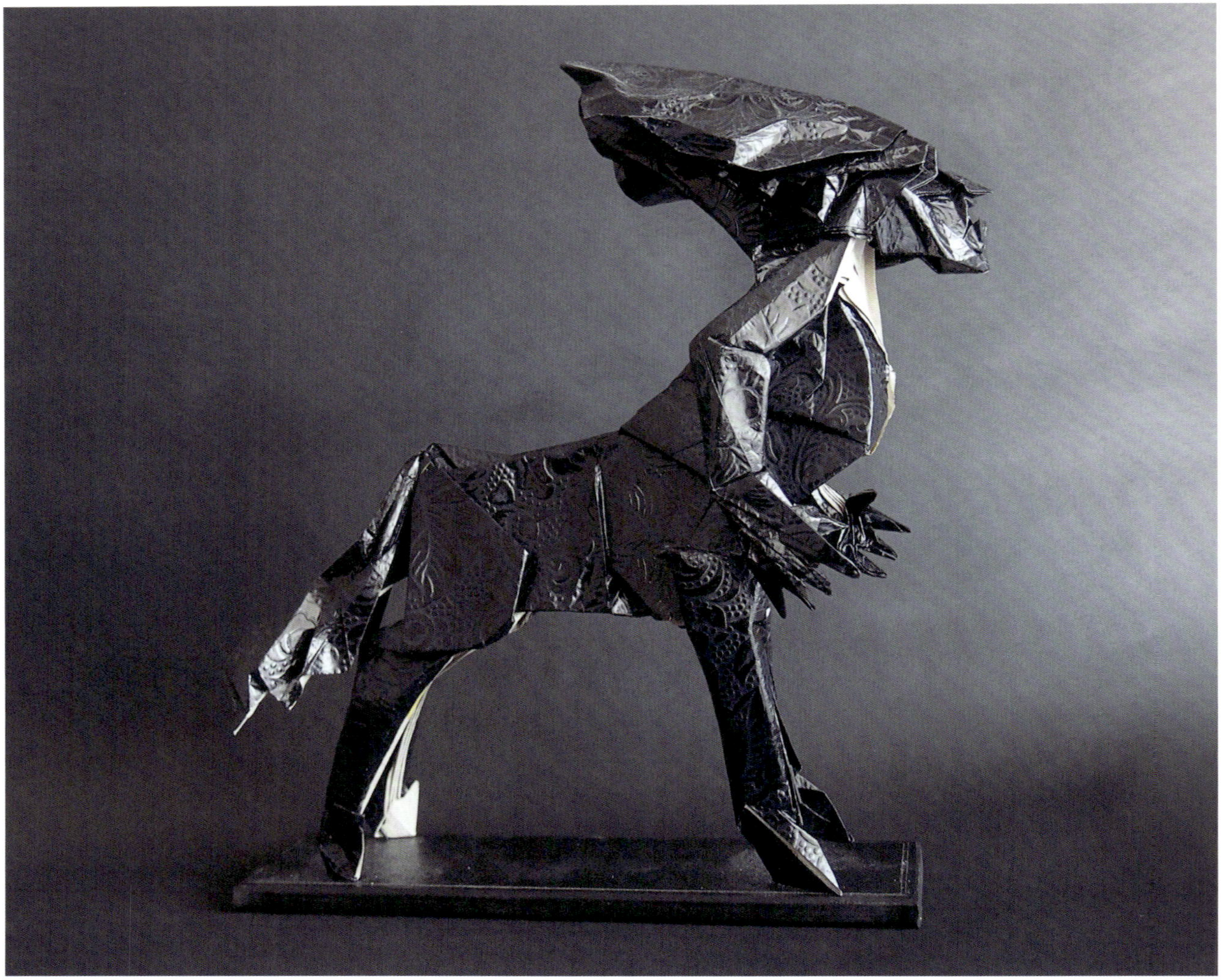

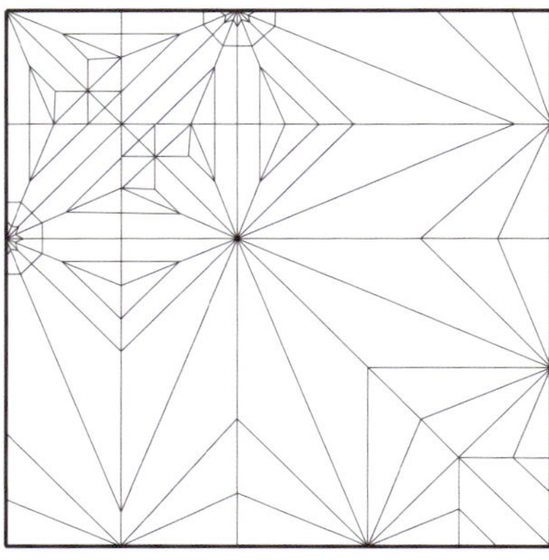

Nishida Shatner

Centaurus
Japan, 2021
urushi-Lackpapier *urushi* paper
36 × 14 × 26

Alien (H. R. Giger)
Japan, 2020
urushi-Lackpapier *urushi* paper
50 × 21 × 33

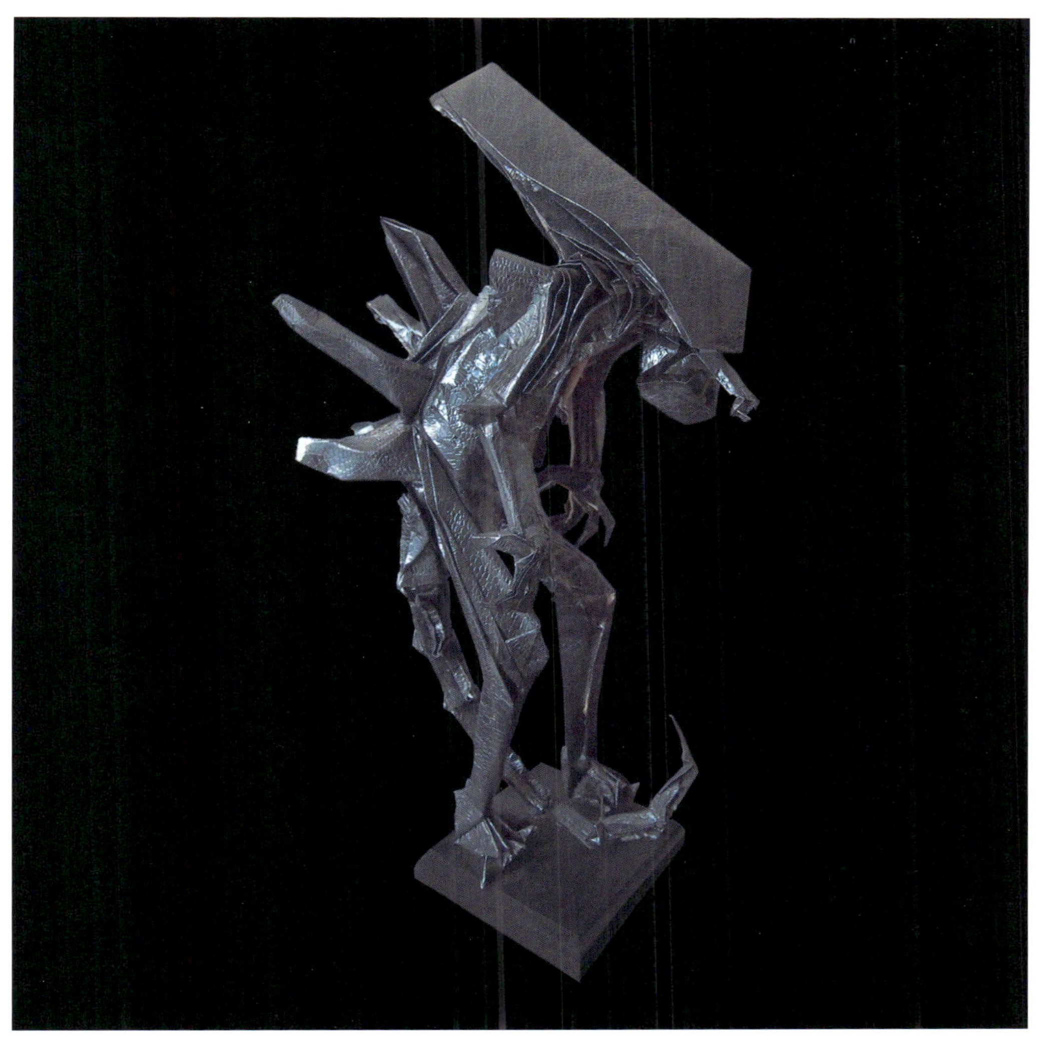

Faltmuster Crease patterns *Centaurus* (links left)
und and *Alien* (rechts right)

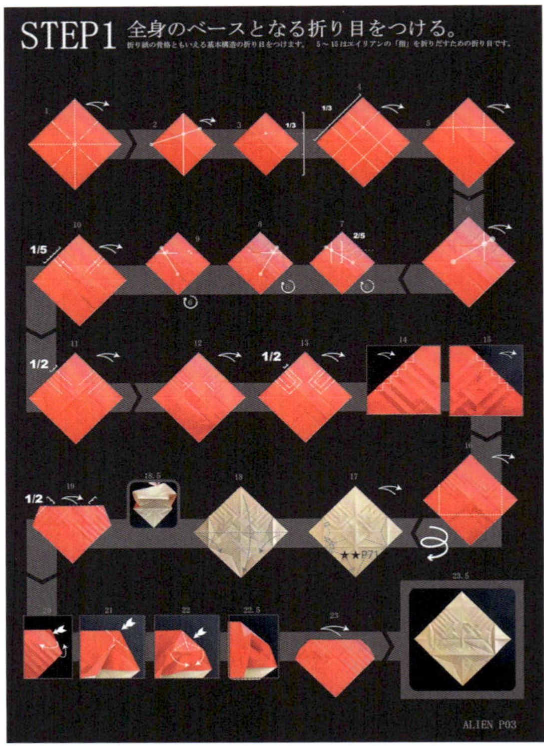

STEP1 全身のベースとなる折り目をつける。

折り紙の骨格ともいえる基本構造の折り目をつけます。　5〜15はエイリアンの「指」を折りだすための折り目です。

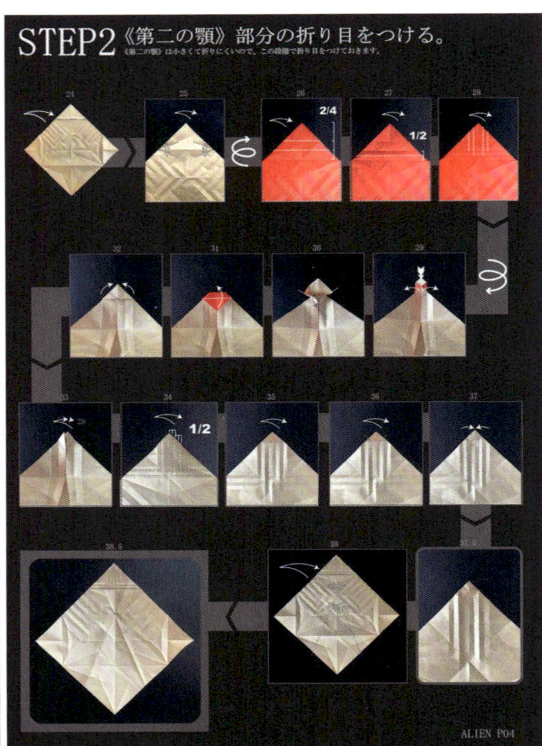

STEP2 《第二の顎》部分の折り目をつける。

《第二の顎》は小さくて折りにくいので、この段階で折り目をつけておきます。

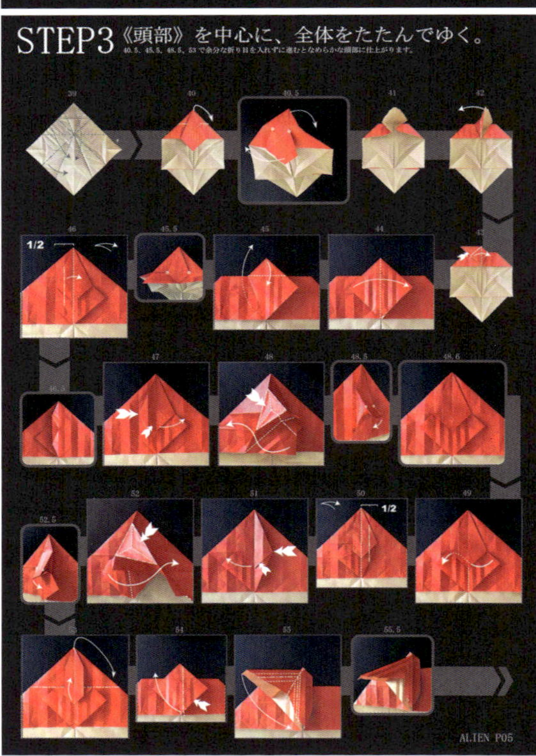

STEP3 《頭部》を中心に、全体をたたんでゆく。

40.5、45.5、48.5、53で余分な折り目を入れずに進むとなめらかな頭部に仕上がります。

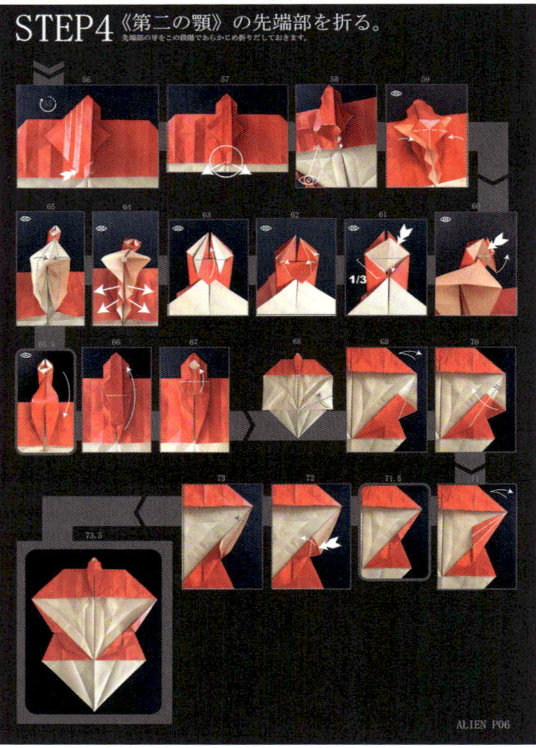

STEP4 《第二の顎》の先端部を折る。

先端部の牙をこの段階であらかじめ折りだしておきます。

Diagramm mit Visualisierung der einzelnen Arbeitsschritte zur Herstellung des Origami-Kunstwerks *Alien* (die Abbildungen zeigen Schritt 1–4 von 16)
Diagram with visualization of the individual work steps to produce the origami artwork *Alien* (the illustrations show steps 1–4 of 16)

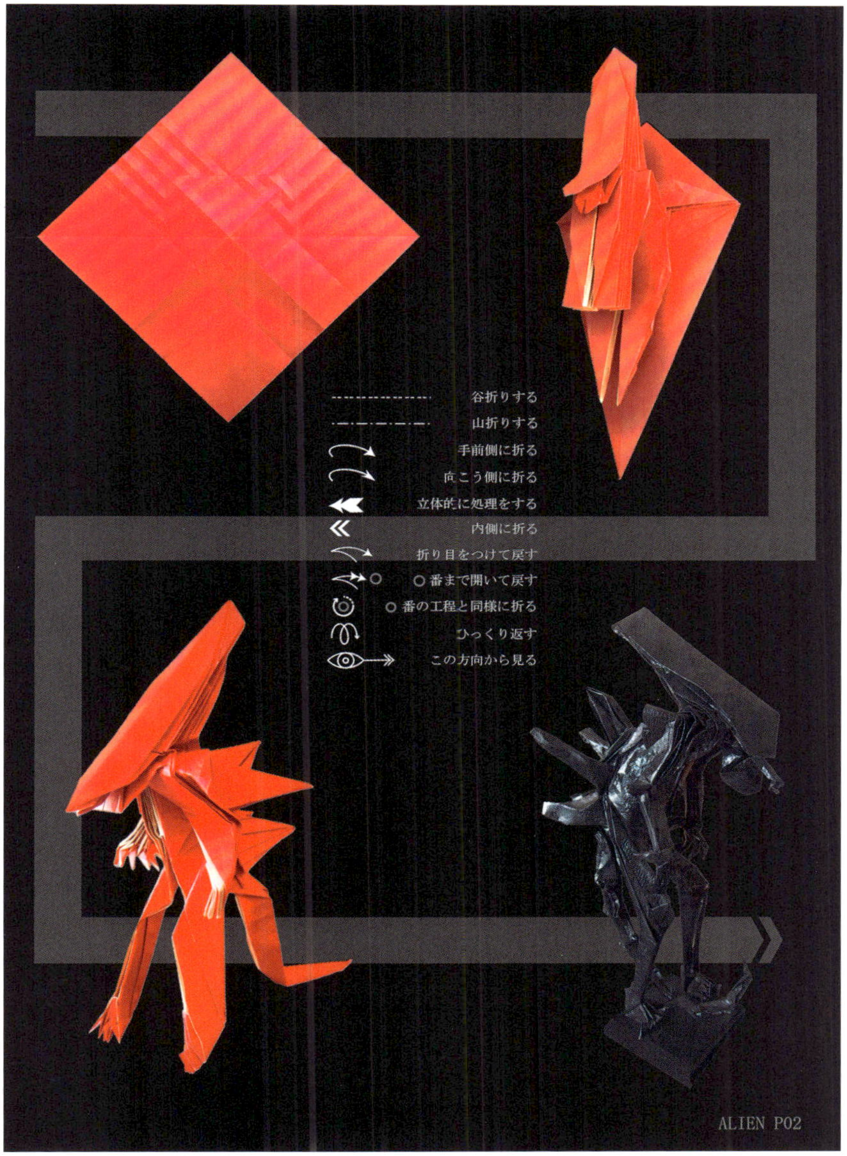

Der Origami-Künstler Nishida Shatner aus Tokyo kreiert zeitgenössische Origami-Werke nach eigenen Entwürfen. Jedes Objekt entsteht aus einem einzigen Blatt Papier, das mehr als einen Quadratmeter groß ist, ohne dass das Papier jemals geschnitten wird. Die hier gezeigten Arbeiten resultieren aus einem mehrwöchigen Entwurfsprozess und einer mehrtägigen praktischen Ausführung, in der Hunderte von Faltungen vorgenommen wurden.

The Tokyo origami artist Nishida Shatner creates contemporary origami works he designs himself. Each object is made out of a single sheet of paper measuring more than one square metre, without the paper ever being cut. The works shown here were designed over several weeks and executed over several days, during which the paper was folded hundreds of times.

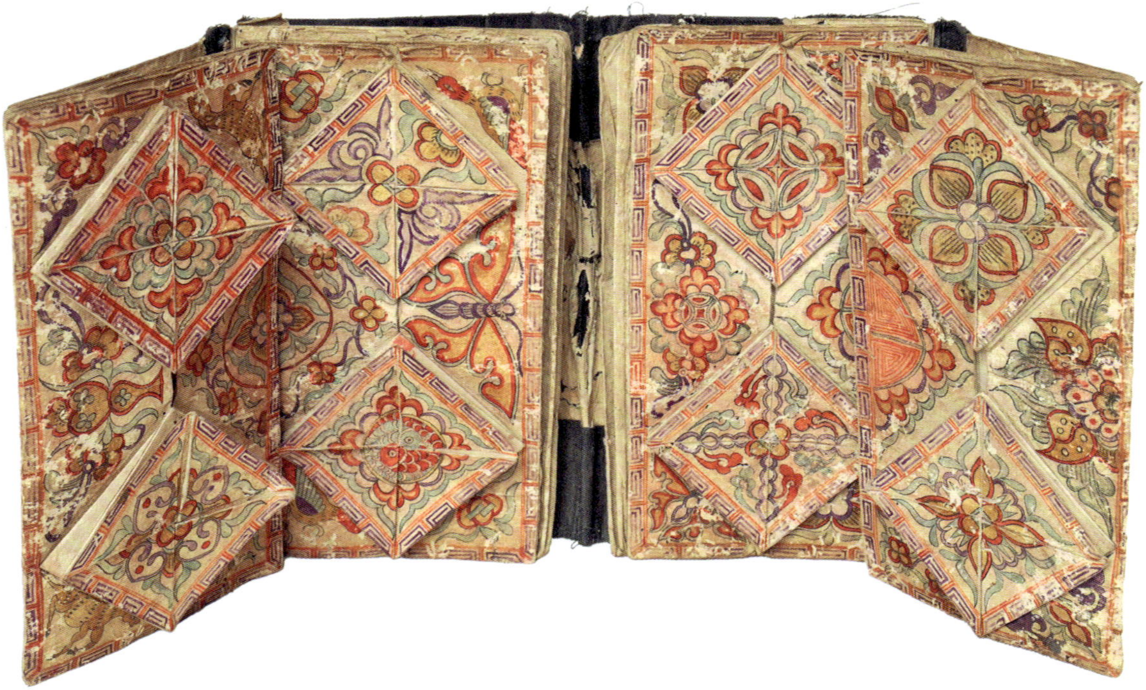

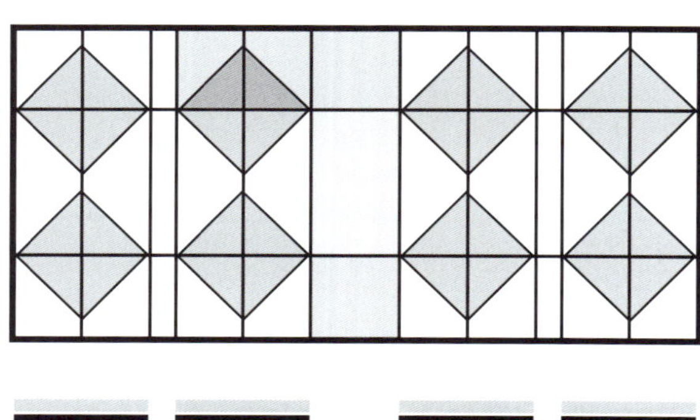

Schema der Anordnung des Zentrums und Querschnitt der Konstruktion Diagram showing the center layout and a cross section of the construction

Dong-Drachenbuch mit 21 Fächern
Dong dragon book with 21 compartments
China, 2008
Handgeschöpftes Papier mit gemaltem Dekor, schwarzer Baumwollbezug aus Twill Handmade paper with painted decoration, black cotton twill cover
66 × 27 (geöffnet open), 27 × 18 (geschlossen closed)
Privatsammlung Private collection

Zhen xian bao („Nadel-Faden-Tasche")
mit 24 Fächern
Zhen xian bao ("needle-and-thread wallet") with 24 compartments
China, 2011
Papier, bedruckter Stoffbezug Paper, printed cloth cover
30 × 86 (geöffnet open), 30 × 21,5 (geschlossen closed)
Privatsammlung Private collection

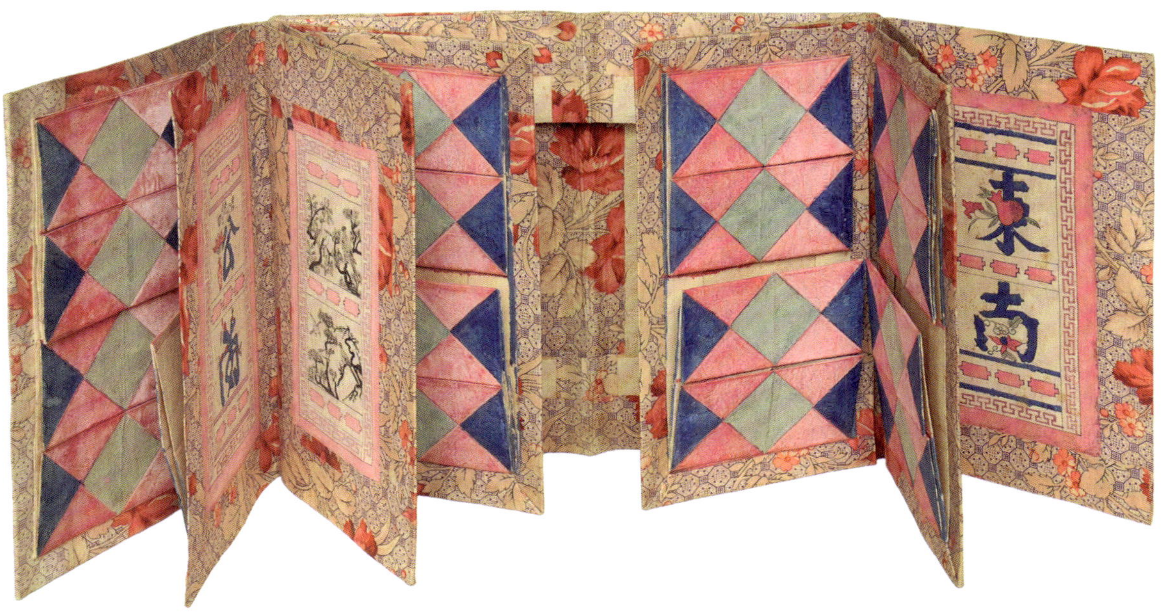

Zhen xian bao sind Faltmappen aus handgeschöpftem, strapazierfähigem Papier, die eine erstaunlich große Anzahl unterschiedlich großer Falttäschchen enthalten. Alle Fächer werden einzeln angefertigt und in mehreren Schichten übereinander geklebt. Öffnet man eine obere Lage, so öffnet sich auch das darunter liegende Fach. Das funktioniert auf mehreren Ebenen.

Diese Papier-Etuis aus gefaltetem Papier wurden von chinesischen Minderheiten aus den ländlichen, gebirgigen Provinzen Yunnan und Guizhou im Südwesten Chinas sowie im Nordosten Chinas hergestellt. Sie dienen der Aufbewahrung von kleinen Alltagsgegenständen sowie Nähzubehör wie Nadeln und Fäden, mit denen Festtracht bestickt wird. In der Provinz Guizhou wurden diese Mappen in der landwirtschaftlichen Nebensaison auch von Männern hergestellt, die sie dann auf dem Markt verkauften oder auch als Verlobungsgeschenk überreichten.

Zhen xian bao are folded wallets constructed of durable hand-made paper that contain an astonishingly large number of different-sized pockets organized in layers. The pockets are individually made and then stuck together to form the layers. If one opens an uppermost layer, the pocket underneath opens too. The wallet functions thus through its several layers.

These folded paper wallets are made by ethnic minorities in the rural mountainous districts of Yunnan and Guizhou in southwestern China as well as in the northwest of the country. They serve to store sewing accessories such as needles and thread used to embroider festive costumes or small objects of everyday use. In the province of Guizhou, men also made these wallets in the agricultural off-season, selling them at markets or giving them as betrothal gifts.

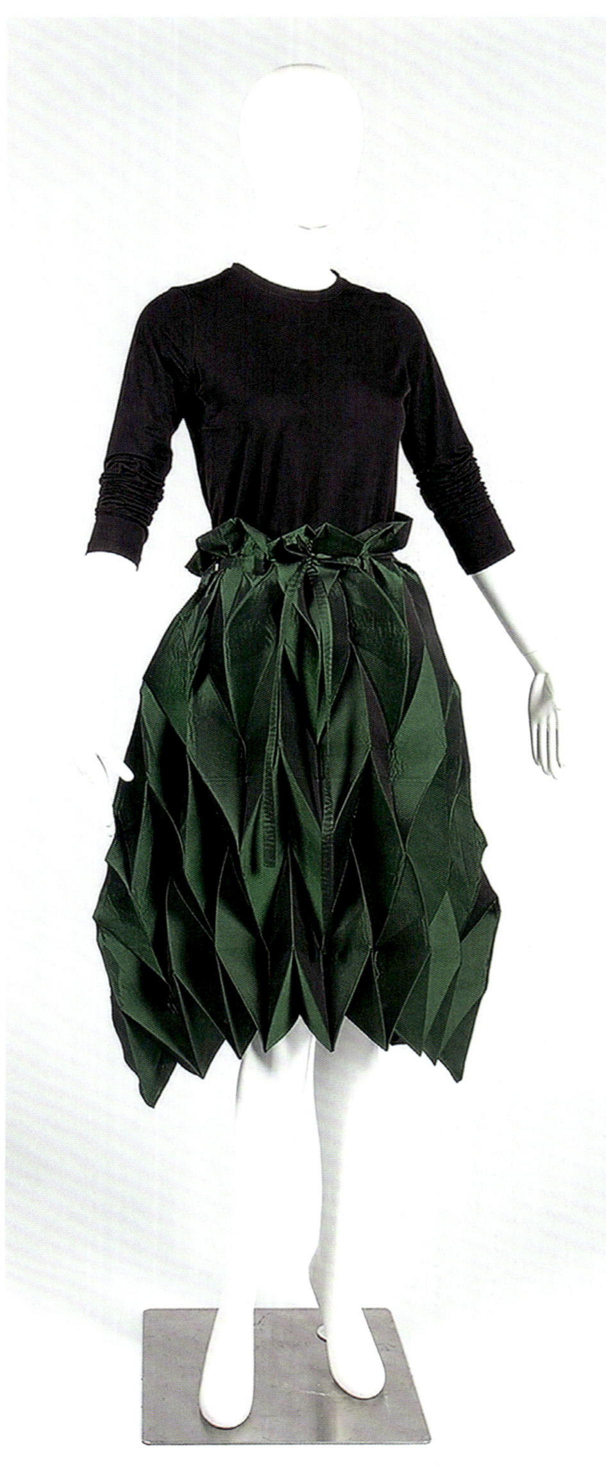

Fujiwara Dai
Rock aus der Kollektion *ISSEY MIYAKE FÊTE*
Skirt from the *ISSEY MIYAKE FÊTE* collection
2007
Polyester
H 68 × 7 (gefaltet folded)
Privatsammlung Private collection

Issey Miyake (1938–2022), bekannt für seine skulpturalen Modedesigns, hat die Tradition des Plissierens neu interpretiert. Ideenreich eingesetzte Plissiertechniken ermöglichen dramatische Silhouetten und fließende Bewegungen des Stoffs, der den Körper der Träger*innen umspielt.
Issey Miyake ließ Kunststoff aus speziell für ihn entwickelten Kunstfasern mit einer Wärmepresse bearbeiten, sodass dauerhafte Falten entstehen. Während Kleidungsstücke traditionell aus bereits plissiertem Stoff gefertigt werden, machte es Issey Miyake genau andersrum: Erst nach der Fertigstellung des Kleidungsstückes wird es plissiert. Durch diese Methode werden Falten nicht mehr mit Nähten, sondern mit einer Wärmepresse erzeugt. Miyakes Experimente mit Falten begründeten seinen Durchbruch als innovativer Designer.

Issey Miyake (1938–2022), famed for his sculptural fashion designs, has reinterpreted the art of pleating. Imaginative pleating techniques enable the creation of dramatic silhouettes combined with the fluid movement of material around the wearer's body.
Using a heating press, Issey Miyake created permanent folds in a plastic material composed of synthetic fibers specially manufactured to his requirements. Whereas clothes are traditionally made of already pleated material, Issey Miyake takes the opposite approach: only after the piece of clothing is finished is it pleated, folds being created not by sewing seams but, precisely, by using a heating press. Miyake's experiments with pleating established his reputation as an innovative designer.

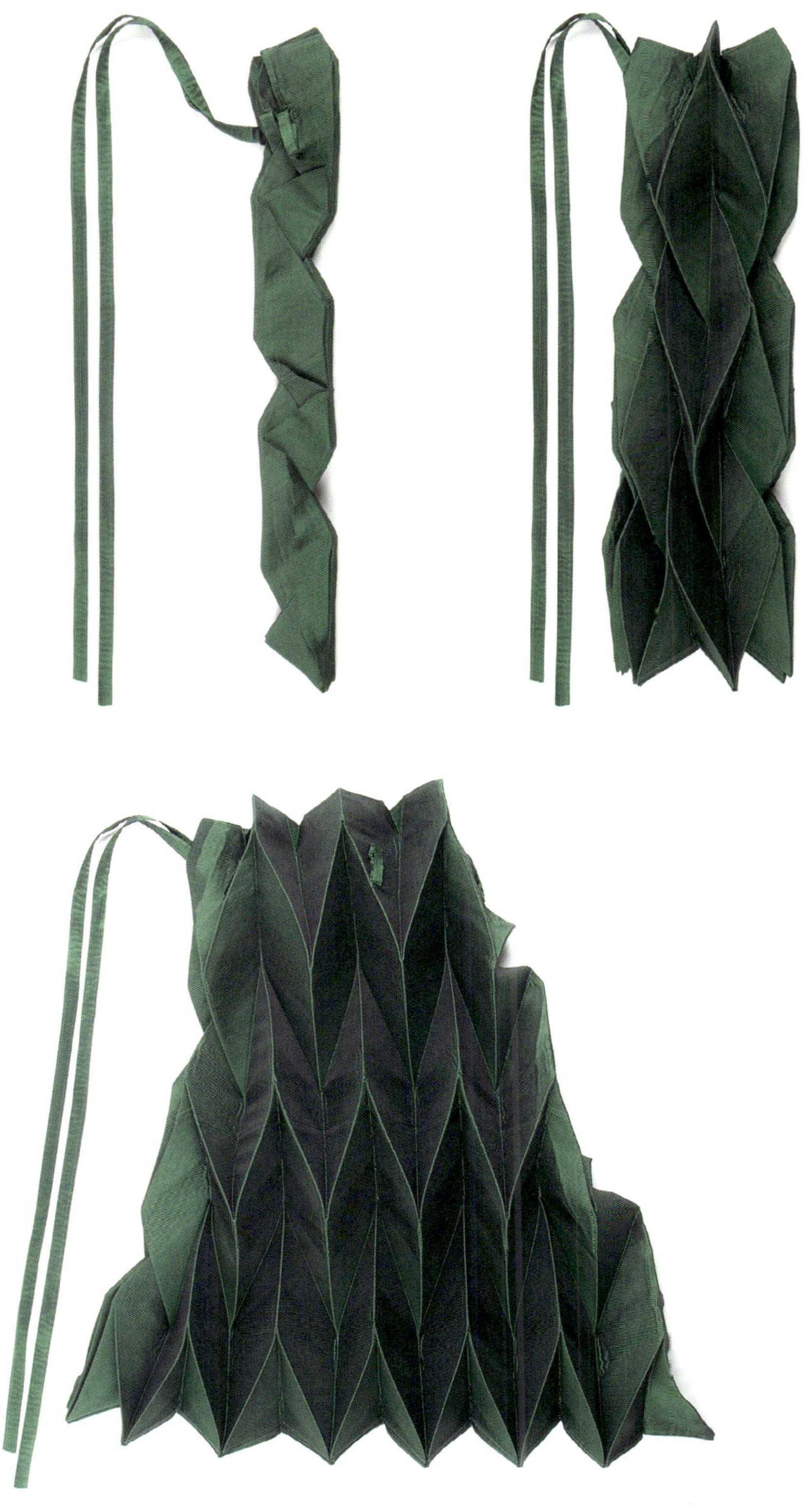

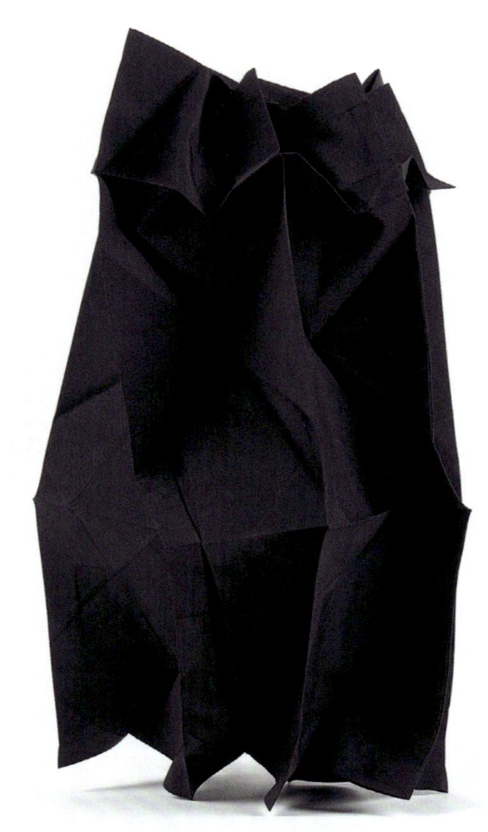

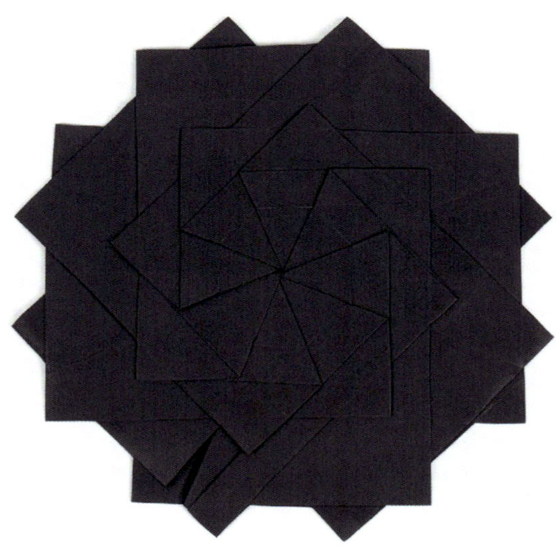

Issey Miyake/Reality Lab.
No. 3 (Shirt) aus der Kollektion
132 5. ISSEY MIYAKE
No. 3 (Shirt) from the
132 5. ISSEY MIYAKE collection
2010/2015
Polyester
ø 35,5
Privatsammlung Private collection

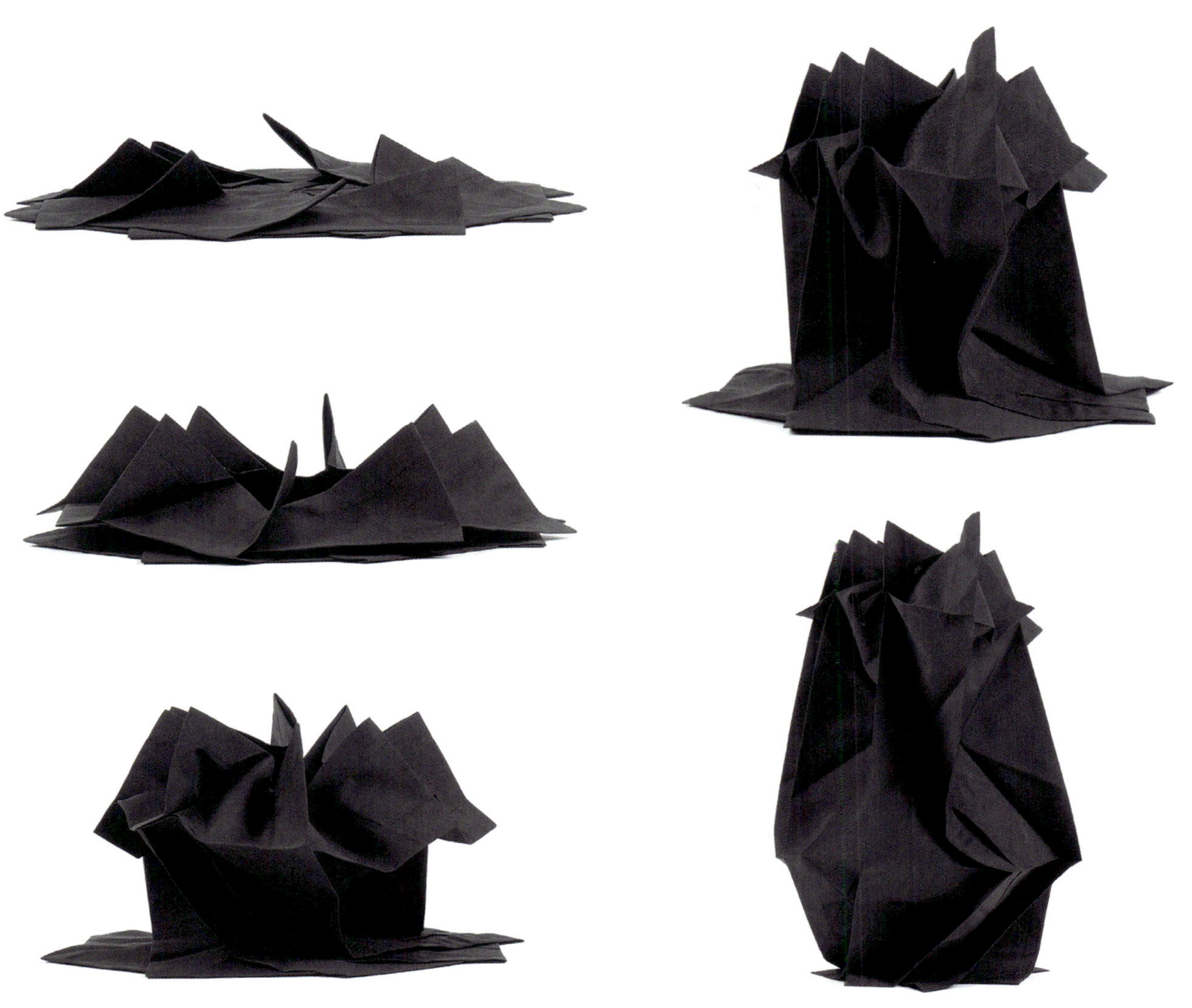

Issey Miyakes Kollektion *132 5* bewegt sich an der Schnittstelle zwischen Mathematik und Mode. In Zusammenarbeit mit einem Informatik-Forscher beschäftigte sich Miyake mit dem Konzept, aus einem Stück Stoff ein dreidimensionales Kleidungsstück zu schaffen, das sich in eine flache, zweidimensionale Form falten lässt. Aus einem nach dem Origami-Prinzip geometrisch gefalteten Stück Stoff entfalten sich Taschen, Röcke, Jacken, Kleider, Blusen oder Hosen mit skulpturaler Faltenoptik.

Issey Miyake's *132 5* collection exists on the interface between mathematics and fashion. In cooperation with a computer science researcher, Miyake worked on creating a three-dimensional piece of clothing from a piece of material that could be folded into a flat, two-dimensional form. From a piece of material geometrically folded according to the principles of origami, bags, skirts, jackets, dresses, blouses, and trousers unfold with pleated sculptural elegance.

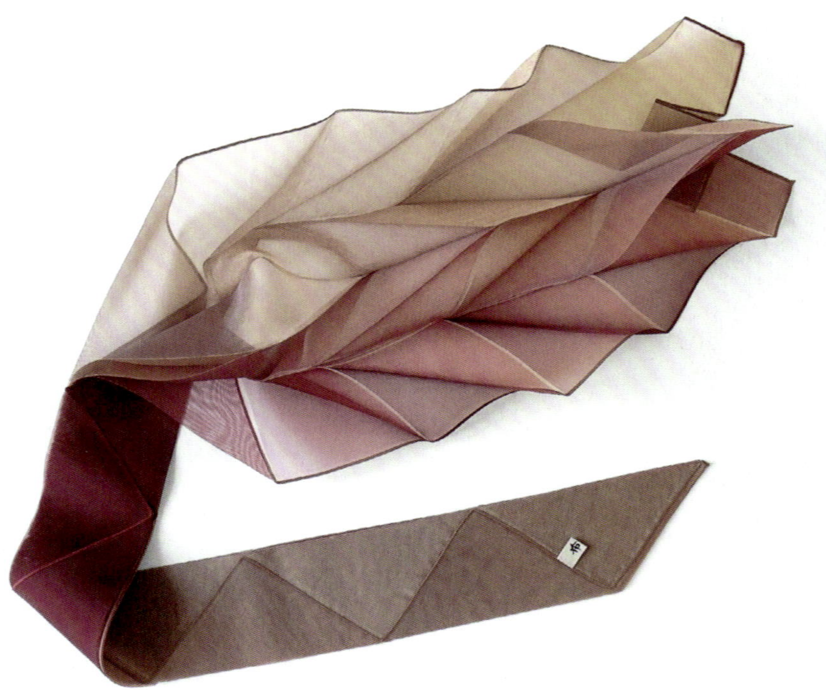

Sudō Reiko
Origami Pleat Scarf
1997
Polyester, plissiert, bedruckt
Polyester, pleated, printed
114 × 42
MAK, T 14618

Ursi Fürtler
Bluebird
2013
Seide, plissiert, bedruckt
Silk, pleated, printed
105 × 27
MAK, T 14917

Die Beschaffenheit von Stofffalten kann sehr unterschiedlich sein, so auch die Nuancen, die sich aus ihrer künstlerischen Interpretation ergeben.
Sudō Reikos *Origami Pleat Scarf* zeigt die skulpturale Qualität eines dreidimensionalen Objekts mit polygonalen Facetten. Dadurch, dass der Stoff in Origami-Technik gefaltet und beidseitig bedruckt ist – eine Seite dunkelrot, die andere beige – entstehen raffinierte Farbverläufe.
Ursi Fürtlers Schal *Bluebird* greift die dreidimensionale Qualität von plissiertem Stoff anders auf, indem sie nur die äußeren Kanten der Falten bedruckt. Durch die unterschiedlich positionierte Struktur des Stoffes ergeben sich Muster-, Kompositions- und Farbvarianten, je nachdem, wie die Plissees auf- oder zugefaltet werden.

The composition of pleated materials can differ greatly, as can the nuances of artistic interpretation to which they give rise.
Sudō Reiko's *Origami Pleat Scarf* manifests the sculptural quality of a three-dimensional object with polygonal facets. The material is folded according to the principles of origami and printed on both sides—one side being dark red and the other beige—creating sophisticated color gradients.
Ursi Fürtler's scarf *Bluebird* makes different use of the three-dimensional quality of pleated material by printing only the outer edges of the pleats. The diversely positioned structure of the material creates variations in pattern, composition, and color depending on whether the pleats are closed or unfolded.

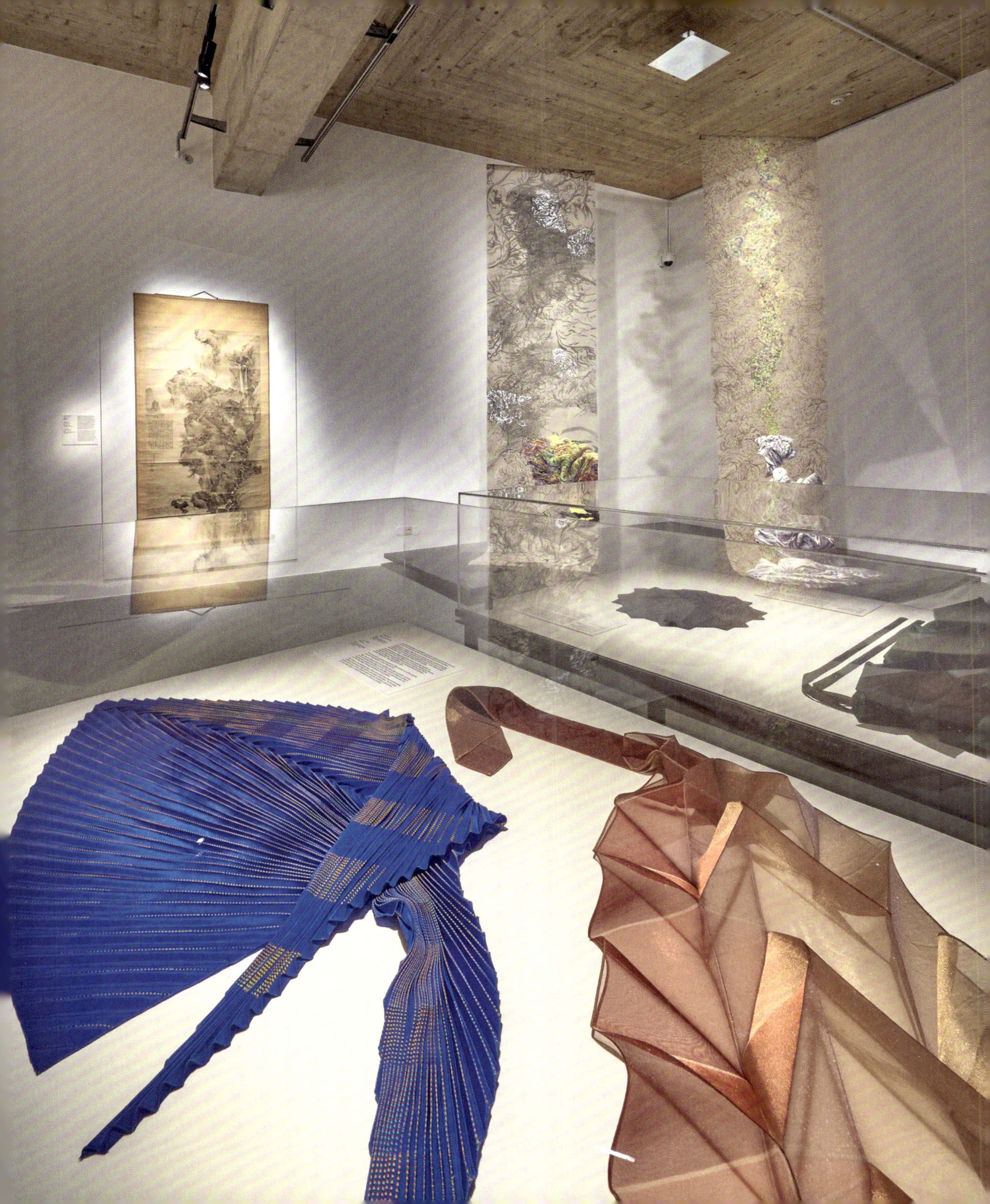

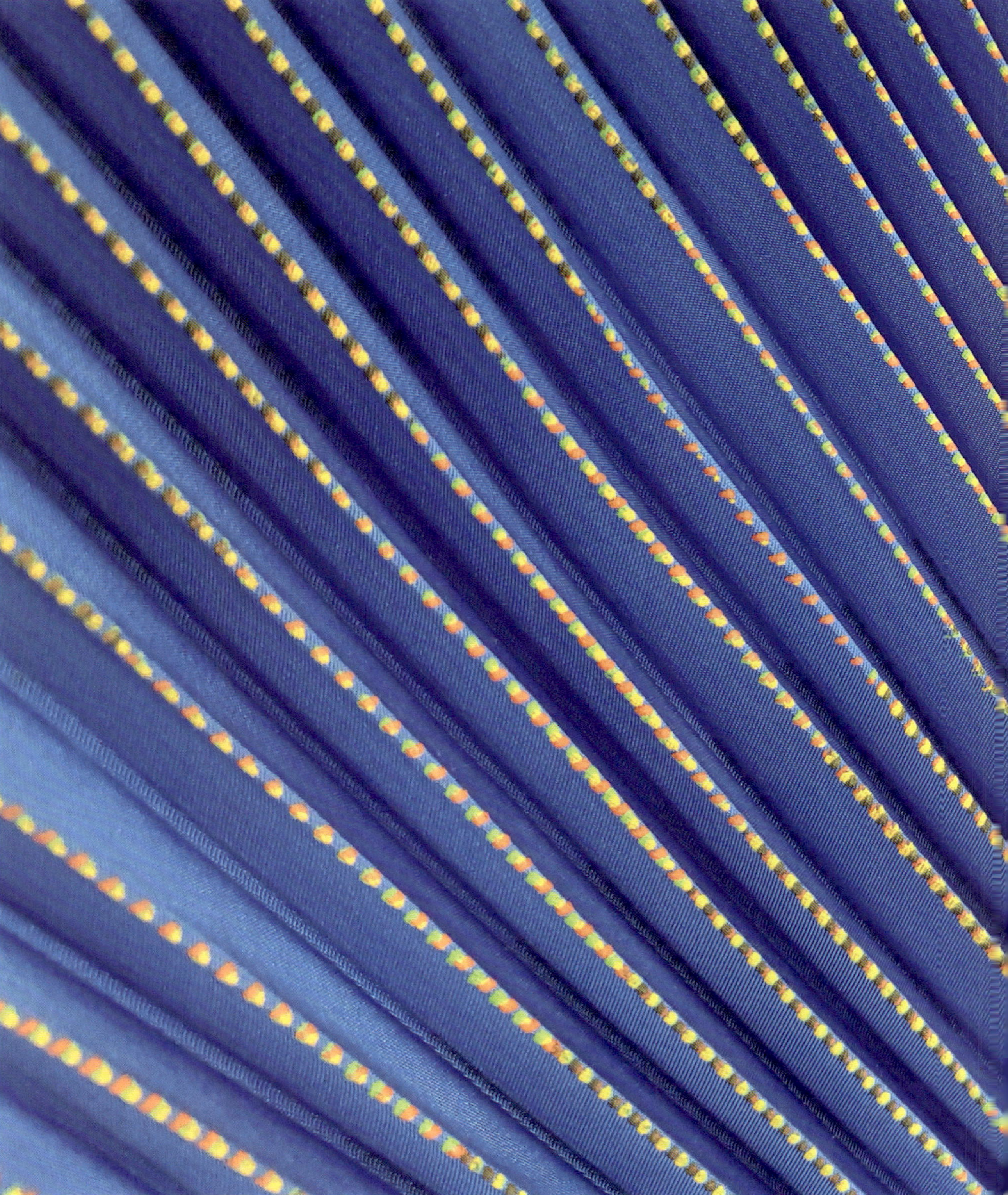

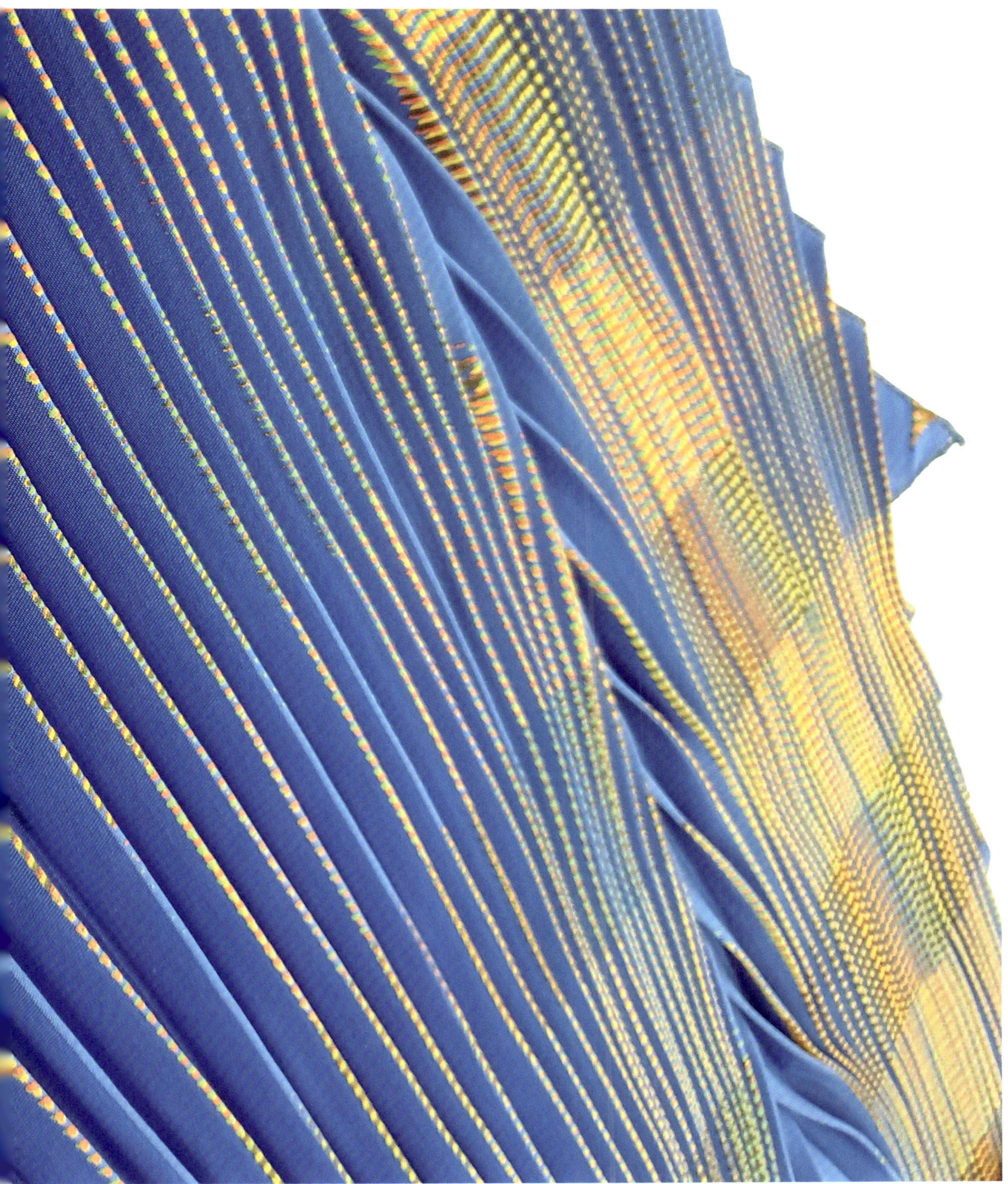

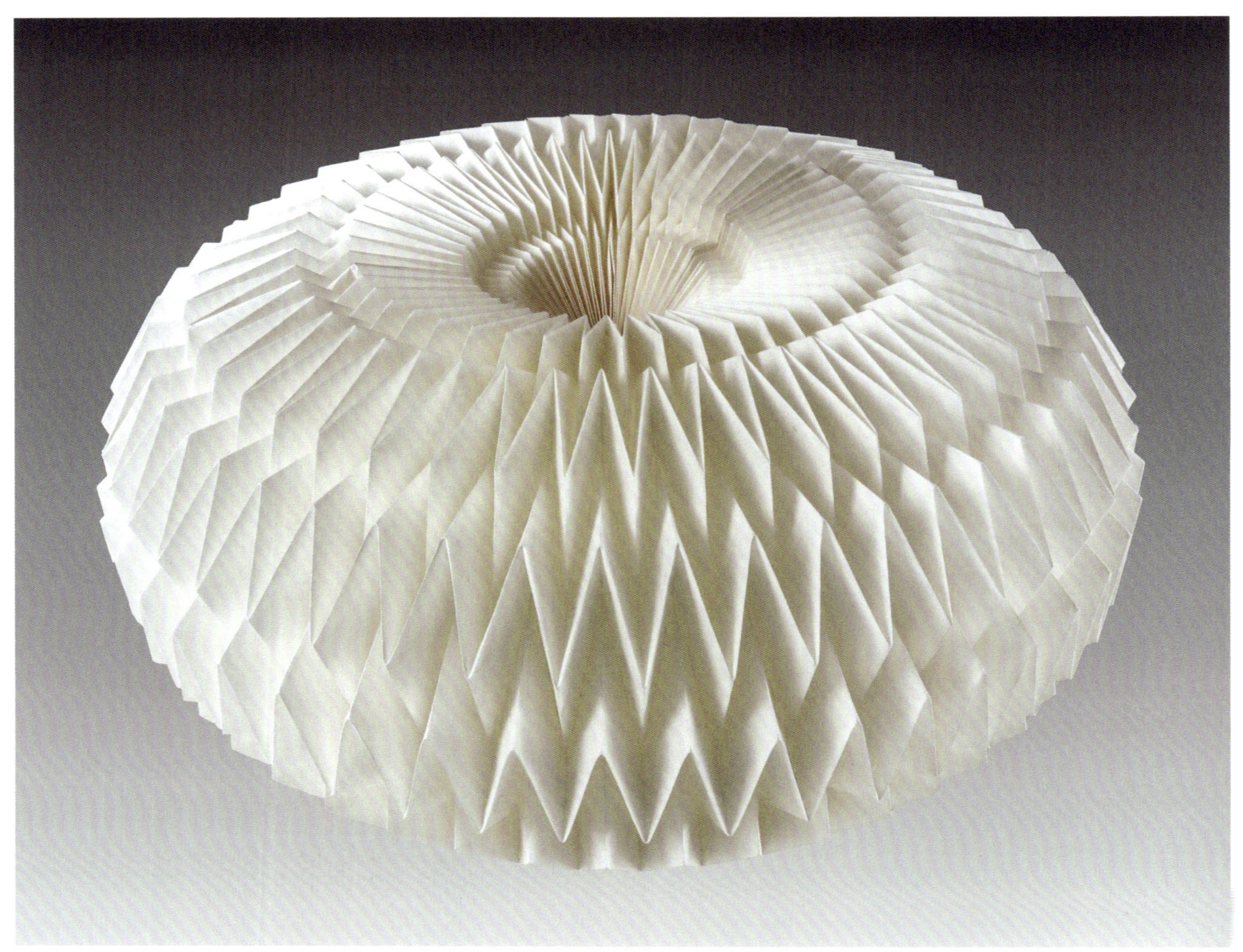

Fuse Tomoko

Coil Fold – Turnip
2014
Shoji-Papier Shoji paper
ø 50, H 25

Biribiri 6/12/36
2015
Westliches Papier Western paper
30 × 27

Privatsammlung Private collection

Fuse Tomoko gilt als eine der weltweit führenden Origami-Künstler*innen. Ihr Schaffen orientiert sich an geometrischen Formen und weist durch Berührungspunkte mit weiteren Feldern wie Mathematik und Design über den rein gestalterischen Aspekt hinaus.
Ihre in der Wickel-Falttechnik angefertigten Zylinder sind äußerst biegsam und können beliebig auseinander- und zusammengezogen werden. Die Struktur der Falten stützt das dreidimensional geformte Papier und stabilisiert das Ganze ohne innere Stütze.
Bei diesen Arbeiten sind zwei unterschiedliche Zylinder-Varianten in Spiral-Falttechnik (*coil fold*) im Spiel. Ihre Ä -

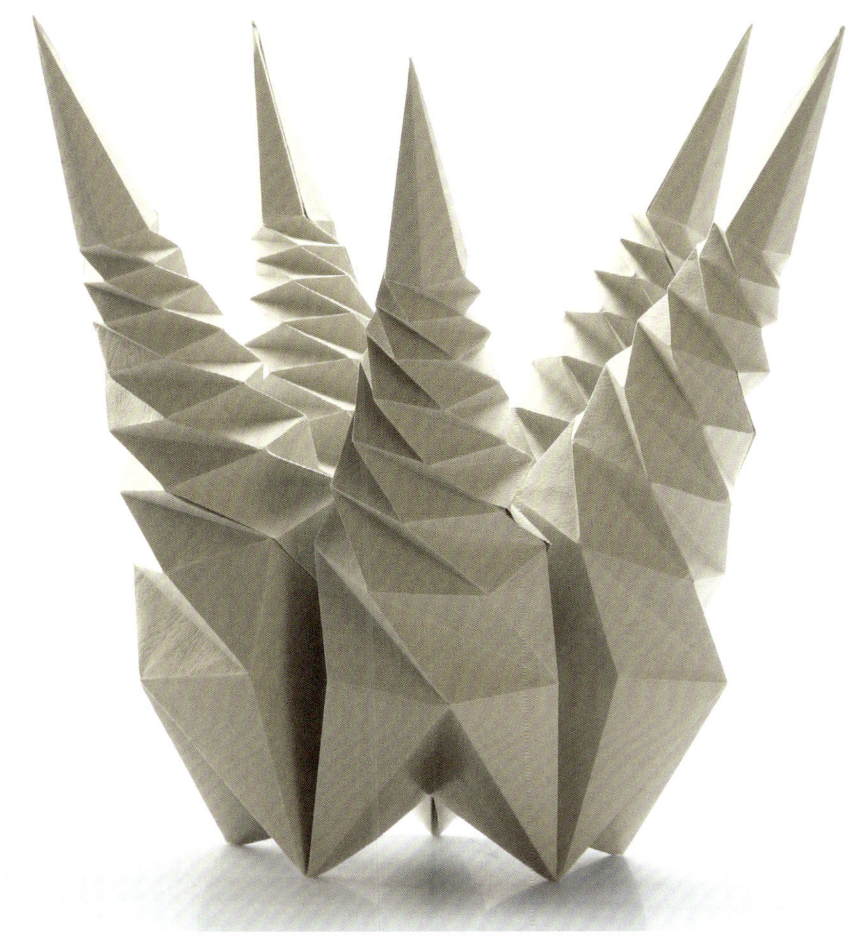

thetik und ihr Formenspiel verändern sich im geöffneten Zustand. Mit der raffinierten Weiterentwicklung der sogenannten Whirlpool-Spiral-Falttechnik erschafft Fuse eine bemerkenswerte vieleckige Struktur. Ihre *Biribiri*-Objekte, bestehend aus mehreren dieser Vielecke, sind nach ihrem eindrucksvollen Erscheinungsbild benannt – sie erinnern an elektrische Blitze.

Fuse Tomoko is considered one of the world's leading origami artists. Her creations are based on geometrical forms and, through their links with fields such as mathematics and design, are more than purely works of art.

Created using a wrap-and-fold technique, her cylinders are extremely flexible and can be extended and compressed at will. The structure of the folds reinforces each three-dimensional paper cylinder and stabilizes it without interior supports.

These works feature two different varieties of cylinder made using the coil fold technique. Their formal aesthetics changes playfully when they are extended. By refining the so-called whirlpool-spiral technique, Fuse creates a remarkable polygonal structure. Her *biribiri* objects, consisting of several of these polygonals, are named for their impressive appearance—they are reminiscent of lightning flashes.

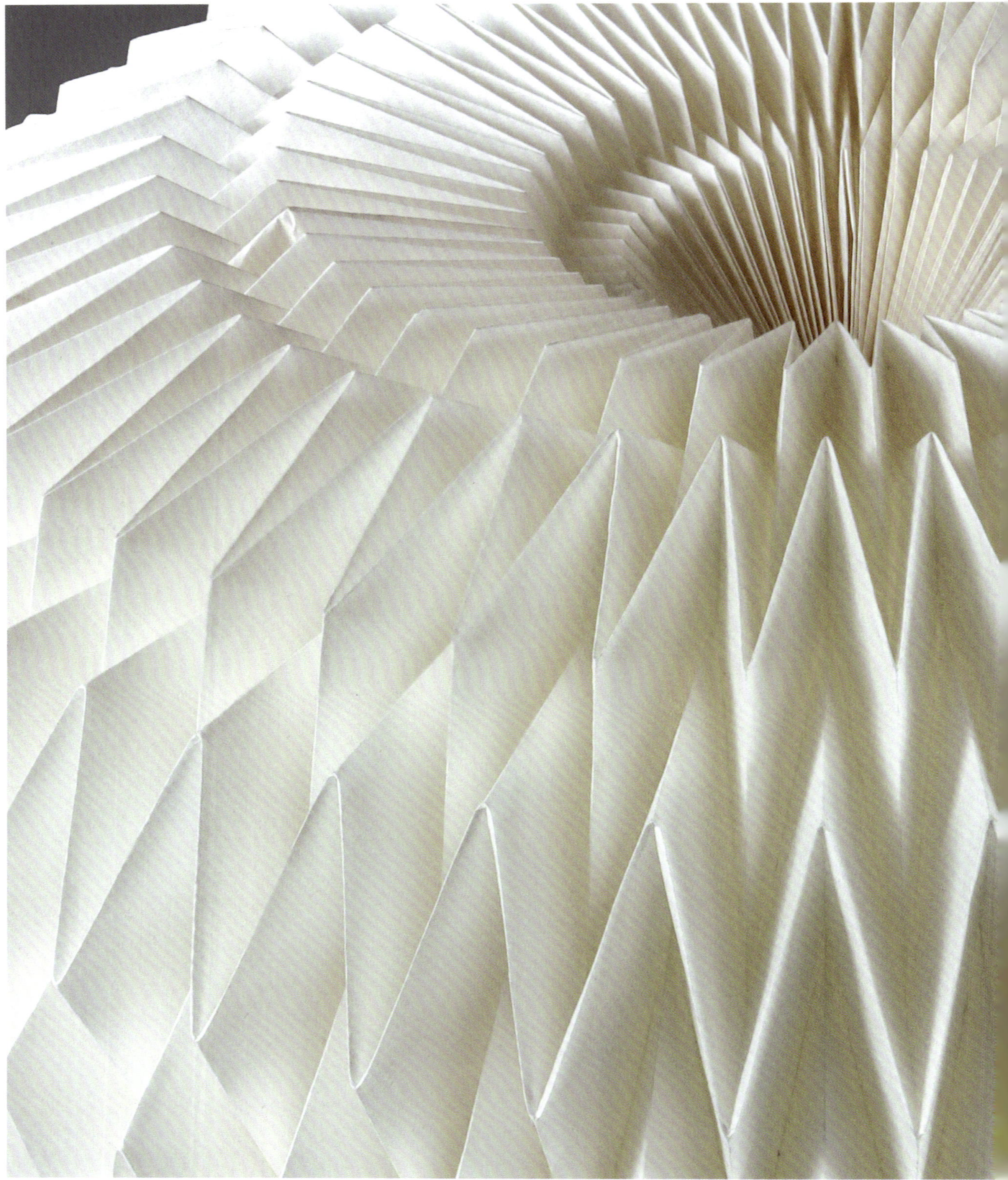

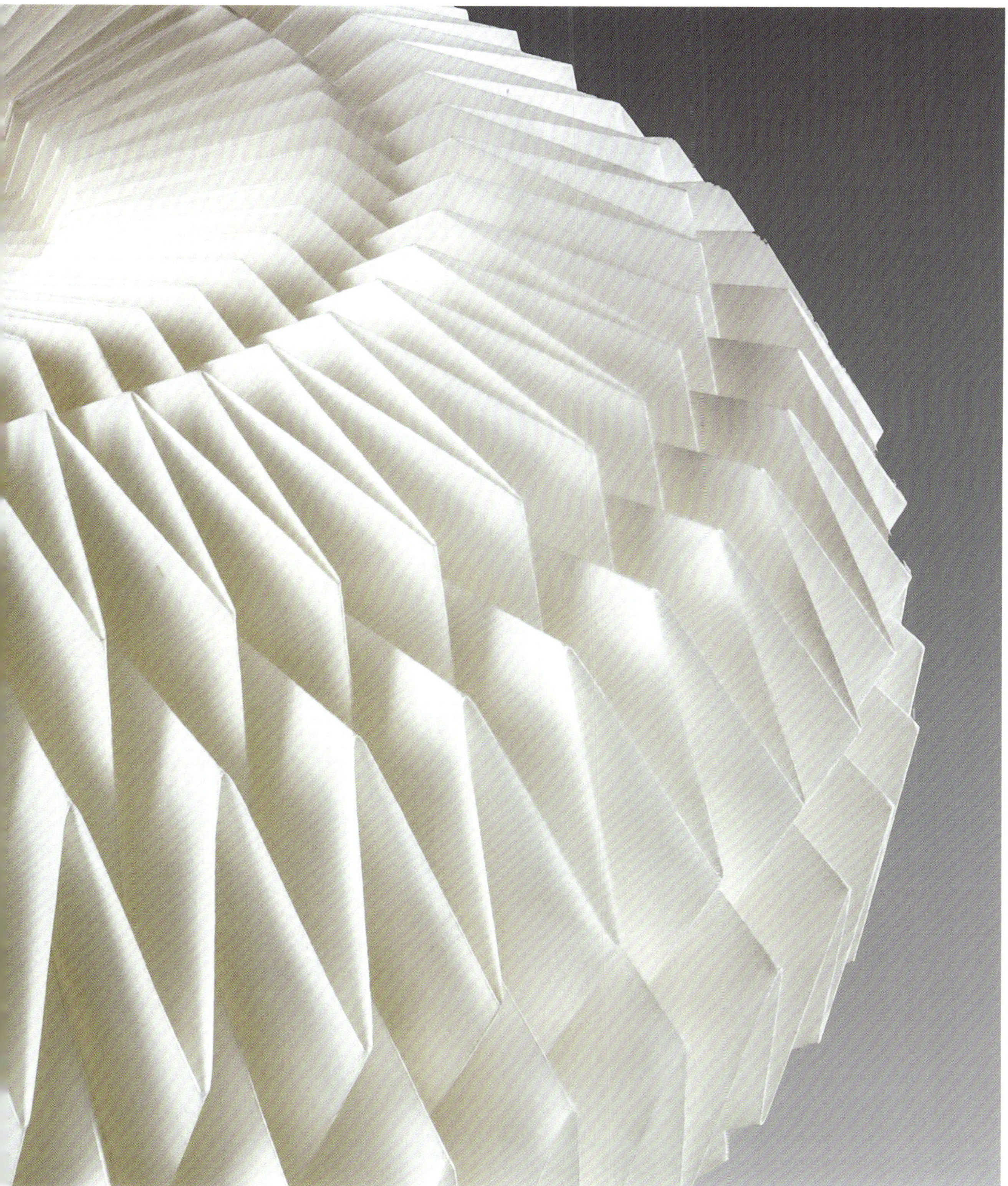

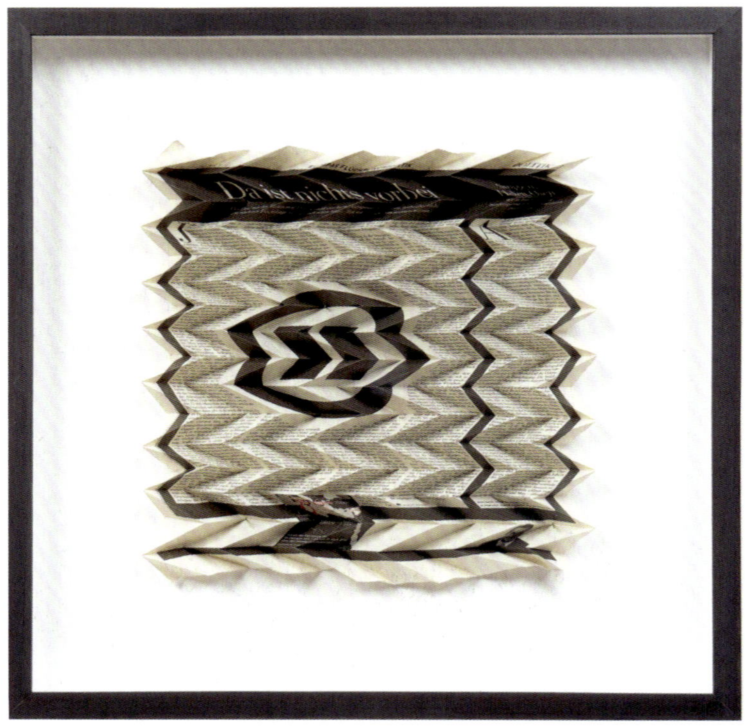

Peter Sandbichler

DIE ZEIT, ÖSTERREICH,
7. JANUAR 2016
DIE ZEIT, AUSTRIA, 7 JANUARY
2016
2016
Zeitungen, Stahl, Museumsglas
Newspapers, steel, museum glass
50 × 50 × 5

DIE ZEIT, POLITIK 3,
21. APRIL 2016
DIE ZEIT, POLITICS 3,
21 APRIL 2016
2018
Zeitungen, Stahl, Museumsglas
Newspapers, steel, museum glass
52 × 52 × 5,5

DIE ZEIT, POLITIK,
21. APRIL 2016
DIE ZEIT, POLITICS,
21 APRIL 2016
2018
Zeitungen, Stahl, Museumsglas
Newspapers, steel, museum glass
52 × 52 × 5,5

Courtesy Galerie Elisabeth & Klaus Thoman

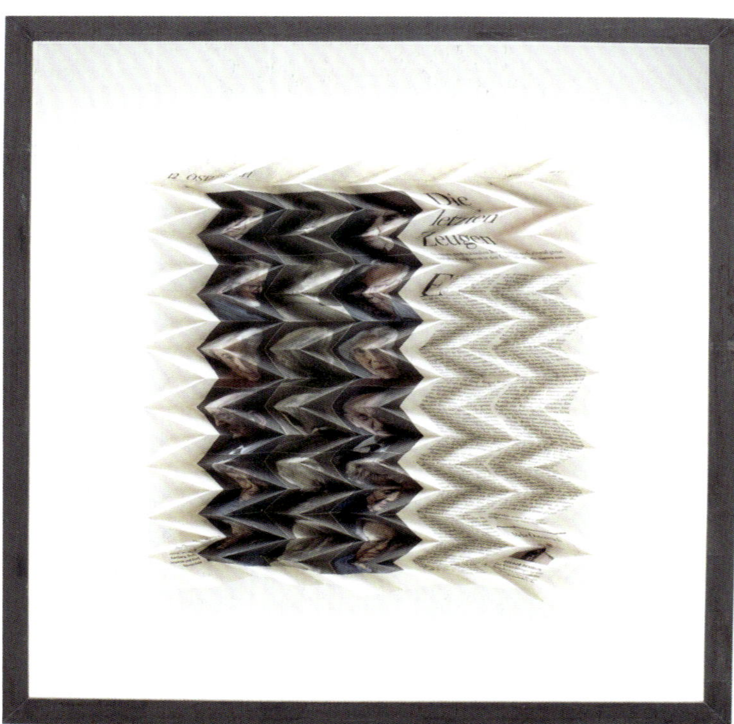

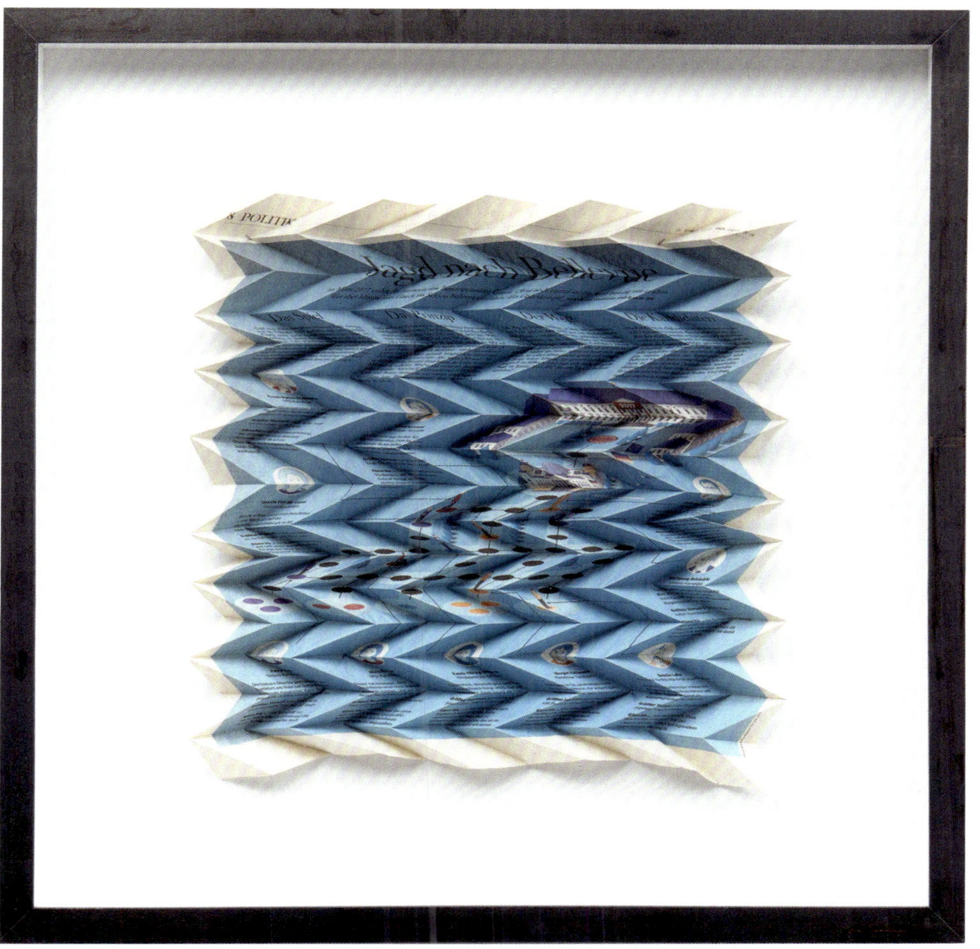

Das Interesse an Falten als Gestaltungsmittel zieht sich durch das gesamte Werk des Wiener Künstlers Peter Sandbichler. In seiner mehrteiligen *ZEIT*-Serie setzt er Falten als Mittel der ästhetischen Intervention ein – spielerisch, jedoch auch radikal. Als optische und physische Störung hindern sie den Zugang zum Zeitungsbericht, sie erzeugen Zerrungen und Zerstückelungen der visuellen und schriftlichen Botschaften. So werden Bilder und Texte zu bloßen inhaltsleeren Signalen verdammt. Die Knicke im Zeitungspapier dekonstruieren den Inhalt der dort kommunizierten Nachrichten und sabotieren somit die gesamte Unternehmung einer Kommunikation. Zurück bleibt nur noch ein geknicktes Papier als falsch ästhetisiertes Ornament und (fast) zynisches Sinnbild für die Unzulänglichkeit unseres Miteinanders.

An interest in folds as a design tool is to be found throughout the work of the Viennese artist Peter Sandbichler. In his multi-part *ZEIT* series, he playfully and yet radically uses folds as a medium of aesthetic intervention. An optical and physical intrusion, they prevent access to newspaper articles, distorting and fragmenting visual and written communication. Images and text are thus reduced to the status of meaningless signs. The folds in the newspaper deconstruct the content of the information transmitted therein and thus sabotage the entire communicative enterprise. What remains is only buckled paper as a falsely aestheticized ornament and (almost) cynical symbol of the deficiencies of our collective existence.

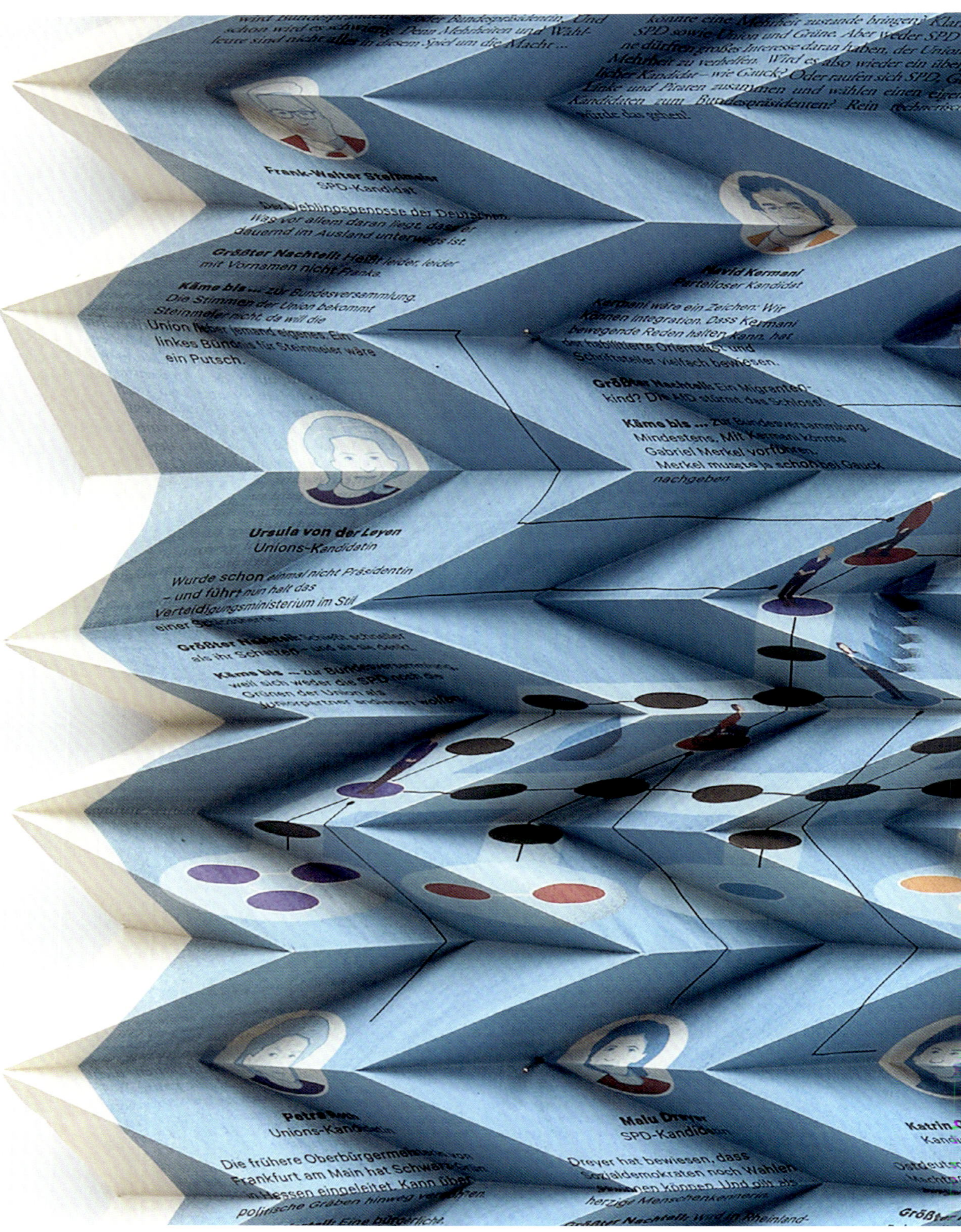

Frank-Walter Steinmeier
SPD-Kandidat

David Kermani
Parteiloser Kandidat

Ursula von der Leyen
Unions-Kandidatin

Petra Roth
Unions-Kandidatin

Malu Dreyer
SPD-Kandidatin

Katrin Göring
Kandidatin

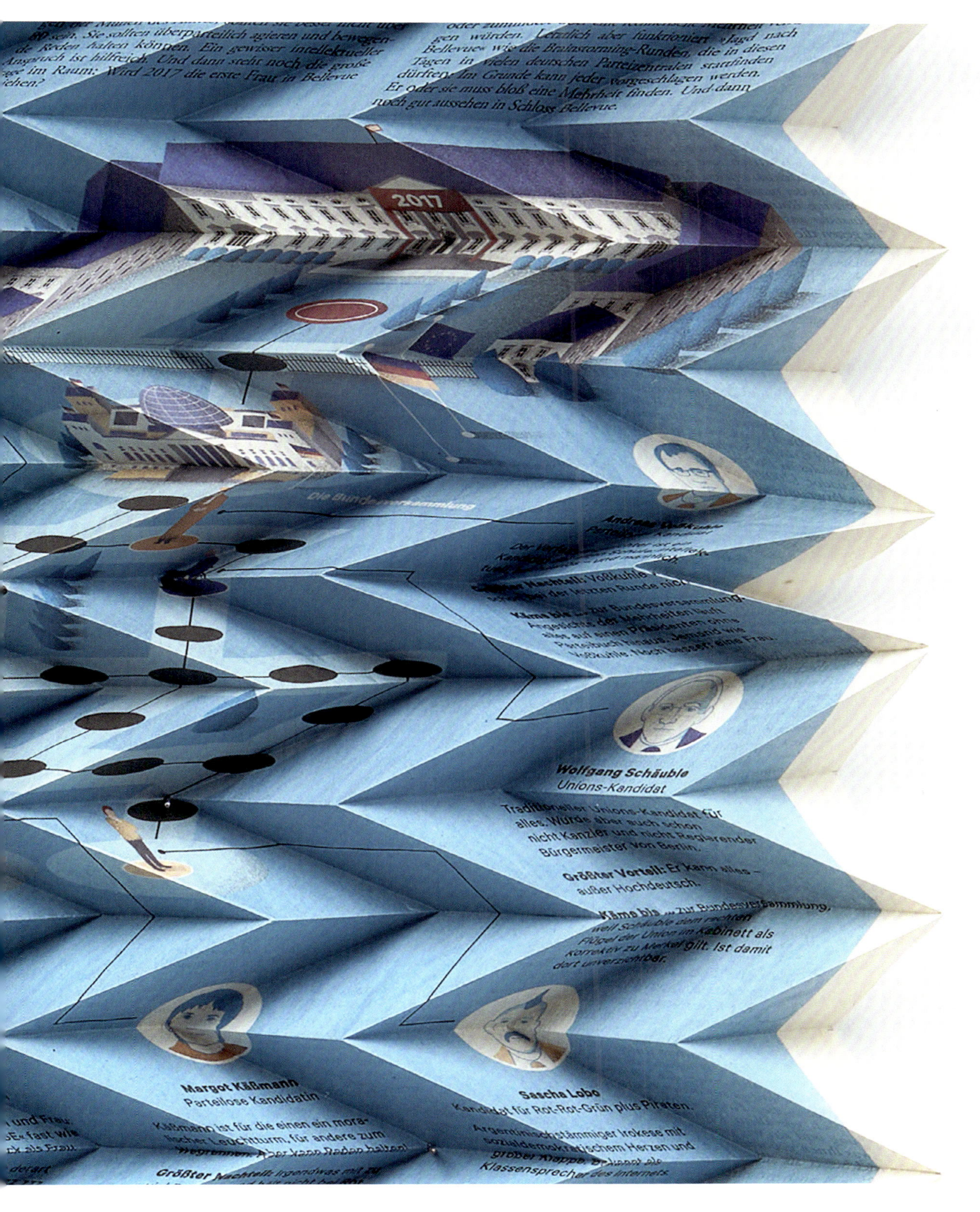
sein. Sie sollten überparteilich agieren und bewegen-
de Reden halten können. Ein gewisser intellektueller
Anspruch ist hilfreich. Und dann steht noch die große
Frage im Raum: Wird 2017 die erste Frau in Bellevue
ziehen?
oder zumindest
gen würden. Letztlich aber funktionieren »Jagd nach
Bellevue« wie die Brainstorming-Runden, die in diesen
Tagen in vielen deutschen Parteizentralen stattfinden
dürften. Im Grunde kann jeder vorgeschlagen werden.
Er oder sie muss bloß eine Mehrheit finden. Und dann
noch gut aussehen in Schloss Bellevue.
2017
Die Bundesversammlung
Andreas Voßkuhle
Parteiloser Kandidat
Wolfgang Schäuble
Unions-Kandidat
Traditioneller Unions-Kandidat für
alles. Würde aber auch schon
nicht Kanzler und nicht Regierender
Bürgermeister von Berlin.
Größter Vorteil: Er kann alles –
außer Hochdeutsch.
Margot Käßmann
Parteilose Kandidatin
Käßmann ist für die einen ein mora-
lischer Leuchtturm, für andere zum
Wegrennen. Aber kann Reden halten.
Größter Nachteil: Irgendwas mit
Sascha Lobo
Kandidat für Rot-Rot-Grün plus Piraten.
Argentinischstämmiger Irokese mit
sozialdemokratischem Herzen und
großer Klappe. Betreibt die
Klassensprecher des Internets.

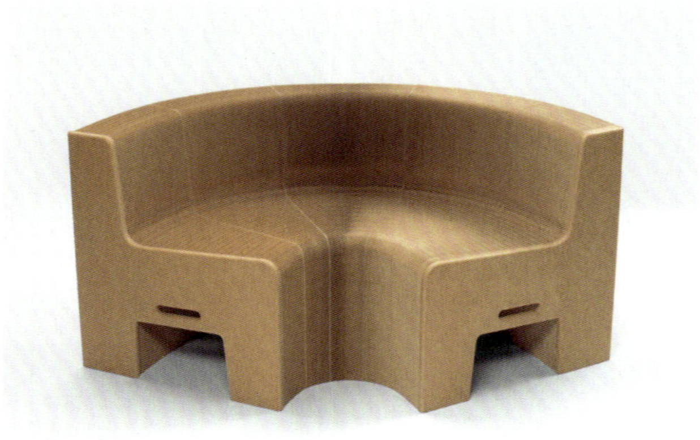
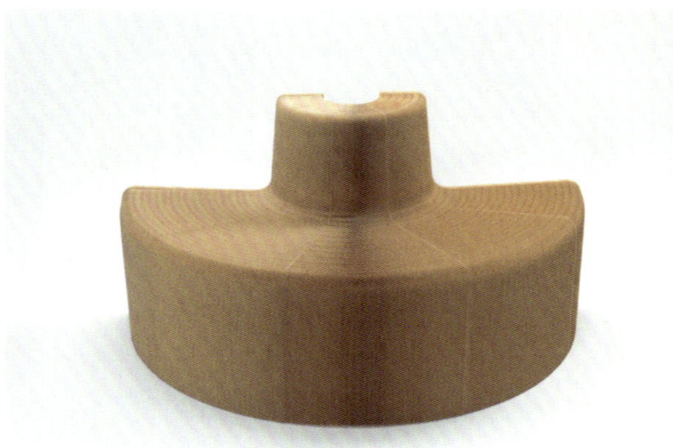
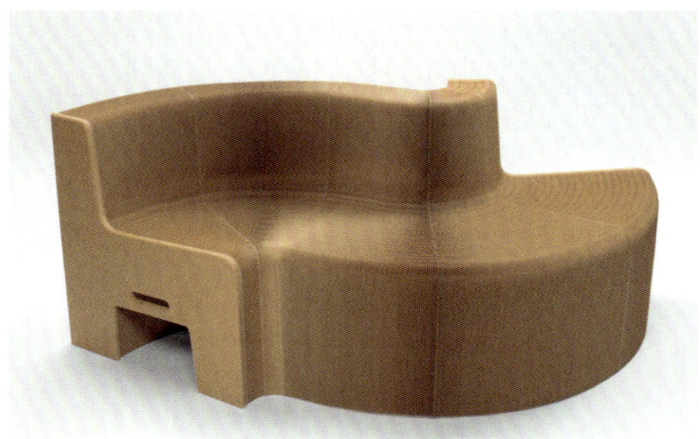
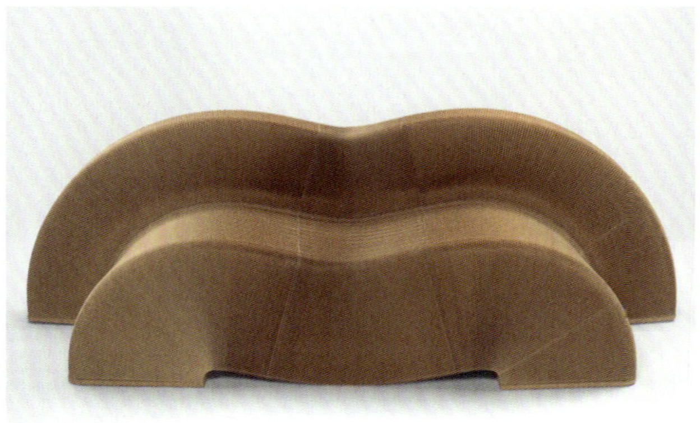

Chishen Shiu
FlexibleLove Earth 8
2005/2012
Papier, Holz und Holzfaserplatte, recycelt
Paper, wood, and fiberboard, recycled
64 × 13,6 bis to 350 × 56
MAK, H 3649

Dieses Sofa aus recyceltem Karton ist erstaunlich flexibel, was der Wabenstruktur des Materials zu verdanken ist. Es lässt sich auf eine Länge von bis zu 300 cm ausziehen und in eine halbrunde, runde oder gewellte Form bringen. Die Struktur des Kartons verleiht dem Sofa gleichzeitig eine hohe Stabilität, wodurch es eine Last von bis zu 1.900 kg tragen kann.

This sofa of recycled cardboard is astonishingly flexible, thanks to the material's honeycomb structure. It can be extended to a length of 300 cm and formed into a semi-circular, circular, or undulating shape. At the same time, the cardboard's structural qualities render it extremely stable, able to bear a load of up to 1,900 kg.

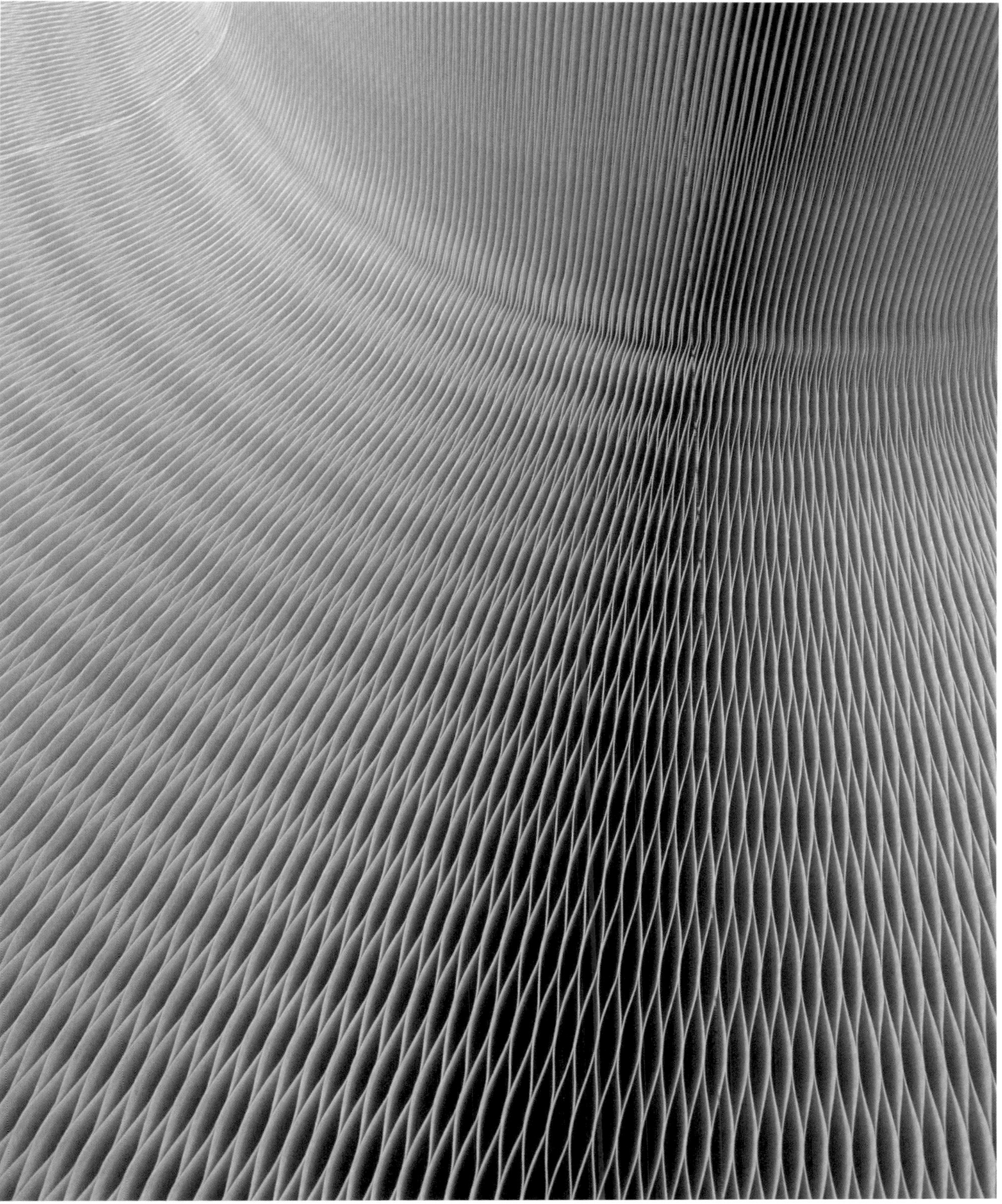

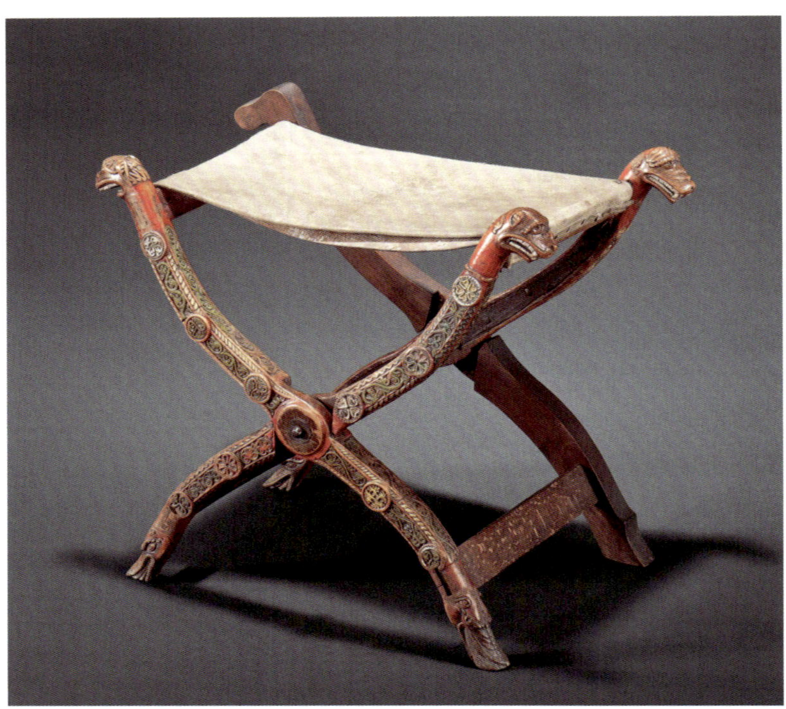

Faltstuhl (Faldistorium)

Folding chair (Faldistorium)

Salzburg, 1201–1210
Birnbaumholz und Leder, geschnitzt und bemalt
Pearwood and leather, carved and painted
61 × 64 × 50
MAK, H 1705

Der Faltstuhl ist ein zusammenklappbares mobiles Sitzmöbel mit Ursprung im Vorderen Orient. Dieser Stuhltyp verbreitete sich im antiken Mittelmeerraum, wurde im bronzezeitlichen Europa übernommen und fand in der römischen Antike sowie im Mittelalter Einzug. Der Faltstuhl hatte stets eine repräsentative Funktion und zeigte den sozialen Rang der sitzenden Person an. Er war weltlichen und religiösen Würdenträgern sowie der gesellschaftlichen Oberschicht vorbehalten.

Der hier gezeigte Faltstuhl wurde aus dem Benediktinerstift Admont erworben, dessen Äbten er neben Mitra, Ring, Brustkreuz und Hirtenstab als Insignie der Macht diente. Als solche steht er in der Tradition der römischen *sella curulis* (Amtsstuhl von hohen Beamten). Er ist neben dem Faltstuhl aus der Benediktinerinnenabtei Nonnberg in Salzburg das älteste in Österreich erhaltene Sitzmöbel.

The folding chair is a collapsible, transportable piece of furniture originating in the Near East. It spread throughout the Mediterranean in Antiquity, was adopted in Bronze-age Europe, and flourished in Roman times and the Middle Ages. Such a folding chair always had a representative function and denoted the sitter's high social rank, being reserved for religious and secular dignitaries as well as for members of the upper classes.

The folding chair shown here was acquired from the Benedictine Monastery of Admont; it was one of the abbot's insignia of power, together with his miter, ring, breast cross, and crosier. As such it stands in the tradition of the Roman *sella curulis*, the chair of office of a high-ranking administrator. After the folding chair from the Benedictine Nunnery of Nonnberg in Salzburg, this chair is the oldest piece of seating furniture in Austria.

Verner Panton
S-Stuhl 275

1956–1965
Ausführung: A. Sommer für
Thonet Frankenberg, um 1967
Execution: A. Sommer for
Thonet Frankenberg, ca. 1967
Sperrholz Plywood
81 × 43 × 50, SH 44
MAK, H 3738

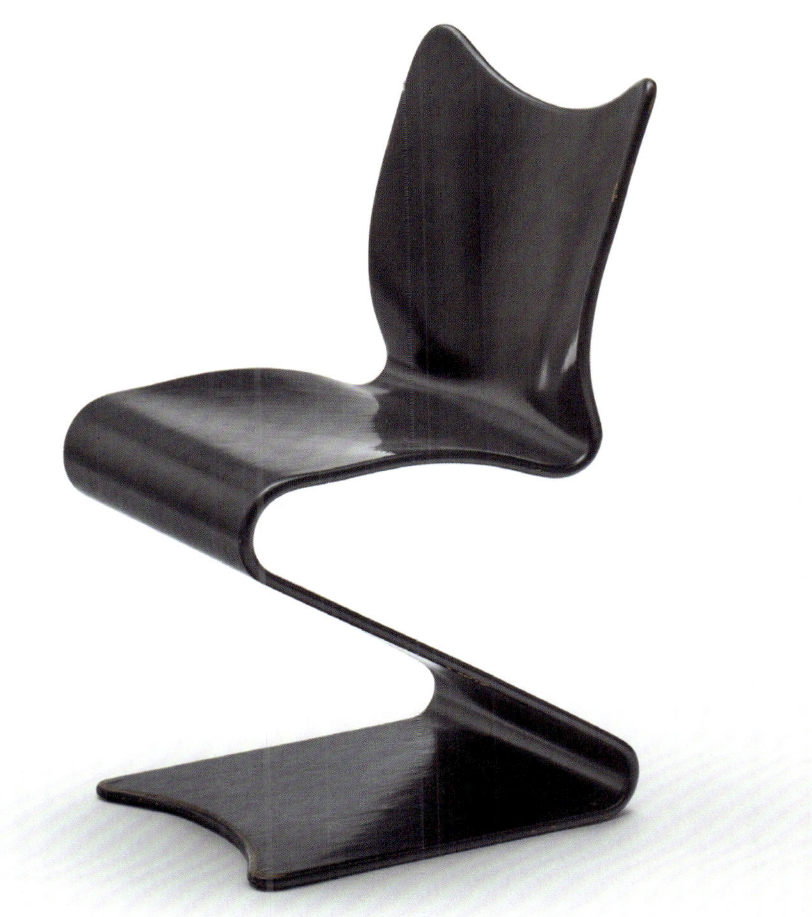

Nachdem die ersten Freischwinger aus gebogenem Metallrohr bereits 1927 Aufsehen erregt hatten, wurde der Stuhltypus ohne Hinterbeine im Laufe der Jahrzehnte immer wieder zum Fixpunkt der Überlegungen von Gestalter*innen. Für den *S-Stuhl 275* verband Verner Panton das frei kragende Stuhlmodell mit seiner ästhetisch-rationalen Formensprache. Als erster Freischwinger, der aus einer einzigen, plastisch gebogenen Sperrholzplatte besteht, weist der *S-Stuhl 275* die elegante Form eines gefalteten Streifens auf. Erst nach aufwendigen Biegeexperimenten gelang die Produktion dieses Schichtholz-Freischwingers. Aufgrund des großen Produktionsaufwands und der hohen Kosten konnte er allerdings nur in geringer Stückzahl realisiert werden.

After the first cantilever chairs formed of bent metal tubing caused a sensation back in 1927, over the decades this type of chair without back legs has continued to challenge designers' skills. For his *S-Chair 275*, Verner Panton combined the free-standing original with his own aesthetically rational form language. The first cantilever chair to consist of a single curved sheet of plywood, the *S-Chair 275* possesses the elegance of a folded strip. However, only after many time-consuming experiments did Panton succeed in making his plywood cantilever chair work. Because of the immense cost and effort involved in its production, the chair was manufactured only in a limited edition.

Olivier Leblois
Fauteuil Carton Marqué FC
1993–2003
Karton, Holz
Cardboard, wood
71 × 71 × 71, SH 35
MAK, H 3805

Dieser Sessel besteht aus zwei recycelbaren Kartonbögen mit Faltmarkierungen, ist extrem leicht zu transportieren und kann eine Last von bis zu 200 kg tragen. Durch das Falten und die Steckverbindungen wird der flache Karton zum dreidimensionalen komfortablen Sitzmöbel. Die tragende Wirkung der Faltung und die Stabilität der Wellpappe, die durch die Biegefaltung der inneren Kartonschicht Ähnlichkeiten mit einer Leichtbaukonstruktion aufweist, sorgen für eine gute Belastbarkeit.

Olivier Leblois' Kartonsessel war Mitte der 1990er Jahre kommerziell sehr erfolgreich, was insofern spannend ist, als die Idee, Kartonmöbel zu entwerfen, auf die Kapitalismuskritik der 1960er Jahre zurückgeht und mit einem demokratisch-ökologischen Designgedanken verbunden ist. Der österreichisch-amerikanische Designer Victor Papanek ist einer der Vertreter*innen dieser Bewegung: Seine Publikation *Nomadic Furniture* von 1973 ist als DIY-Handbuch für die Herstellung von transportablen, wandelbaren und recycelbaren Möbelstücken aus Karton und anderen Ausgangsmaterialien angelegt.

Papaneks geistiges Erbe ist in Leblois' Designphilosophie spürbar zu erkennen, auch wenn sein Sessel kommerziell vertrieben wurde: Das Material Karton ermöglicht eine einfache Handhabung und das Falten als eine der ältesten Kulturtechniken der Menschheit lädt uns ein, am Gestaltungsprozess eines Möbelstücks mitzuwirken.

This chair consists of two recyclable sheets of cardboard scored with fold marks, is extremely light and easy to transport, and can bear a load of up to 200 kg. By folding the flat pieces of cardboard and slotting them together, a comfortable three-dimensional armchair is created. The load-bearing qualities of the folds and the stability of the corrugated cardboard—whose inner undulations evoke comparisons with other lightweight construction materials—guarantee a high level of robustness.

Olivier Leblois's cardboard armchair was commercially successful in the mid-1990s—a remarkable fact, considering that the idea of designing cardboard furniture originated with the anticapitalism of the 1960s and is thus part of a democratic, ecological design philosophy. The Austro-American designer Victor Papanek was a representative of this movement. His 1973 publication *Nomadic Furniture* is a DIY handbook for creating transportable, convertible, and recyclable furniture out of cardboard and other basic materials.

Papanek's spiritual legacy is manifest in Leblois's design philosophy, even though his chair was commercially distributed. As a material, cardboard is easy to manipulate, and the art of folding—one of humanity's earliest cultural techniques—invites us here to participate in the creation of a piece of furniture.

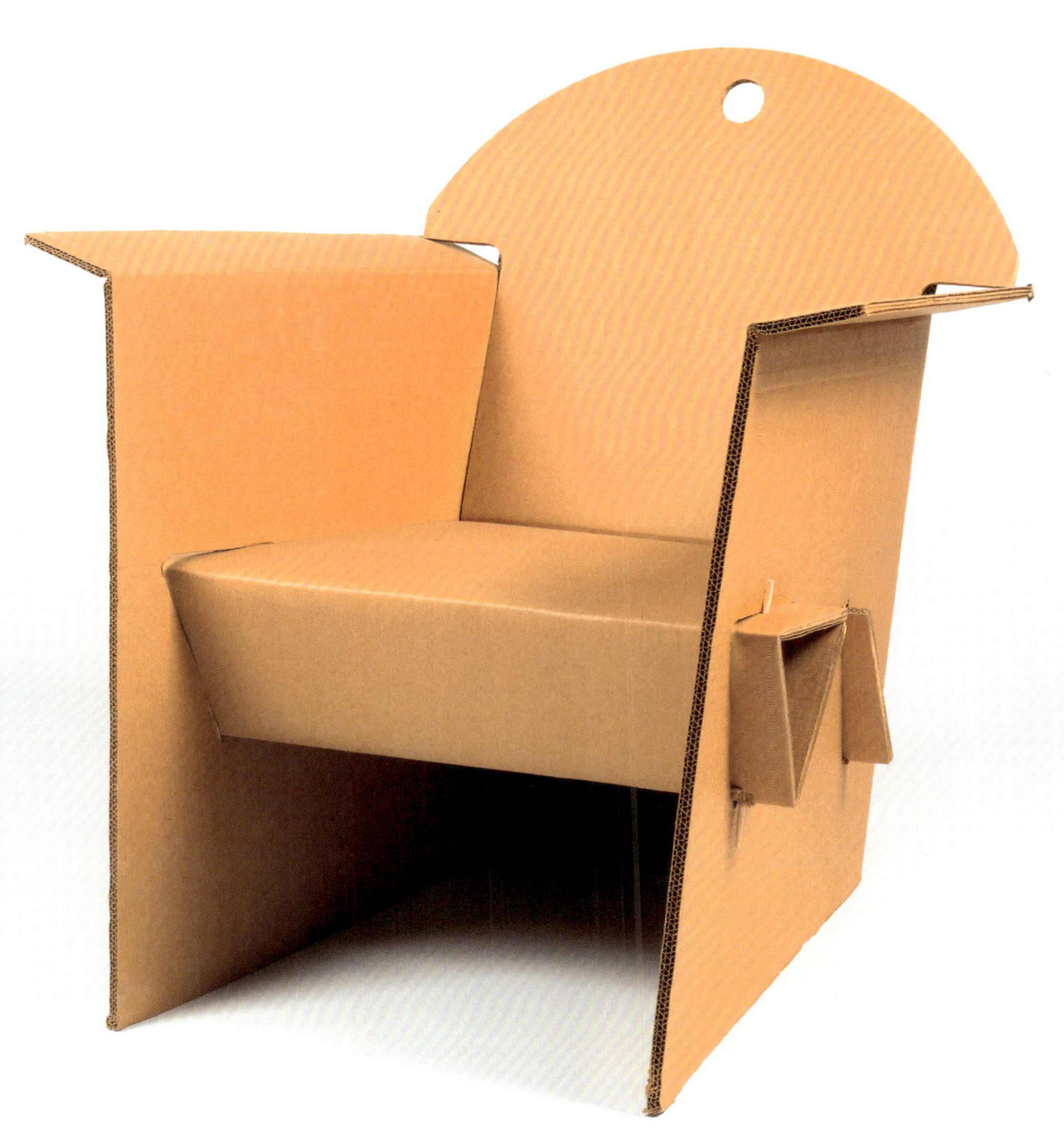

Klappstuhl Folding chair *Cricket*
1977
Ausführung Execution: Brown Jordan Co.
Metall und Textil, lackiert
Metal and textile, lacquered
65 × 68 × 88, SH 43
MAK, H 3268-2

Gastone Rinaldi
Klappstuhl Folding chair *Daphne*
1979
Ausführung Execution: THEMA
Metallrahmen, Sitzfläche aus gebogenem Sperrholz, blau lackiert
Metal frame, seat of curved plywood, lacquered blue
80 × 35,5 × 35, SH 46
MAK, H 2766

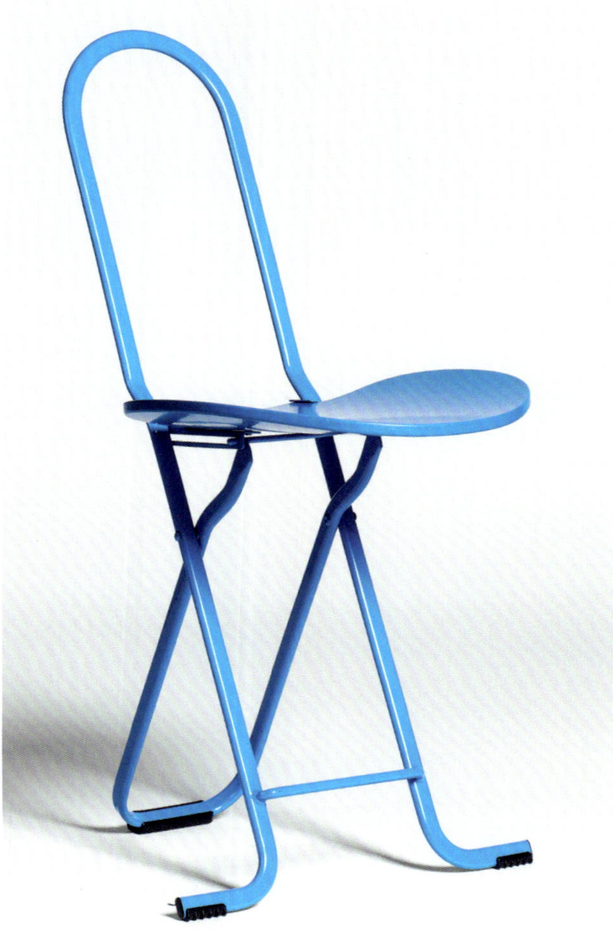

Beweglichkeit, flexible Raumnutzung und eine einfache Handhabung haben das Produktdesign seit Beginn des 20. Jahrhunderts geprägt. Auch Gastone Rinaldis Klappstuhl *Daphne* entspricht diesen Grundsätzen: Nur aus einem lackierten Metallrahmen und einer Sitzfläche aus gebogenem Sperrholz bestehend, lässt er sich bis auf wenige Zentimeter zusammenfalten. Die elegante und gleichzeitig materialsparende Gestaltung dieses Stuhls ist eine unkonventionelle Antwort auf tradierte (Möbel-)Formen, eine Tendenz, die der Kunsthistoriker Hans Wichmann als charakteristisch für das italienische Möbeldesign nach 1945 bezeichnet. Hier ist eine radikale Transformation des Faltstuhls und seiner funktionalen, sozialen und kulturellen Bedeutung festzustellen – vom repräsentativen Prunkmöbel mit Ursprung im Vorderen Orient zum Inbegriff einer auf Spontaneität bedachten und mobilen Kultur der 1960er und 1970er Jahre.

Since the beginning of the 20th century, product design has been characterized by mobility, the flexible utilization of space, and ease of use. Gastone Rinaldi's folding chair *Daphne* also meets these criteria. Consisting only of a lacquered metal frame and a seat of curved plywood, it can be folded to a thickness of just a few centimeters. The elegant and at the same time material-saving design of the chair is an unconventional riposte to traditional forms of furniture—a trend that art historian Hans Wichmann has described as characteristic of Italian furniture design since 1945. Here one can witness a radical transformation of the folding chair and its functional, social, and cultural significance—from a ceremonial piece of furniture originating in the Near East to this epitome of 1960's and 1970's mobile culture committed to spontaneity.

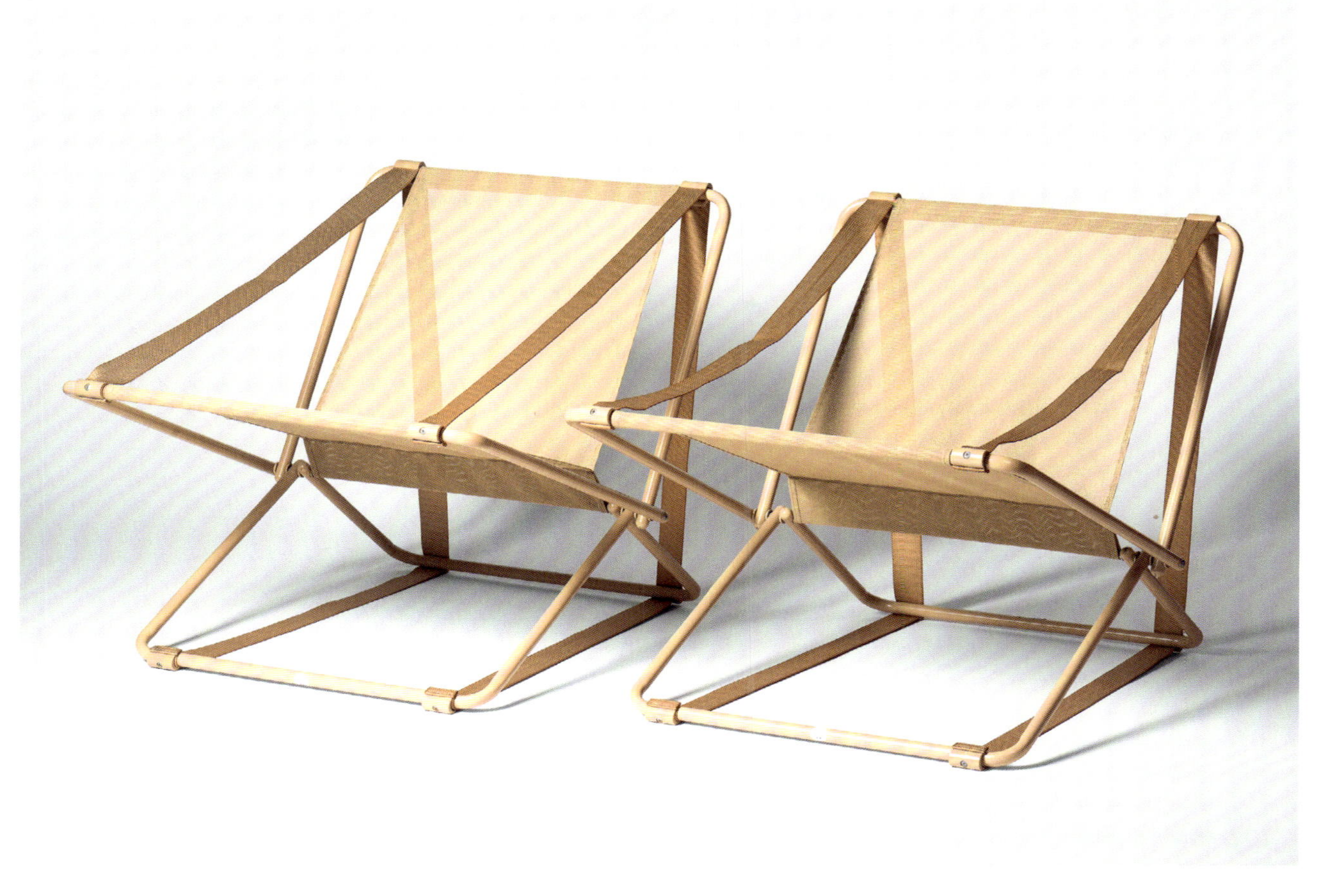

Der in Wien gebürtige US-amerikanische Architekt und Industriedesigner Henry Peter Glass (1911–2003) konnte sich 1941 mit seinen „Hairpin Leg"-Möbeln aus gebogenem Metall in der US-Designszene schlagartig einen Namen machen. Die speziell für die Kollektion *American Ways* des Designers Russel Wright entworfenen Möbel zeichnen sich durch ihre innovative Formensprache aus: Für die filigranen Möbelbeine wird jeweils ein einziges Stück Stahl in Haarnadel-Form gebogen. Mit äußerst sparsamem Materialeinsatz wird hier eine hochwertig-moderne Wirkung erzielt.
Wie seine raffinierten Möbeldesignentwürfe seit den 1940er Jahren, die dem Effizienz-Prinzip verpflichtet waren, ist auch der Outdoor-Klappstuhl *Cricket* aus sehr stabilen Ausgangsmaterialien gefertigt und dennoch sehr leicht im Gewicht. Das Besondere ist, dass er sich äußerst platzsparend zusammenklappen und stapeln lässt.

In 1941, the American architect and industrial designer Henry Peter Glass (1911–2003), who was born in Vienna, achieved instant fame in the US designer scene with his bent metal Hairpin Leg furniture. Created exclusively for the *American Ways* collection of designer Russel Wright, Glass's furniture is distinguished by its innovative form language: to make the filigree legs of his furniture, a single piece of steel is bent into a hairpin form. Through its extremely sparing use of material, Glass's chair appears both modern and of high quality.
Like all Glass's sophisticated furniture designs since the 1940s, this outdoor folding chair *Cricket* is committed to the principle of efficiency. Constructed of exceptionally stable basic materials, it is nevertheless very lightweight. Its special quality is that it is extremely space-saving—easy to fold and to stack.

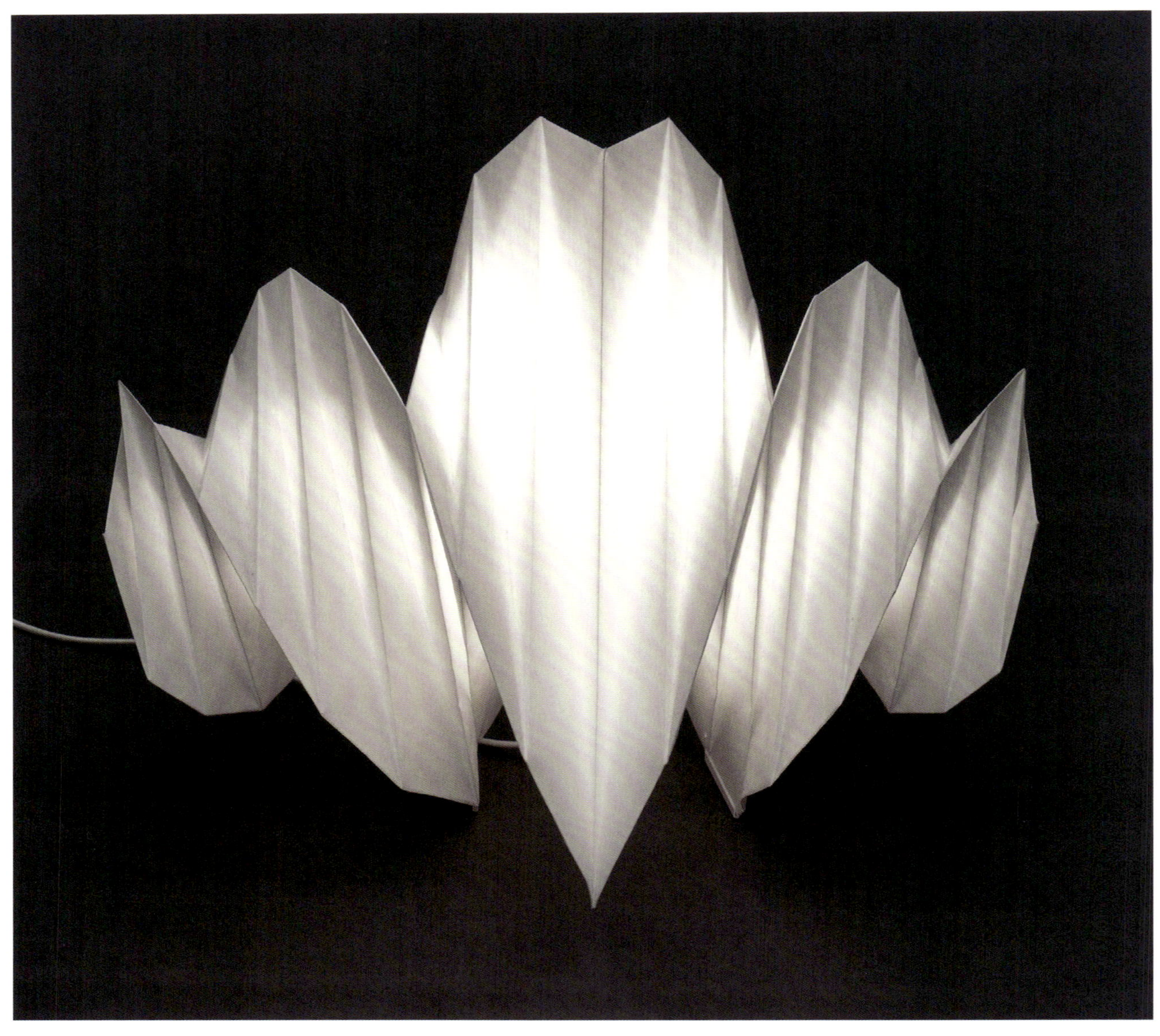

Issey Miyake/Reality Lab.
Mendori aus der Serie *IN-EI*
Mendori from the series *IN-EI*
2012
Recycling-Textilgewebe aus Polyester, elektronische Bauteile
Recycled polyester textile fabric, electronic components
44 × 48 × 50
MAK, DS 170

Dieser skulpturale Origami-Lampenschirm ist aus einem einzigen Stück Stoff gefaltet. Mittels geometrischer 3D-Grundsätze entsteht aus einem komplett flach gefalteten zweidimensionalen Stück Stoff eine dreidimensionale Form, die von einem speziellen Mathematikprogramm berechnet wird und durch eine besondere Behandlung der Stoffoberfläche ohne zusätzliche Innenstütze stabil bleibt. Die Struktur erzeugt eine beeindruckende Wechselwirkung von Licht und Schatten.

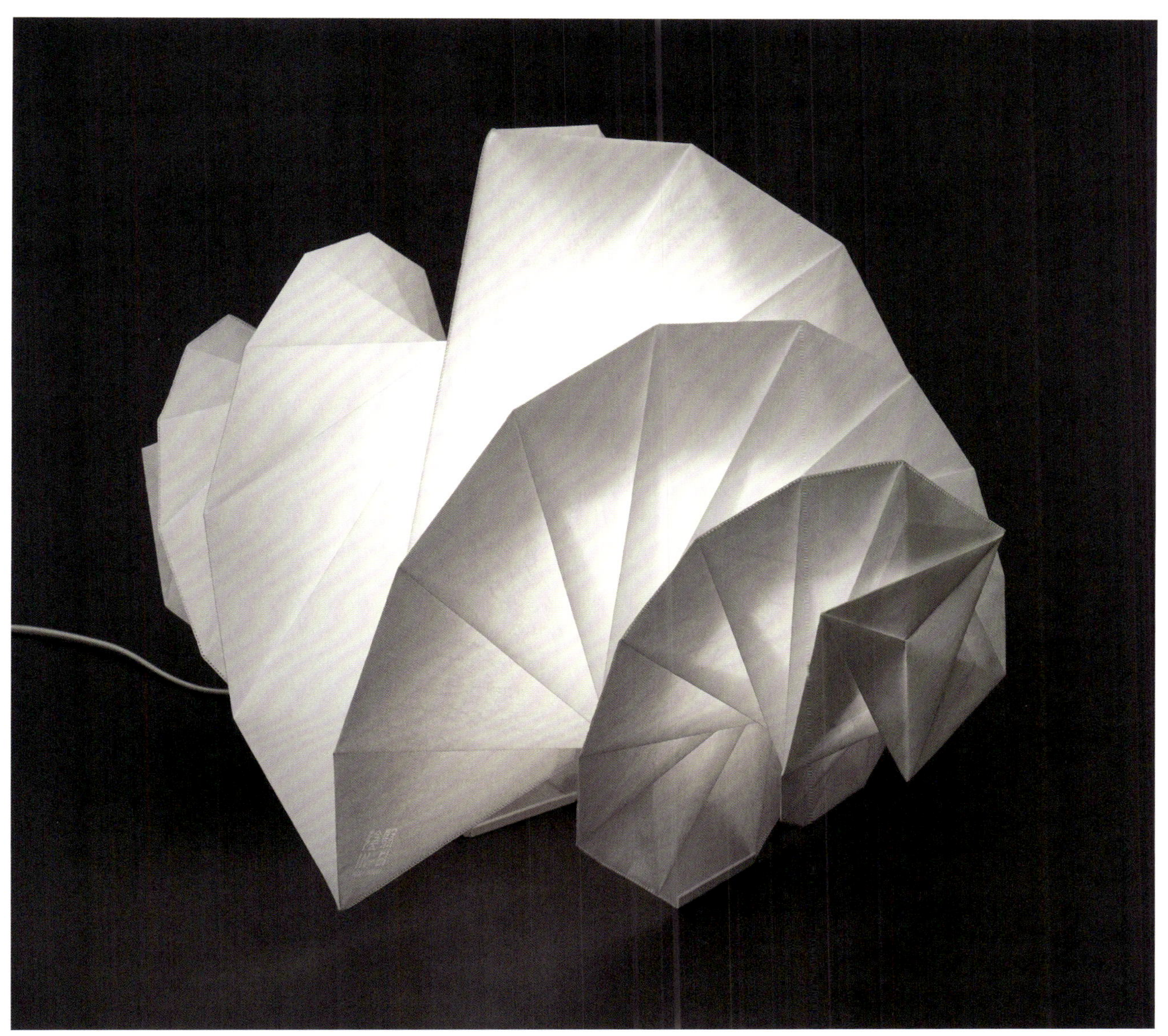

This sculptural origami lampshade is folded out of a single piece of material. Using principles derived from trigonometry, a two-dimensional piece of folded cloth is transformed into a three-dimensional object. The lampshade's form is calculated by a computer program and stabilized by special treatment of the material's surface—dispensing with the need for interior supports. The resulting interplay of light and shadow generated by the structure is truly impressive.

MATERIE, SEELE, FALTEN

Als biologisches Lebewesen unterliegt unser physischer Körper einer ständigen Metamorphose. Kurz vor der Geburt entfaltet sich unsere Lunge, und der Prozess des Alterns ist mit der Entstehung von Falten in unserer Haut verbunden. Falten am menschlichen Körper sind dabei so individuell, dass sie als persönliche Signatur dienen können.

Die Art und Weise, wie sich unsere gegenwärtige Gesellschaft mit etwas so Grundlegendem wie den Falten unserer Haut beschäftigt, nimmt zunehmend obsessive Züge an. Bei genauerer Betrachtung der kulturellen Praktiken zeigt sich allerdings ein viel differenzierteres Spektrum an Begrifflichkeiten und Konzepten. Unsere soziokulturellen – und nicht zuletzt geschlechtsspezifischen – Normen und Verhaltenscodes, ja sogar die Ideologien, die das heutige Gesellschaftssystem konstituieren, werden sichtbar im Spannungsverhältnis zwischen unserem Körper und seiner äußeren Hülle sowie zwischen unserem allzu menschlichen Bedürfnis nach Ordnung und der Unordnung der Welt.

Unser äußerst ambivalentes Verhältnis zu Falten ist ein Beleg dafür, dass es sich dabei um ein Konstrukt handelt. Es zeigt, wie eng die Beziehung zwischen Menschen und Falten mit den zeit- und kulturspezifischen Ausprägungen unserer Weltansichten verknüpft ist.

MATERIAL, SOUL, FOLDS

As biological creatures, our physical bodies are subject to constant metamorphosis. Shortly before birth, our lungs unfold, and the process of aging is accompanied by a wrinkling of our skin. The folds and wrinkles on each human body are also unique and may serve as a personal signature.

Our contemporary society's preoccupation with something as elementary as the wrinkles on our skin is increasingly becoming an obsession. But a closer look at cultural practices yields a much more differentiated range of terminologies and concepts. Our sociocultural, and not least our gender-specific, norms and codes of conduct—indeed, even the ideologies constituting our contemporary social system—are apparent in our strained relationship between our body and its outer shell, and between our all-to-human yearning for order and an entropic universe.

Our highly ambivalent attitude towards wrinkles is evidence of its being a construct. It shows how closely connected the relationship between people and folds is to the temporally and culturally specific terms through which we express our understanding of the world.

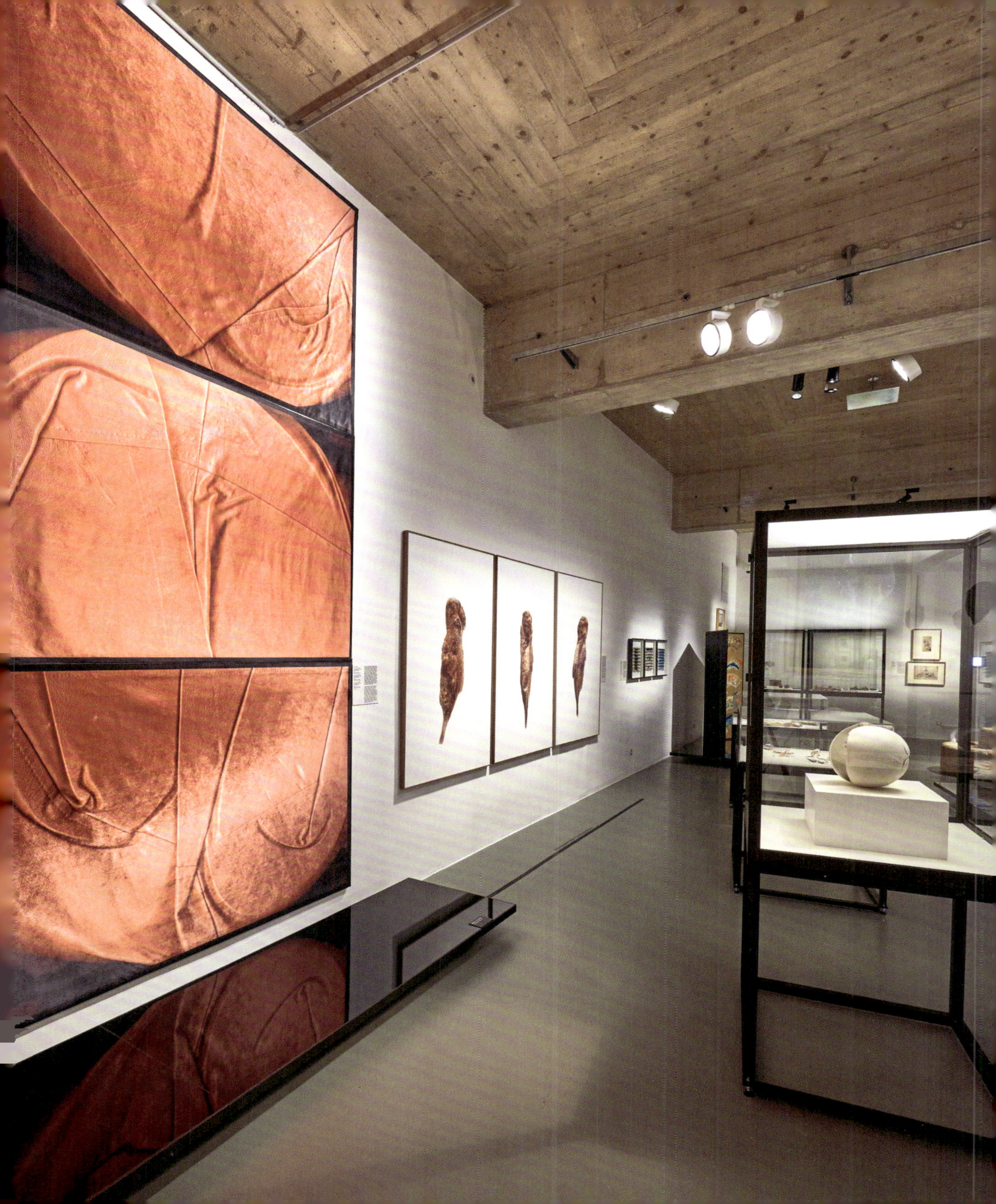

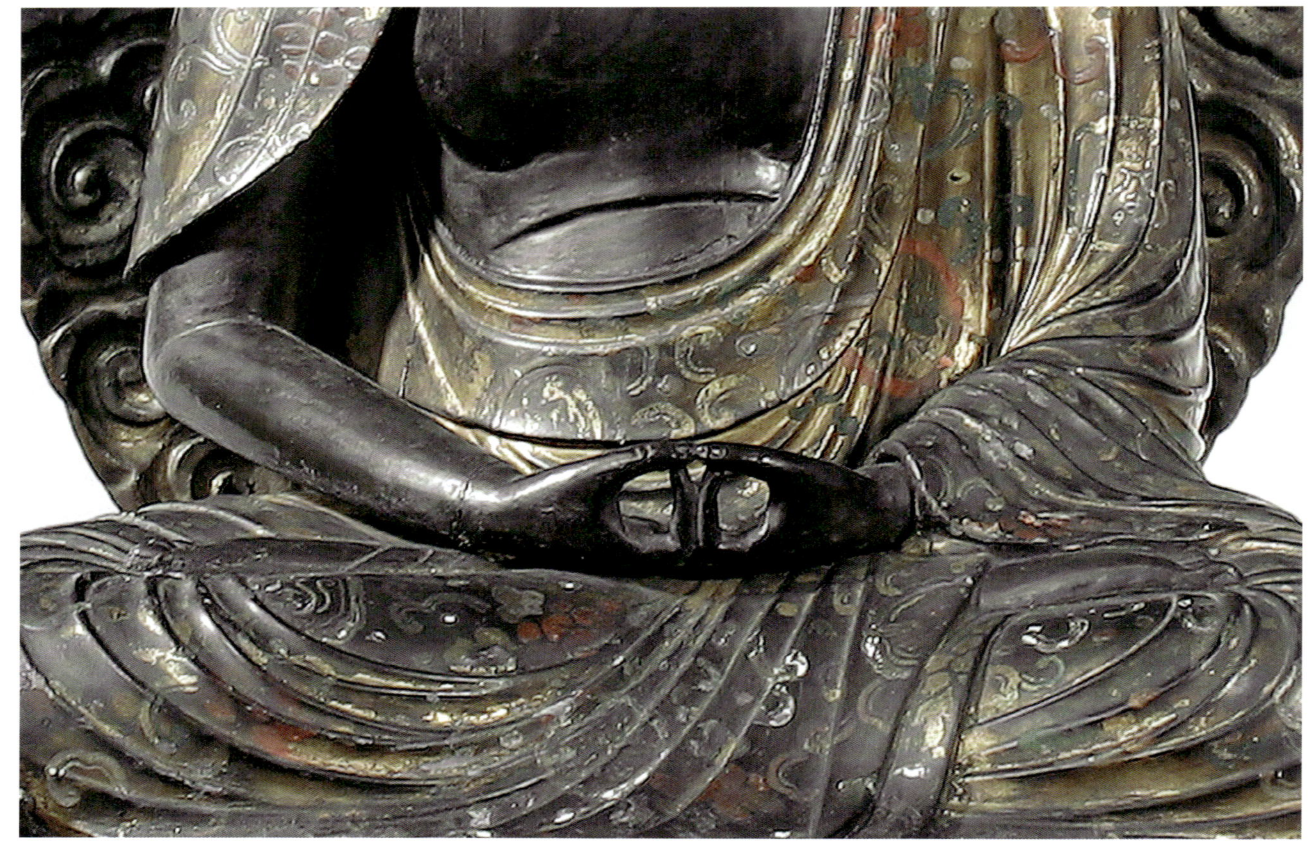

Amida nyorai (Sanskrit *Buddha Amitabha*)

Japan, 18. Jh. 18th c.
Holz, lackiert, Gold- und Rotlackbemalung
Wood, lacquered, gold and red lacquer painting
78 × 58 × 51
MAK, OR 3860

Buddhistische Gläubige erhoffen sich, nach ihrem Ableben Einlass in das „Westliche Paradies" des Buddha Amitabha (Japanisch *Amida nyorai*) zu erlangen, da sie sonst den qualvollen Weg der Reinkarnation auf sich nehmen müssen. Laut der Lehrmeinung der *jōdo*-Schule (Schule des Reinen Landes) tragen die Visualisierung von Buddha Amitabhas Erscheinungsbild sowie die Anrufung seines Namens dazu bei, in sein Paradies zu gelangen. Auch die Stiftung oder Anbetung einer solchen Skulptur – wie der hier gezeigten – sollte den Gläubigen helfen, aus dem qualvollen karmischen Kreislauf herauszukommen. *Amida nyorais* friedvolle Ruhe und Vollkommenheit spiegelt sich in der sanften Gestaltung des Faltenwurfs wider.

After their death, the Buddhist faithful hope to enter the "Western Paradise" of the Buddha Amitabha (in Japanese *Amida nyorai*); otherwise, they must undergo the distressing process of reincarnation. According to the teachings of the *jōdo* school (the School of the Pure Land), visualizing Buddha Amitabha's appearance and calling out his name can help one enter his paradise. Donations or worshiping such sculptures as the one shown here are also supposed to help the faithful to break free from the harrowing karmic cycle of rebirth. *Amida nyorai's* tranquility and spiritual perfection is reflected in the gentle folds of his robe.

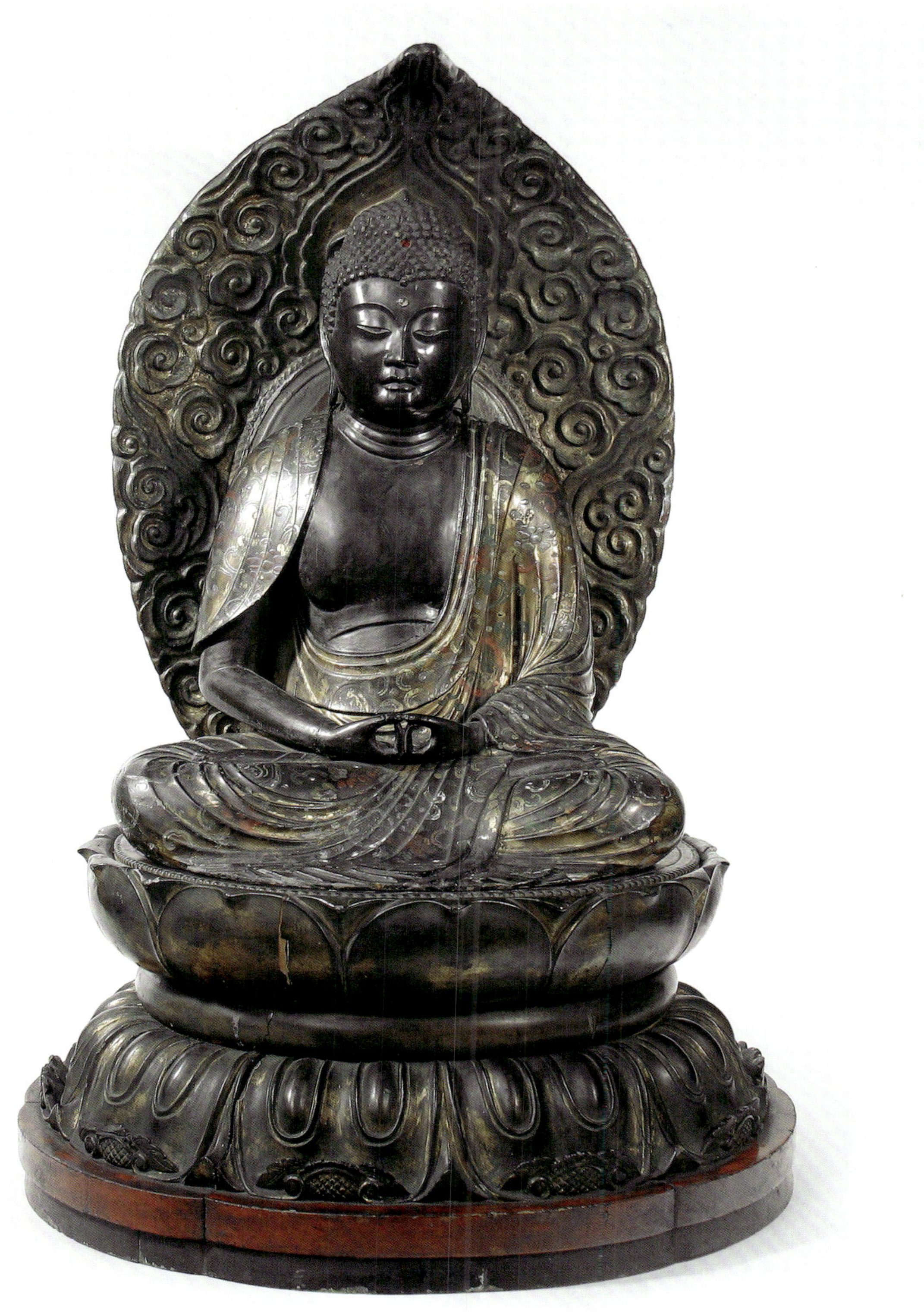

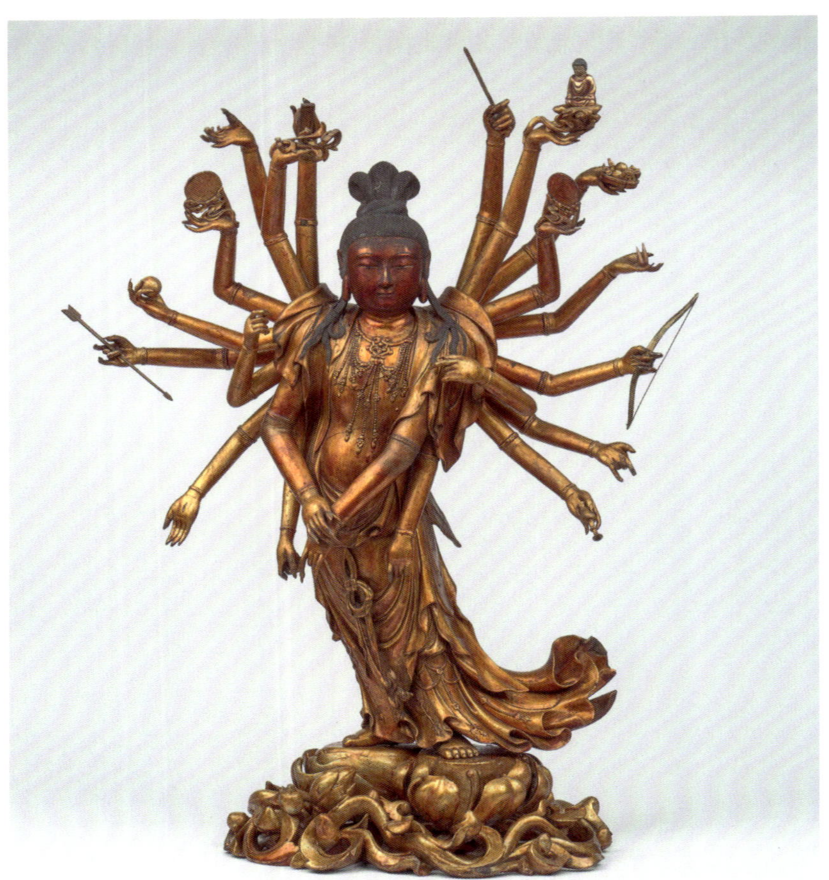

Bodhisattva „tausendarmiger Avalokiteshvara"
Thousand-armed Bodhisattva Avalokiteshvara

China, 18. Jh. 18th c.
Holz, vergoldet Wood, gilded, 95 × 72 × 33
MAK, PL 878

Der Bodhisattva (Chinesisch *Guanyin*, Japanisch *Kannon*) ist die buddhistische Gottheit des Mitgefühls, die Gläubigen zur Erleuchtung verhelfen möchte. Die Hilfsbereitschaft des Bodhisattva wird bereits durch seine stehende, bewegte Haltung signalisiert (im Gegensatz zu Buddha Amitabha in Meditationshaltung!). Die Mehrarmigkeit des sogenannten „Bodhisattva mit Tausenden Händen" verkörpert seine Barmherzigkeit: Mit seinen vielen Armen fängt er die karmisch belasteten Normalsterblichen auf und sucht energisch nach Möglichkeiten, sie zu retten. Die wehenden Faltenwürfe bilden seine große Tatkräftigkeit ab.

The Bodhisattva (Chinese *Guanyin*, Japanese *Kannon*) is the Buddhist deity of compassion who desires to help the faithful achieve enlightenment. The Bodhisattva's willingness to help others is indicated by his standing, concerned posture (in contrast to the Buddha Amitabha's meditative posture!). The many arms of the so-called "Bodhisattva of the Thousand Hands" symbolize his compassionate nature: with his plethora of arms, he embraces ordinary mortals burdened by bad karma and energetically seeks for ways to redeem them. The billowing draperies represent his enormous vigour.

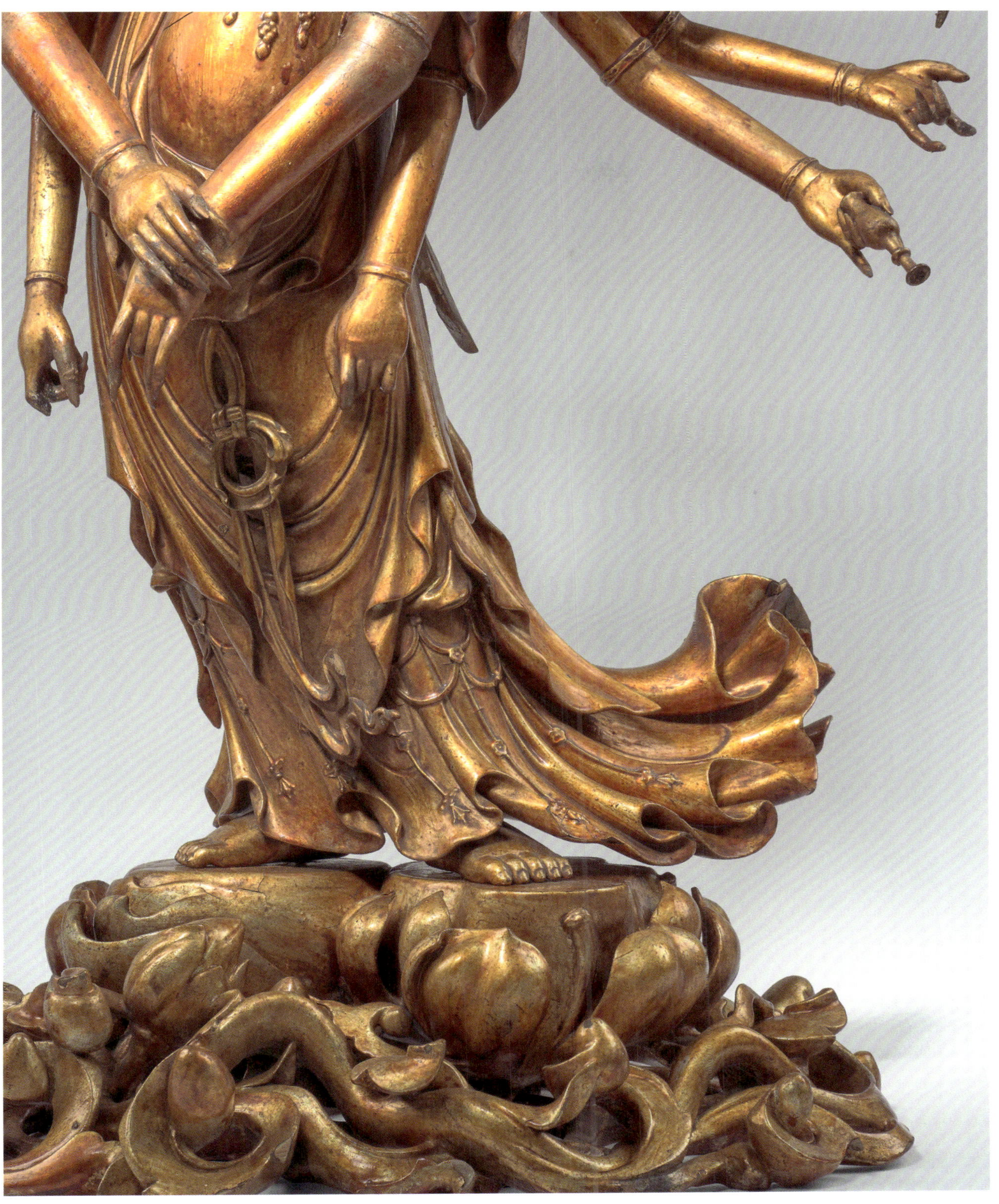

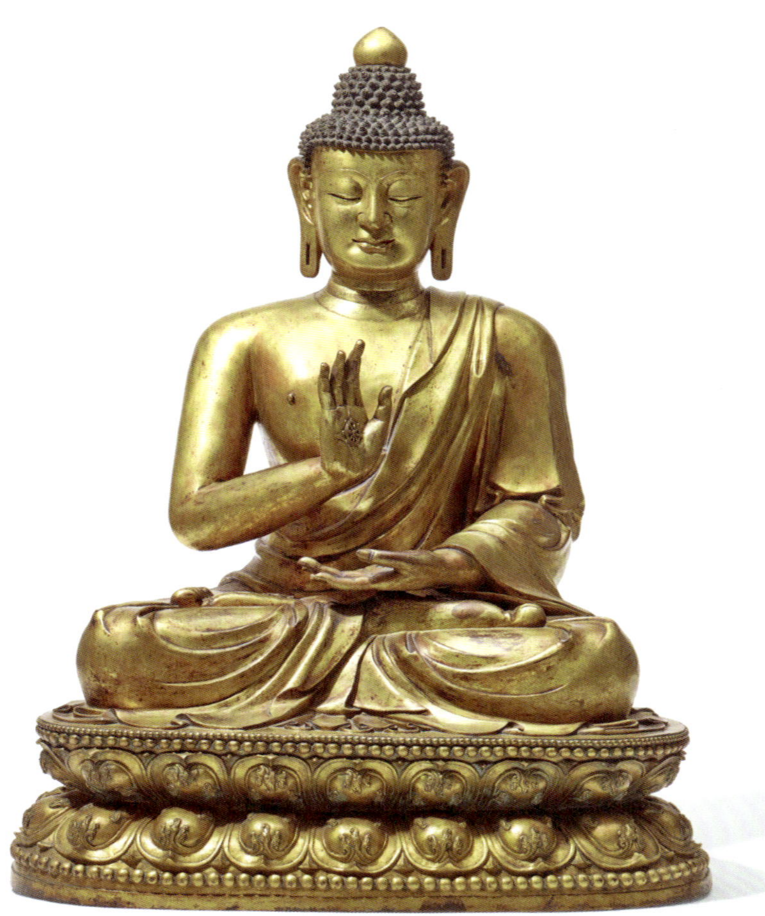

Zum ikonografischen Repertoire bei der Darstellung Buddhas gehören neben dem Plattfuß, dem Schädelauswuchs und dem Mal an der Stirn auch drei Falten am Hals. Sie zählen zu den Merkmalen, durch die sich jeder Buddha rein äußerlich von Normalsterblichen unterscheidet. Alle 32 großen und 80 kleineren Merkmale Buddhas sind in kanonischen Schriften festgehalten.

The iconographic repertoire of Buddha images includes—besides his flat foot, the growth on his skull, and the birthmark on his forehead—three wrinkles on his neck. These attributes outwardly distinguish him from ordinary mortals. All of Buddha's 32 major and 80 minor physical characteristics are set down in canonical texts.

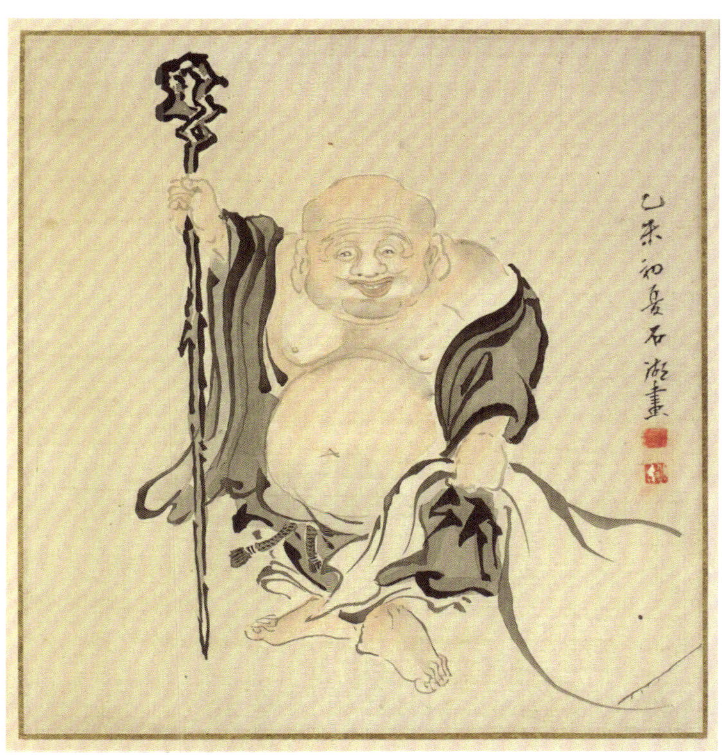

Hotei (Glücksgott)
Hotei (god of good fortune)
Japan, 19. Jh. 19th c.
Tusche und Farbe auf Seide
Ink and color on silk
23 × 21,5
MAK, KI 14989-25

Eine Ikone der Body Positivity aus einer alten Zeit ist der japanische Glücksgott Hotei (Chinesisch *Budai*) mit seiner Körperfülle und der entsprechenden Vielzahl an Falten. Der auch als „lachender Buddha" bekannte Gott geht ursprünglich auf eine historische Person aus China zurück, den Bettelmönch Qici aus dem späten 9. Jahrhundert. Trotz seiner körperlichen, sprachlichen und motorischen Auffälligkeiten (u. a. Stottern, Dickbäuchigkeit und Schlafsucht) war Qici der Legende nach magisch wie hellseherisch höchst begabt. Im Chan- bzw. Zen-Buddhismus erreichte er aufgrund seiner Exzentrik einen besonderen kultischen Status.

Außergewöhnliche körperliche und persönlichkeitsbezogene Merkmale wurden in der langen Geschichte der Menschheit keinesfalls immer als Defizit oder Mangel verstanden. Wie David Graeber und David Wengrow in ihrer bahnbrechenden Publikation *The Dawn of Everything* (2021) darlegen, waren es gerade diese Eigenschaften, die politische, gesellschaftliche und religiöse Autoritäten ab dem Jungpaläolithikum (vor gut 30.000 Jahren) und an manchen Orten der Erde noch bis ins frühe 20. Jahrhundert auszeichneten – Abweichungen von der Norm waren positiv besetzt und essenziell für die Gesellschaft.

With his physique and plethora of skinfolds, the Japanese god of good fortune, Hotei (Chinese *Budai*), is the icon of the body positivity movement of days gone by. Also known as the "laughing Budcha," this god is based on a real historical personage from China: the late 9th-century begging monk Qici. Despite his bodily, linguistic, and motoric anomalies (stutter, huge belly, and hypersomnia), according to legend Qici was a very talented magician and clairvoyant. In Chan or Zen Buddhism, his eccentricity gave him cult status.

In the long history of humanity, extraordinary physical or psychological characteristics have by no means always been interpreted negatively—as deficits. As David Graeber and David Wengrow demonstrate in their groundbreaking publication *The Dawn of Everything* (2021), it was precisely these characteristics that distinguished individuals of political, social, and religious authority starting in the Upper Paleolithic (at least 30,000 years ago)—in many locations up into the early 20th century. Abnormality was seen positively and essential for society.

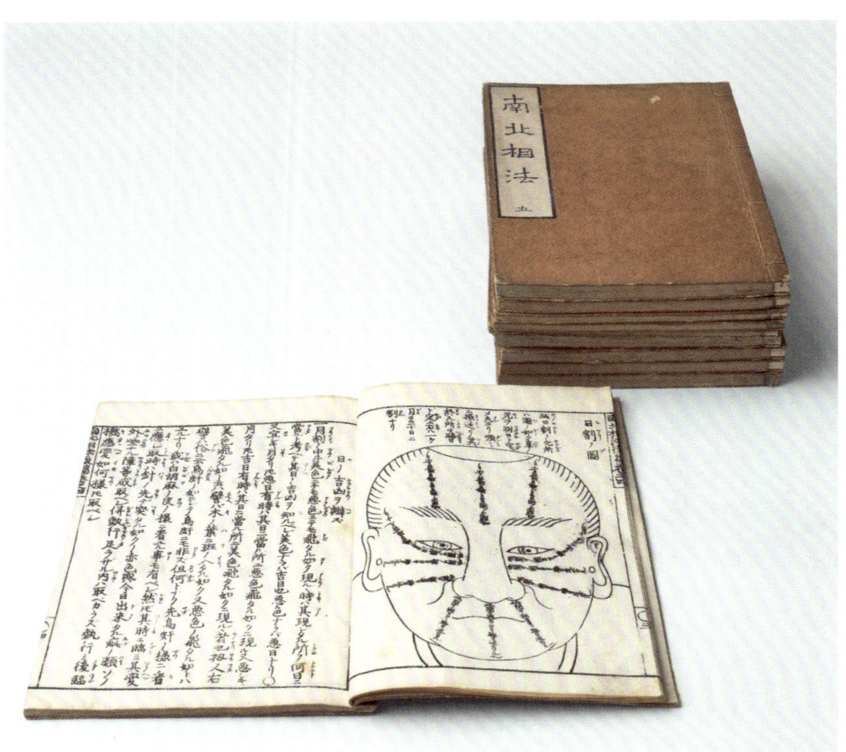

Mizuno Nanboku
Nanboku sōhō [Physiognomi-
sche Studien von Nanboku]
Nanboku sōhō [Physiognomic
Studies of Nanboku]
10 Bde. (zwei Serien), Tenpō Shoin,
1830–1890er Jahre (?)
10 vols. (two series), Tenpō Shoin,
1830s–1890s (?)
Holzschnitt Woodblock print
22,1 × 15,3
MAK, I 1648/1-5, I 1649/1-5

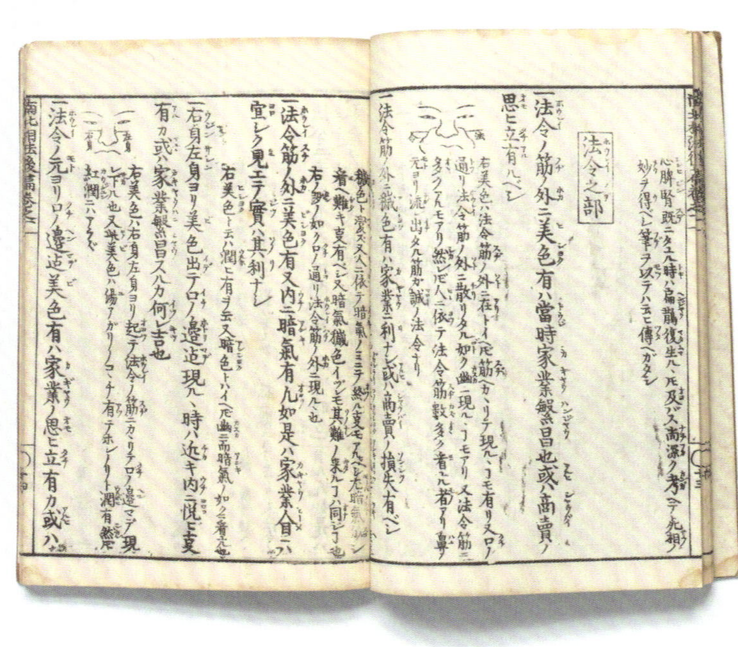

Physiognomische Studien aus China waren teilweise bis ins 20. Jahrhundert fester Bestandteil des ostasiatischen Wissenskosmos. Sie dienten dazu, die physische wie metaphysische Welt als Ganzes zu verstehen und vermittelten Methoden, wie sich an einzelnen Merkmalen des Menschen in seiner Gesamtheit – dazu zählen Körper, Stimme und Qi (Lebenskraft) – sowohl Charakterzüge und Krankheiten als auch das Schicksal und die Zukunft ermitteln und voraussagen lassen. Der Einfluss dieser Studien zeigt sich u. a. in historischen Ritual- und Festmasken, in der Porträtmalerei, in Darstellungen von Personen im populären japanischen Ukiyoe-Farbholzschnitt und in der Literatur.

Mizuno Nanboku (1760–1834) galt zu seinen Lebzeiten als der beste Gelehrte auf diesem Gebiet in Japan. Falten sind in seinem Werk eine komplexe Angelegenheit: So geben die Stellen, an denen sie in Erscheinung treten, Aufschluss über das Schicksal, das einen erwartet. Aber auch Form und Beschaffenheit der Falten und ihrer benachbarten Gesichtspartien sind entscheidend. Hier ist Nanbokus Beschreibung von Falten im Mundbereich zu sehen. Interessant sind dabei die Kriterien, anhand derer sie unterschieden und bewertet werden: u. a. Farbe, Glanz und Ausformung.

Physiognomic studies from China were an integral part of the East Asian cosmos of knowledge, in part right up into the 20th century. They served to elucidate the physical and metaphysical world as a whole, facilitating predictions regarding character types and illnesses, as well as a person's future fate, through the application of methodologies based on individual attributes considered holistically—these included a person's bodily characteristics, voice, and Qi (life force). The influence of such studies is manifested in historical ritual and festival masks, in portrait painting, in representations of individuals in the popular *ukiyoe* color woodblock prints of Japan, and in literature.

Mizuno Nanboku (1760–1834) was considered the leading expert in this field in Japan during his lifetime. Wrinkles are a complex phenomenon in his work: the locations in which they appear provide clues as to the fate that awaits one. But the form and composition of the wrinkles, as well as which parts of the face they border on, are also important. Here we show Nanboku's description of wrinkles around the mouth. Of interest are the criteria by which they are distinguished and assessed, to include color, luster, and shape.

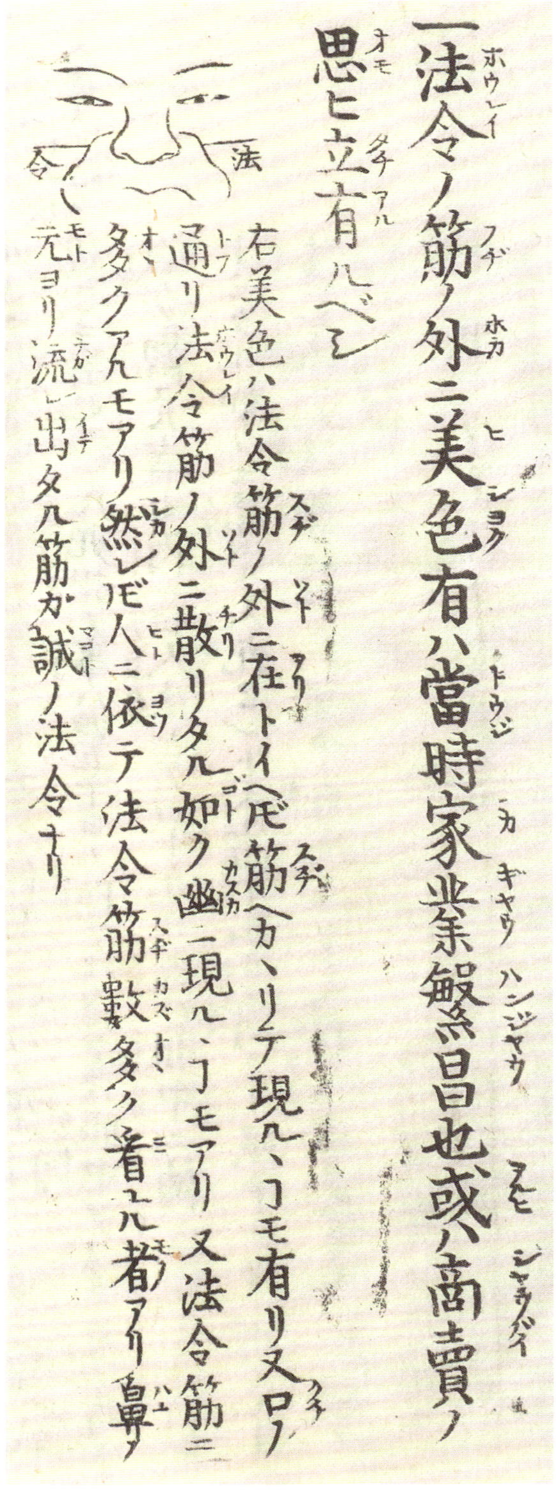

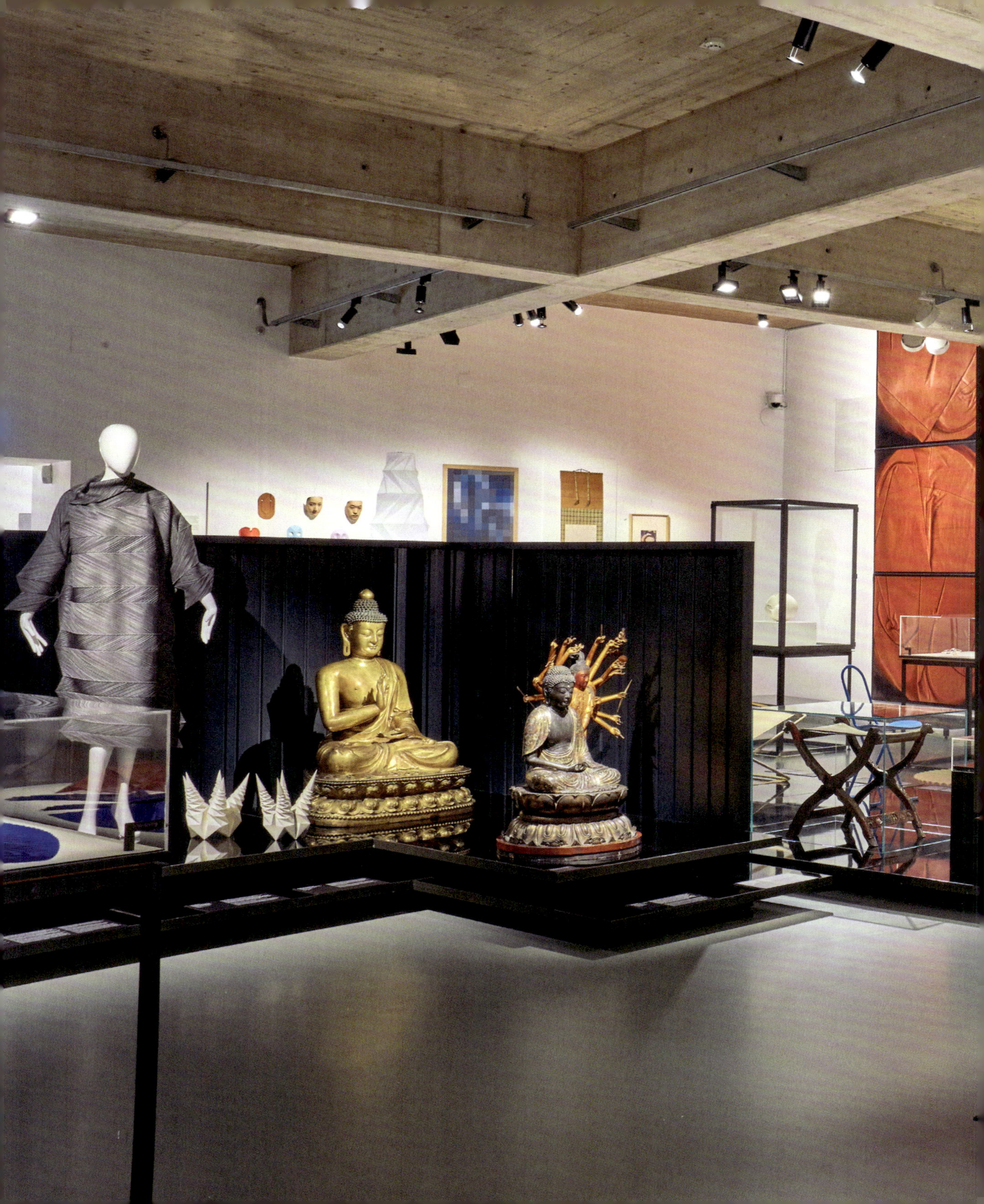

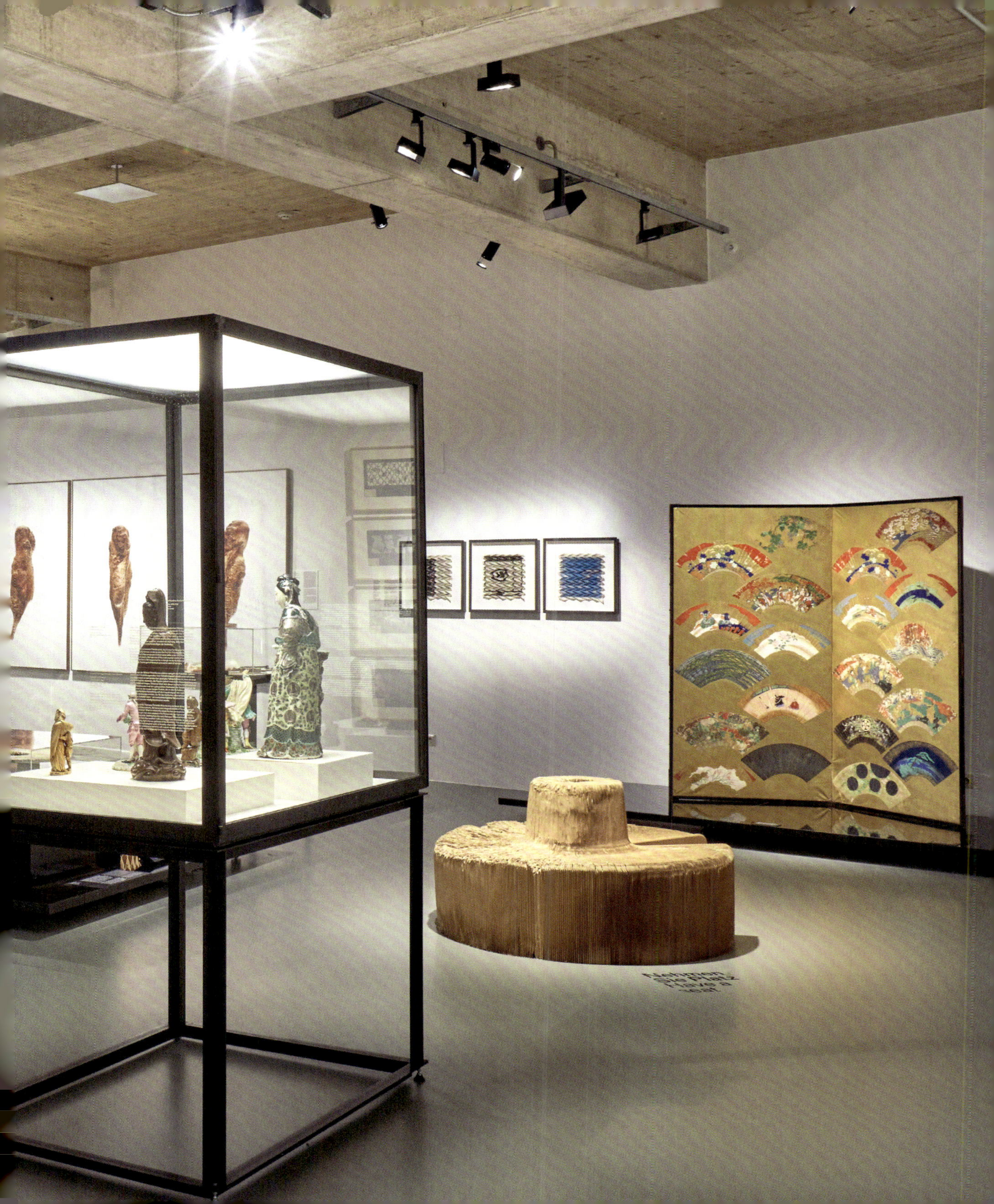

Plakat für den Film Poster for the film
The Lord of the Rings: The Return of the King
(Gollum)
2003
Papier, Farbdruck
Paper, color print
59,4 × 42
Privatsammlung Private collection

Eine der wichtigsten Figuren aus dem Fantasy-Roman *Der Herr der Ringe* (1954/55) des britischen Autors J. R. R. Tolkien – Gollum – ist auf einem der Plakate für die gleichnamige Verfilmung von Peter Jackson (2001–2003) zu sehen. Gollums Obsession für den mächtigen „Herrscherring" und das zeitweise Tragen dieses Rings nehmen ihn mental völlig in Besitz und lassen ihn körperlich verfallen, während nur seine Augen die Besessenheit seiner Seele zum Ausdruck bringen.
Hollywood bedient sich hier teilweise aus klischeehaften Darstellungen von Alter und Wahnsinn: Gollums äußeres Erscheinungsbild – nackt, faltig und abgemagert, aber mit besessenem Blick – ist ein visueller Hinweis auf seine Gier, Verbissenheit und den Drang nach Macht.

One of the most important characters from the fantasy novel *The Lord of the Rings* (1954/55) by the British writer J. R. R. Tolkien—Gollum—can be seen on one of the posters for the film adaptation of the same name by Peter Jackson (2000–2003). His obsession with the powerful "Ruler's Ring" and his wearing the ring for a time have completely taken over his mind to the detriment of his body, while only his eyes glare with the obsession that governs his soul.
Hollywood here partly makes use of stereotyped representations of age and insanity: Gollum's appearance—naked, covered in wrinkles, and emaciated, but with a haunted look in his eyes—is a visual manifestation of his greed, singlemindedness, and thirst for power.

Oshiguma von Kabuki-Schauspieler by Kabuki actor
Nakamura Tokizō III (1895–1959)
Japan, Mitte 20. Jh. mid-20th c.
Hängerolle, Farben auf Textil
Hanging scroll, paint on textile
180 × 47
Privatsammlung Private collection

Abdrücke der Theaterschminke eines Kabuki-Schauspielers (Japanisch *kumadori*) sind nicht nur Kunstwerke. Da sie oft direkt nach der Aufführung eines Theaterstücks gemacht werden, gelten sie verständlicherweise auch als exklusive Fanartikel.
Die *kuma*-Linien, eine Schminktechnik aus dem Kabuki-Theater, sind allerdings keine Gesichtsfalten, sie markieren anschwellende Ader- und Muskelkonturen, um die Gefühlsregungen und Charakterzüge einer Figur plastisch und typisierend abzubilden. Hier sind die sogenannten *chaguma* (braune *kuma*-Linien) zu sehen. Sie sind Rollen vorbehalten, in denen Menschen sich in übernatürliche Wesen wie Geister oder *oni*-Dämonen verwandeln.

The makeup imprinted from a Kabuki actor's face (in Japanese *kumadori*) is not only a work of art. Since it is fabricated directly after a theater performance, it is understandably also considered an exclusive fan article.
However, the *kuma* lines that are part of Kabuki face makeup are not wrinkles but represent swollen veins and muscles, vividly depicting the figure's typical emotions and character traits. Here one can see the so-called *chaguma* (brown *kuma* lines). They are reserved for roles in which people are transformed into supernatural beings such as ghosts or *oni* demons.

新古演劇十種うち内　戻橋乃鬼女を　津らめて

三吾　時蕗

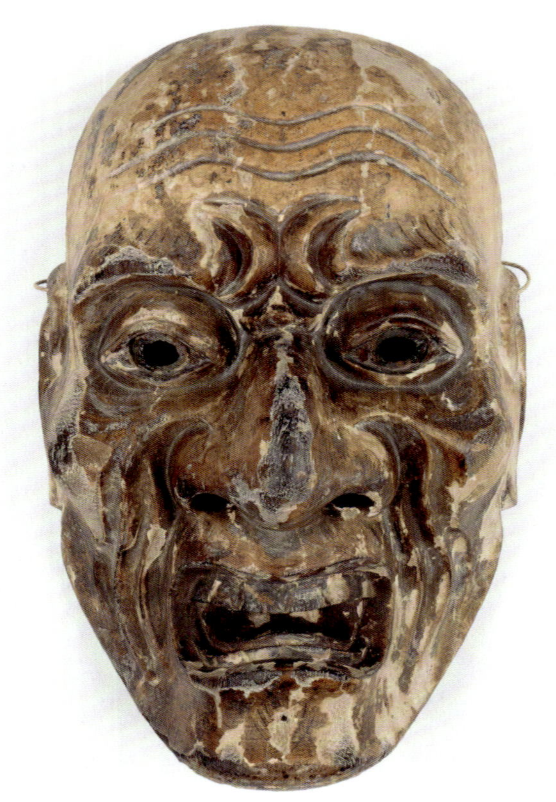

Nō-Maske des Typus *shikami*

Noh mask of the *shikami* type

Japan, 19. Jh. 19th c.
Holz, geschnitzt, bemalt und lackiert
Wood, carved, painted, and lacquered
22 × 15
MAK, PL 650

Masken genießen in Ostasien traditionell eine hohe Wertschätzung. Insbesondere Nō-Masken zeigen eine große Bandbreite typisierter menschlicher Charaktere (unterschiedliche soziale Klassen, Geschlechter und Altersgruppen), die von den Schauspielern belebt werden. Ein einziger Darsteller kann durch einen Maskenwechsel eine oder mehrere Figuren mit diversen Identitäten verkörpern. Künstlerisch sorgt die Maske für die Spannung zwischen der starren plastischen Form und ihrer Belebung durch den Schauspieler.

Bei dieser Maske des japanischen Nō-Theaters handelt es sich um den *shikami*-Typus eines Dämons. Tief eingegrabene Falten zwischen den hochgezogenen Augenbrauen und Zähnefletschen deuten auf seinen bösartigen, brutalen Charakter hin.

In East Asia, masks are traditionally highly valued. Noh masks in particular manifest a broad cross-section of typical human traits—different social classes, genders, and age groups— brought to life by the Noh actors. By changing masks, a single actor can play several roles with different identities. A mask creates tension between its rigid plastic form and its being brought to life by the actor's art.

This Japanese Noh theater mask represents a *shikami* demon. Deep wrinkles between his raised eyebrows and his bared teeth indicate his wicked, brutal character.

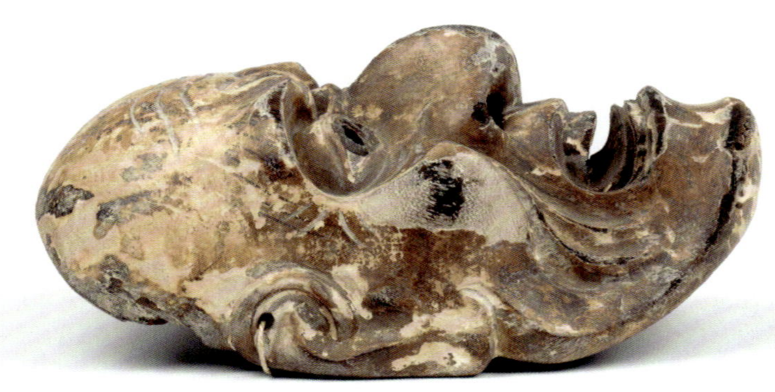

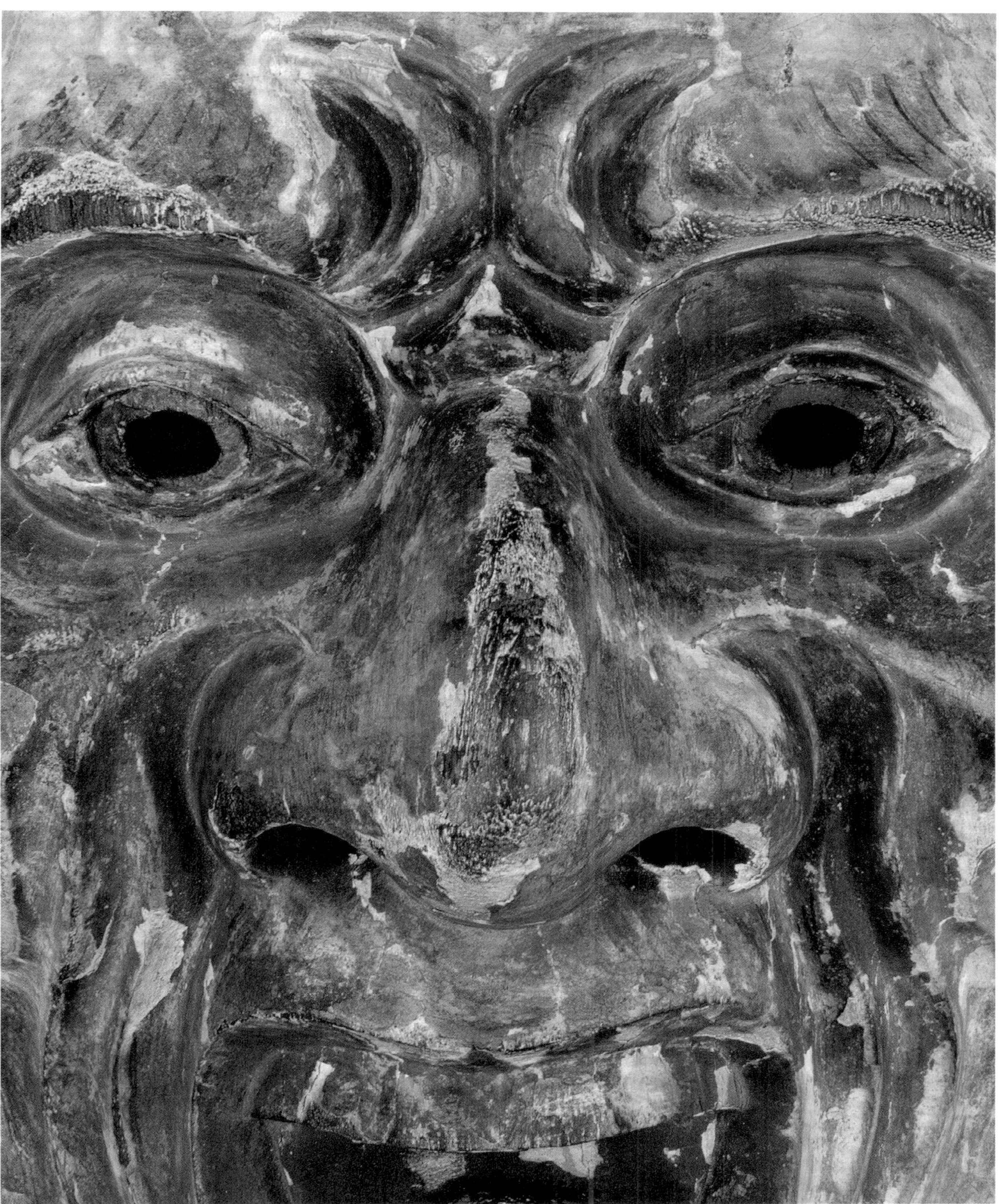

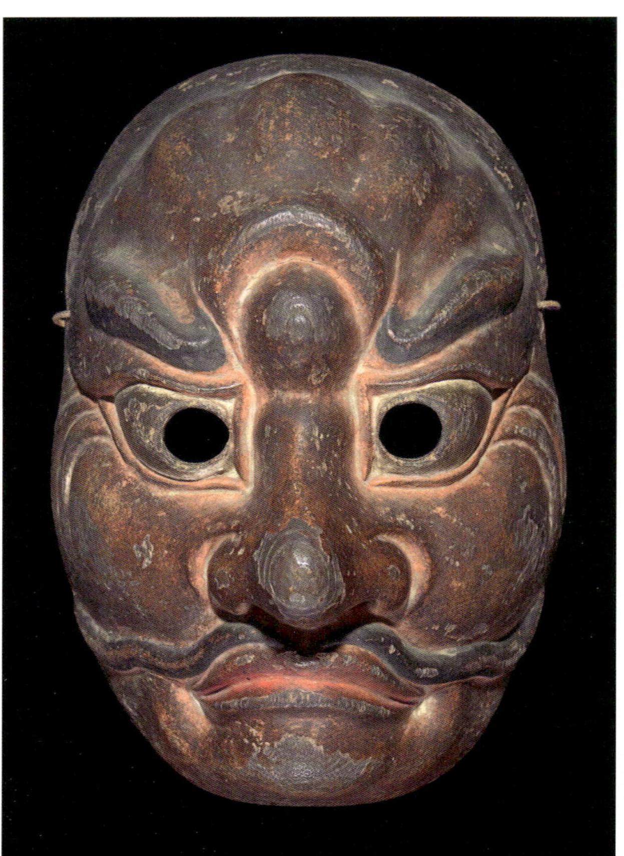

bugaku-Tanzmaske für die Rolle *kitoku*
bugaku dance mask for the role of *kitoku*

Japan, 1. Hälfte 20. Jh. first half 20th c.
Holz, farbig bemalt
Wood, color painted
25 × 17
MAK, PL 646

Bugaku-Tänze entstanden in Japan im 8./9. Jahrhundert im höfischen Kontext, sie wurden aber auch in buddhistischen und shintoistischen Zeremonien aufgeführt. Ihr Ursprung lässt sich auf China, Korea, Indien und Südostasien zurückführen. Masken wurden verwendet, um Figuren mit übernatürlichen Kräften darzustellen.
Kitoku ist ein nordischer (kontinental-chinesischer) Krieger; die Maske zeigt seinen typischen strengen Gesichtsausdruck mit fest geschlossenen Lippen, die Entschlossenheit signalisieren, seine buschigen Augenbrauen und seinen Oberlippenbart.

Bugaku dances began in the Japan of the 8/9th century at the royal court, though they were also performed as part of Buddhist and Shinto rituals. They originated in China, Korea, India, and South-eastern Asia. Masks were used to represent characters with supernatural powers.
Kitoku is a northern warrior from mainland China; the mask shows his typically stern facial expression with lips tightly closed, signaling determination, his bushy eyebrows and mustache.

Okina-Maske
Okina mask

Japan, Edo-Zeit Edo Period
1603–1868
Holz, geschnitzt, bemalt und lackiert
Wood, carved, painted, and lacquered
21,5 × 14,8 × 8
MAK, PL 656

Die *okina*-Maske (*hakushikijō*-Typ) zeigt eine Gottheit in Gestalt eines alten Mannes. Sie wird zusammen mit ihrem schwarzen Pendant in einem speziellen gleichnamigen Nō-Theaterstück verwendet, das zu feierlichen Anlässen wie Neujahr aufgeführt wird. Das faltige Gesicht mit breitem Lächeln, buschigen weißen Augenbrauen und langem Bart geht ikonografisch auf eine daoistische Heiligenfigur zurück und verweist auf Glück und langes Leben.

This *hakushikijō* style *okina* mask depicts a deity in the shape of an old man. It is used, together with its black counterpart, in a special Noh theater play of the same name performed on special occasions such as New Year. The wrinkled face with its broad smile, bushy white eyebrows and long beard has its iconographic roots in a Daost holy man and stands for good fortune and longevity.

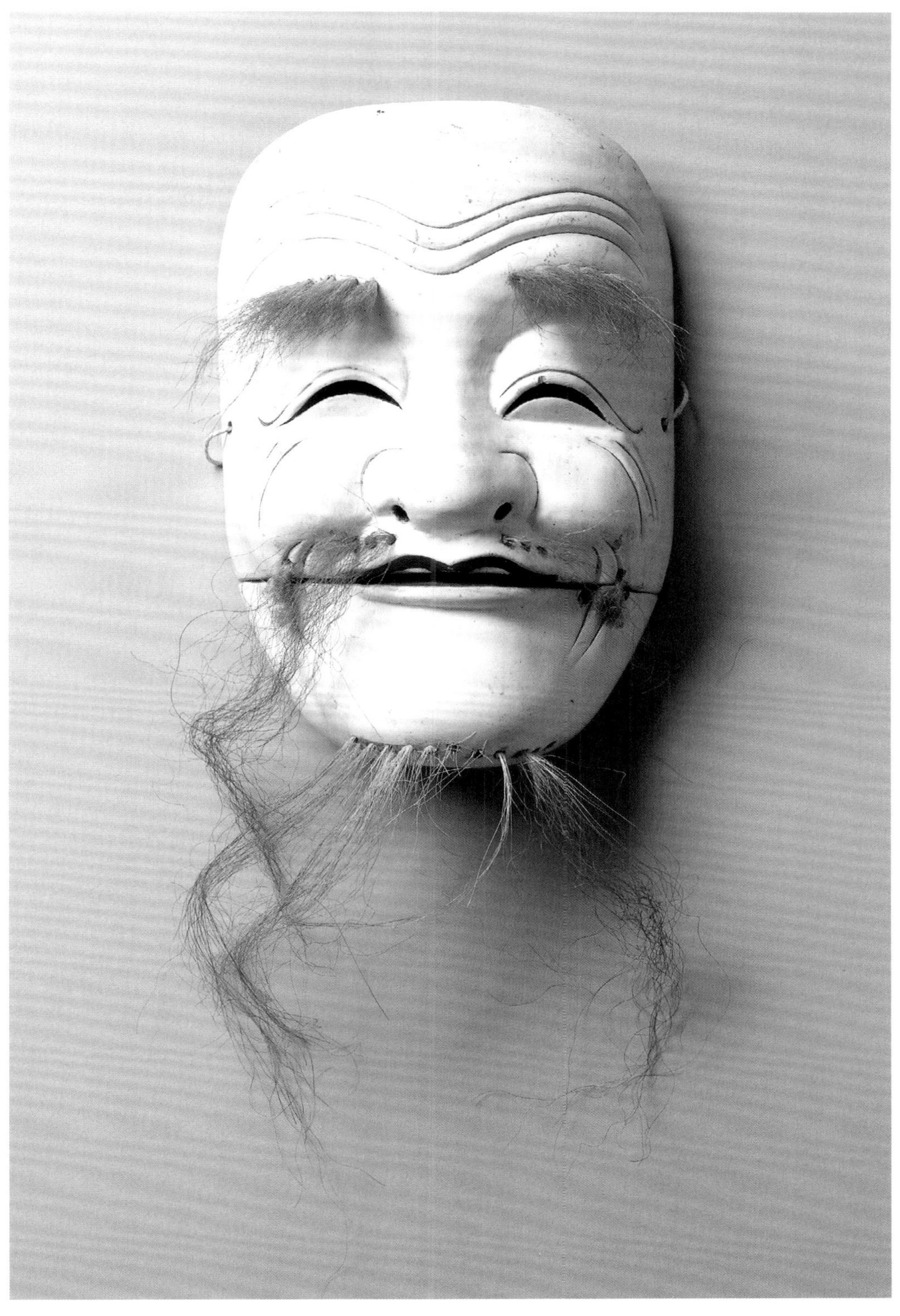

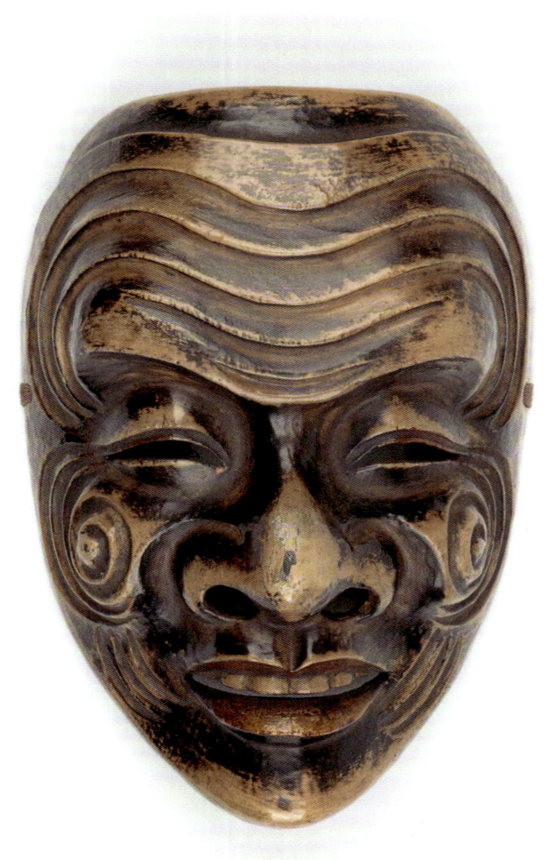

Maske

Mask

Japan, o. D. date unknown
Holz, geschnitzt, Bemalung abgerieben
Wood, carved, painting rubbed off
21,4 × 15,2 × 7,9
MAK, JW 87

Hierbei handelt es sich wahrscheinlich um eine *sanbasō*-Maske, die im rituellen *okina*-Stück des Nō-Theaters getragen wird. Der dunkle Teint, die starke Faltenbildung im Gesicht, speziell die wirbelförmigen Faltenlinien auf den Wangen und die lächelnden Gesichtszüge, sprechen für diese Zuschreibung, allerdings scheint die Maske nicht den vollständigen Herstellungsprozess durchlaufen zu haben, da die Abkopplung des Kinns, der Bart und die Augenbrauen fehlen.

This is probably a *sanbasō* mask worn in a ritual *okina* drama of Noh theater. The dark coloring, the strongly wrinkled face, and in particular the spiral wrinkles on the cheeks and smiling features, speak for this attribution. However, the mask appears to be incompletely made—the deccupling mechanism for the chin and the beard and eyebrows are missing.

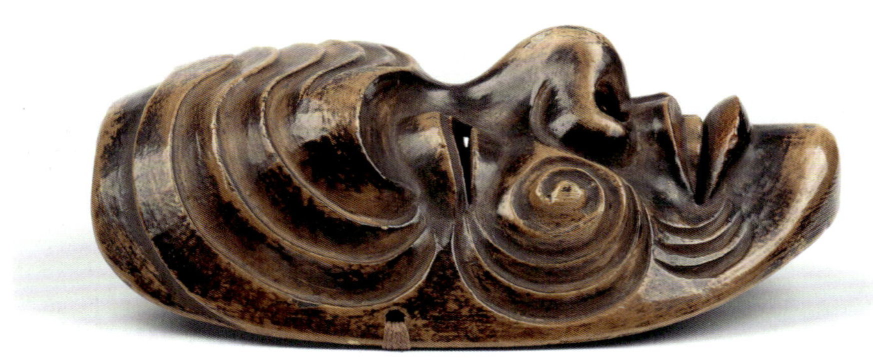

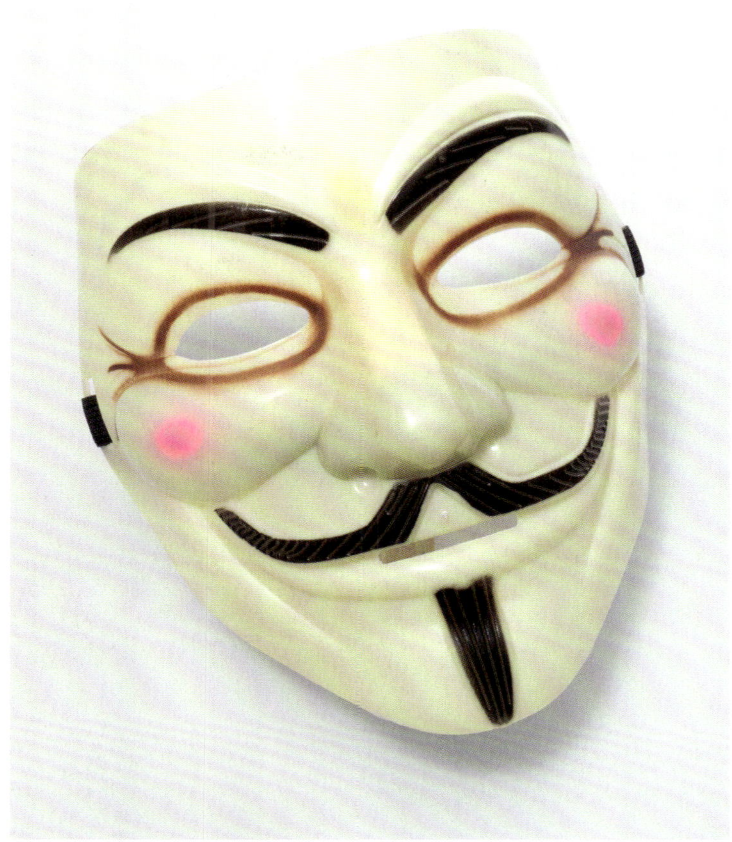

David Lloyd, Guy-Fawkes-Maske
(„Anonymous-Maske")
David Lloyd, Guy Fawkes mask
("Anonymous mask")
1982/2006
Kunststoff, Gummi und Schaumstoff
Plastic, rubber, and foam
21,4 × 17,5 × 10,2
MAK, DS 466

Der britische Comic-Zeichner David Lloyd erschuf in seinem Comic-Roman *V wie Vendetta* (1982–1985/88) das ikonische Maskengesicht des lächelnden Guy Fawkes, eines britischen Revolutionärs aus dem 17. Jahrhundert. Spätestens nach der Verfilmung des Romans (2005) wurde die „Anonymous-Maske" mit dem Gesicht von Guy Fawkes zum Symbol für politischen Protest und den Widerstand gegen Tyrannei – eine globale Ikone der Protestbewegungen und der Populärkultur des frühen 21. Jahrhunderts.

Lloyds Design dieses stilisierten Gesichts verbindet Gegensätzlichkeiten: Entmenschlichung und Starre (abstrahierte Gesichtszüge) treffen auf Vermenschlichung und Lebendigkeit (faltiges Lächeln). Diese Spannung verleiht der Maske viele Nuancen.

In his comic strip novel *V for Vendetta* (1982–85/88), the British comic artist David Lloyd created his iconic mask of the laughing Guy Fawkes, a 17th-century British revolutionary. At the latest after the novel was filmed in 2005, the "Anonymous Mask" of Guy Fawkes's face became a symbol of political protest and resistance to tyranny—an icon of protest movements worldwide and of early 21st-century pop culture.

Lloyd's design of this stylized face is a combination of opposites: it is rigid and dehumanized, and at the same time full of life and humanity, its face creased by a smile. This tension imparts to the mask a richly nuanced aura.

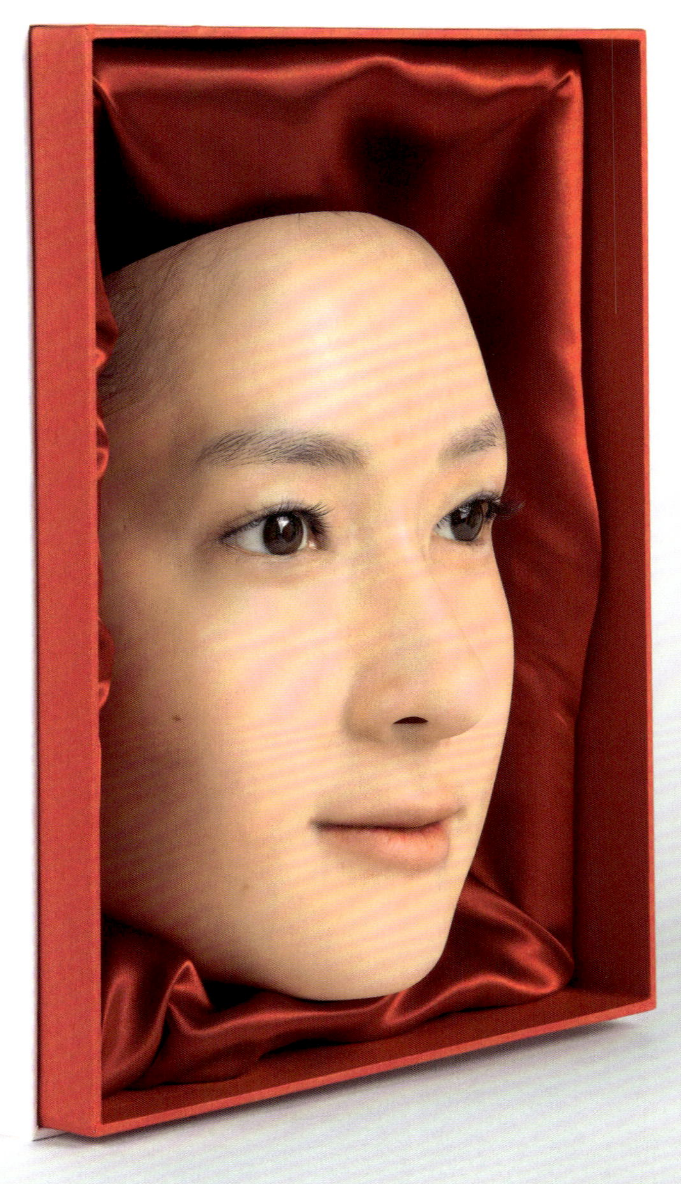

Usono inc. (Tokyo)

ano kao (*That face* project), No. 0
2021
Plastik, 3D-Druck
Plastic, 3D print
19,3 × 14,8 × 8
MAK, PL 1057
>

ano kao (*That face* project), No. 01
2021
Plastik, 3D-Druck
Plastic, 3D print
18,9 × 14,6 × 8,8
MAK, PL 1054
<

Diese hyperrealistischen Masken aus (nachbearbeitetem) Kunststoff, Teil der Projektserie *That face*, basieren auf Daten von gescannten Gesichtern real existierender Menschen und wurden mit einem 3D-Drucker produziert. Das Projekt kauft „das Gesicht" von Menschen, reproduziert es und verkauft es dann als anonymisierte Maske, die als „zweites Gesicht" getragen werden kann. Durch den Einsatz von Reproduktionstechnologien des 21. Jahrhunderts und das glatte Erscheinungsbild lassen sich diese Masken als zeitgenössische Antwort auf die historische Masken-Tradition lesen. Zugleich sind sie auch als eine künstlerische Intervention zu verstehen, die kritische Themen wie Identität, Individualität, Authentizität, Reproduktion oder Käuflichkeit eines menschlichen Gesichts beleuchtet.

These hyper-realistic masks made of (reworked) synthetic material from the *That face* project series are based on data from the scanned faces of real people and were created using a 3D printer. The project purchases people's "faces," reproduces them, and then sells them as anonymized masks that can be worn by anyone as a "second face." In their use of 21st-century reproduction technology and their smooth visual appearance, these masks may be read as a contemporary answer to the historical tradition of mask-making. At the same time, they can also be understood as an artistic intervention shedding light on critical themes such as the identity, individuality, authenticity, reproduction, and the marketability of the human face.

Lex Pott
Family 3 of 7 Paper Characters
2022
Papier Paper
17–24,5 × 13–19,5
MAK, DS 509

Die Papiermasken des Designers Lex Pott aus Rotterdam zeichnen sich durch eine grafisch extrem reduzierte Formensprache und das Spiel mit der Technik des Papierfaltens aus. Diese abstrakten Masken zeigen in sieben Varianten die Grundelemente, die ein Gesicht ausmachen: Löcher und Falten, die die Volumina einzelner Gesichtspartien definieren.

The paper masks of designer Lex Pott from Rotterdam are characterized by a graphically extremely minimal form language and playful use of technology. These abstract masks show in seven variations the basic elements that go to make up a face: the holes and wrinkles that define the dimensions of individual parts of the human countenance.

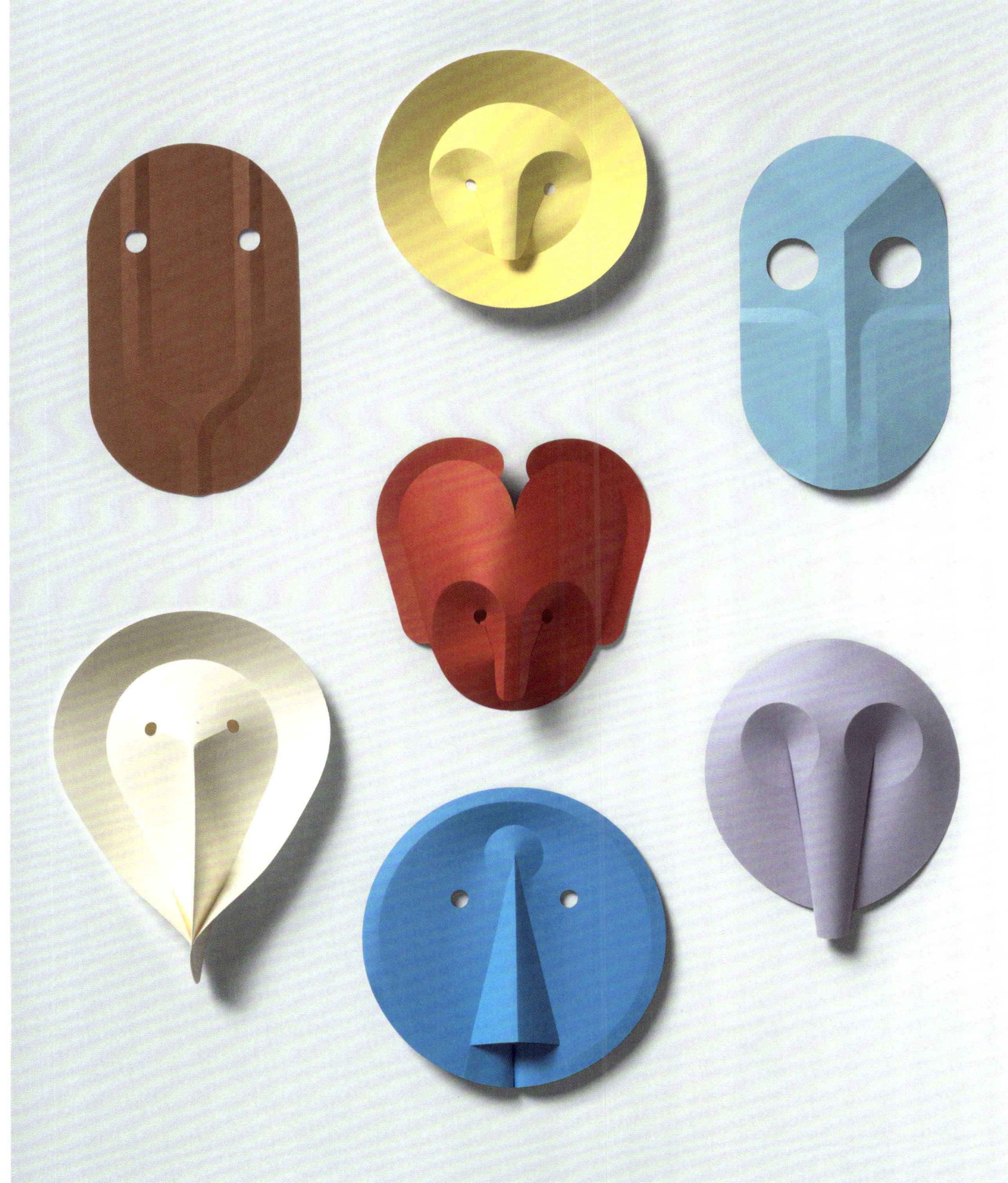

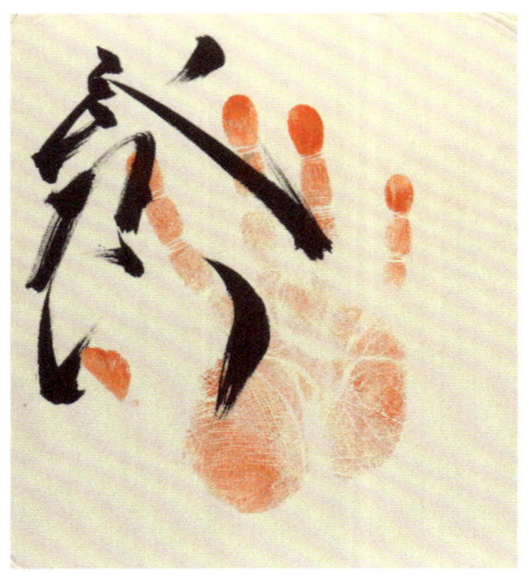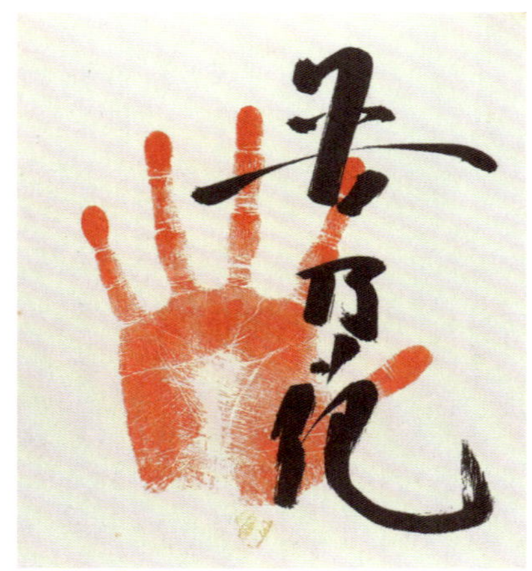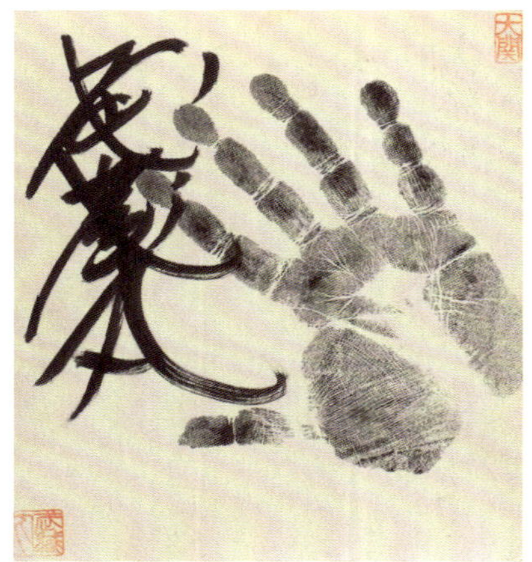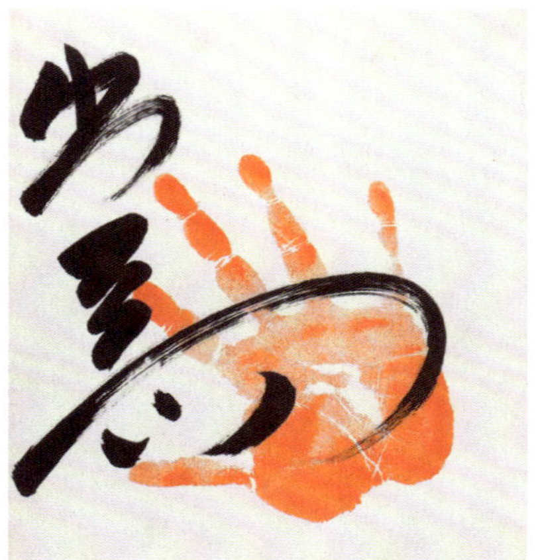

Signierte Handabdrücke von fünf Sumō-Ringern
Signed handprints of five sumo wrestlers
(Musashimaru, Dejima, Konishiki, Wakanohana, Mitoizumi)
Japan, 1990er Jahre 1990s
Farbe auf Papier Paint on paper
27 × 24
Privatsammlung Private collection

Finger- oder Handabdrücke galten bis zum Beginn des Zeitalters der DNA-Analyse als unverwechselbare persönliche Signatur. Da die Linien bzw. Falten auf den Handflächen physisch entstandene Spuren sind, weisen sie einen hohen Echtheitsgrad auf. Handabdrücke von Sumō-Ringern sind allerdings viel mehr als nur Fanartikel mit persönlichem „Touch". Die Verbundenheit von Sumō-Ringern mit Ritualen, ihre Rolle als Kämpfer und Verkörperung von Gottheiten und vor allem ihre kraftvolle Körperlichkeit verleihen ihren Abdrücken magische Kraft, weshalb sie bis heute als Talisman gelten und gerne Förderern als Geschenk übergeben werden.

Until the advent of DNA analysis, fingerprints and handprints were considered distinctive personal signatures. Since the lines or wrinkles on the palm of the hand are physically generated characteristics, they may indeed claim a high degree of authenticity. However, handprints of sumo wrestlers are much more than just fan merchandise with a personal "touch." The connection of sumo wrestlers to rituals, their role as fighters and embodiments of deities and, above all, their powerful physicality lend their prints magical power. They are still regarded as talismans and are used as gifts for patrons.

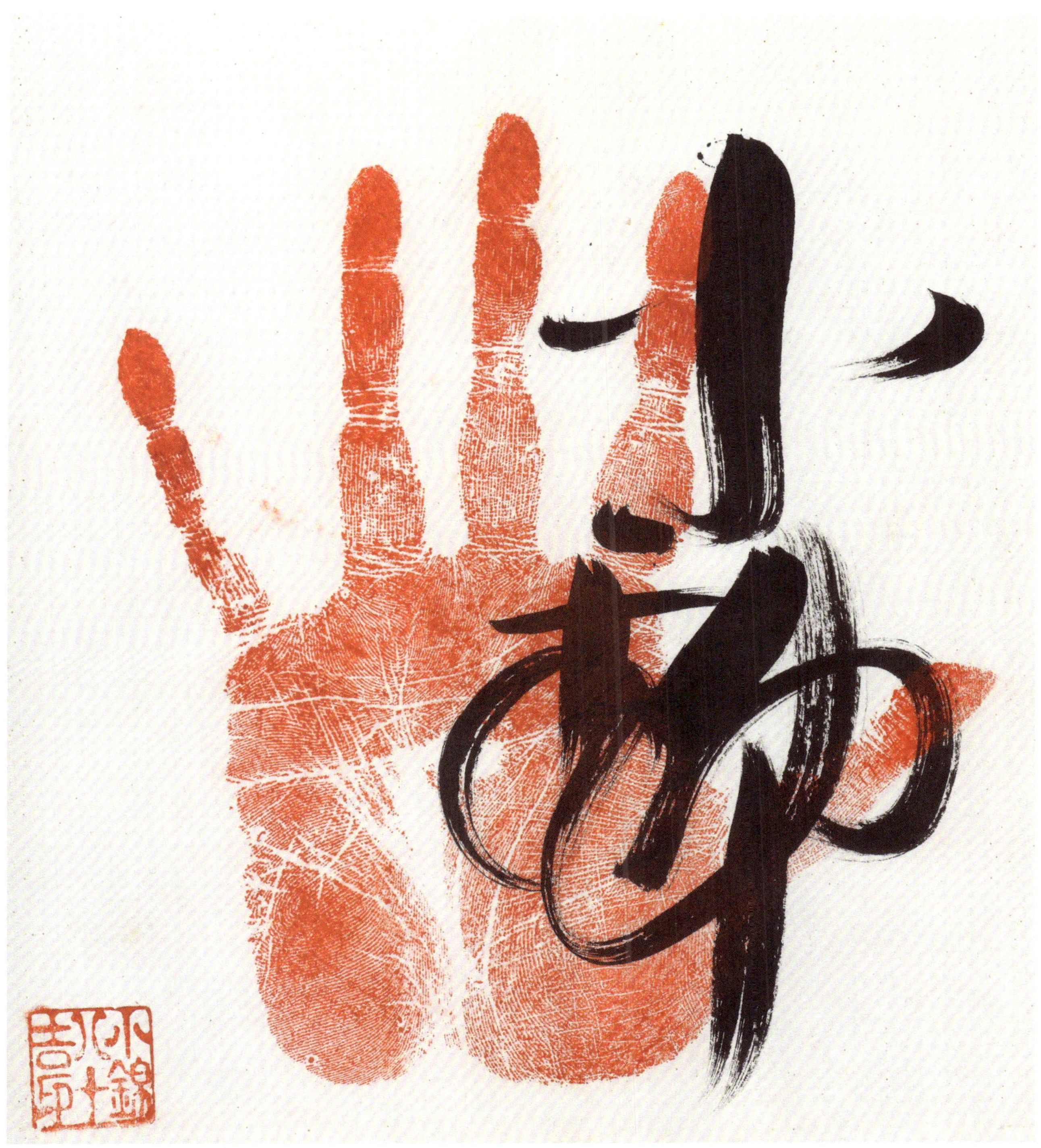

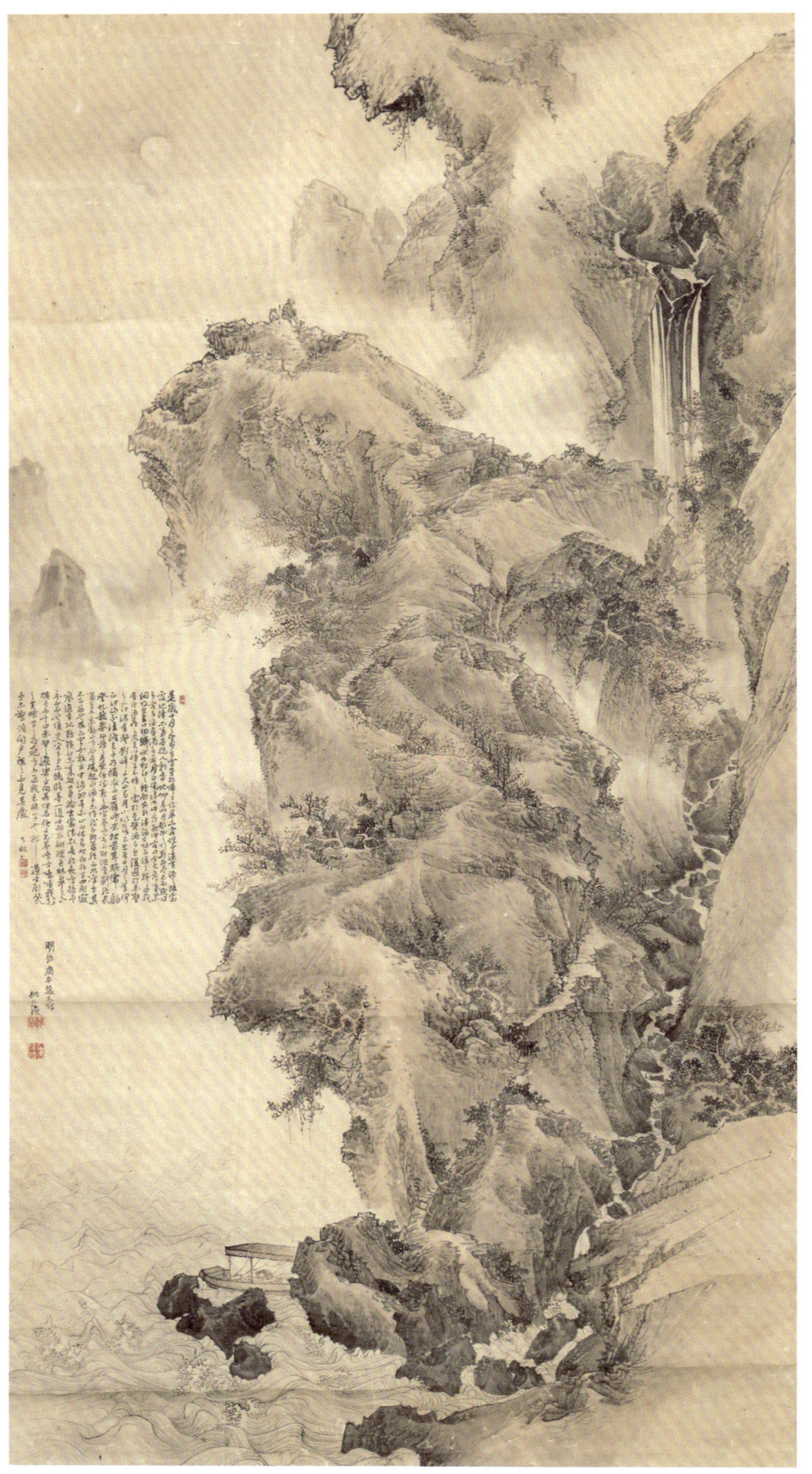

Yamamoto Tōkoku
Ohne Titel Untitled
Japan, 1870
Tusche und Farbe auf Papier
Ink and color on paper
210 × 103,5
MAK, MAL 210

Aika Furukawa

Lost Colours – 02
2021
Sumi-Tusche und Öl auf transparenter
Leinwand
Sumi ink and oil on transparent canvas
420 × 100
Aichi Prefectural Museum of Art

Aika Furukawa
Configuration – 30.8
2018
Öl und Acryl auf transparenter Leinwand
Oil and acrylics on transparent canvas
420 × 104
Aichi Prefectural Museum of Art

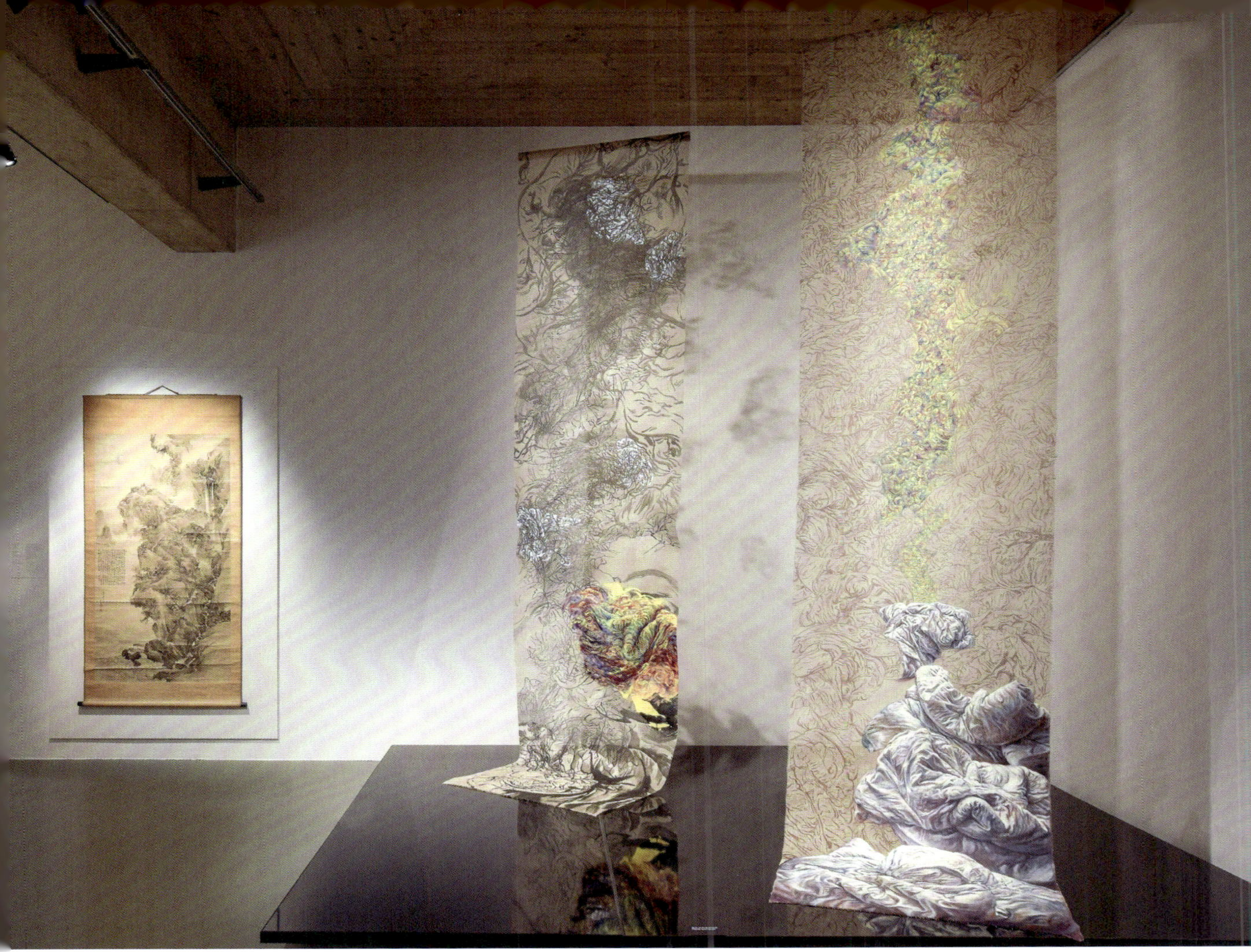

Die beiden Arbeiten der japanischen Künstlerin Aika Furukawa und eine japanische Landschaftsmalerei von 1870 in chinesischem Stil bieten einen spannenden Ansatz zur Frage der Entropie (Unordnung) als Naturgesetz der materiellen Welt. Furukawas Arbeiten *Lost Colours – 02* (2021) und *Configuration – 30.8* (2018) bestehen aus Bild-Collagen von Falten, denen sie immer wieder in ihrem Alltag begegnet ist und die sie zeichnerisch dokumentiert hat. Das vier Meter lange Faltengeflecht zeigt einerseits formell verblüffend deutliche Parallelen zur Literatenmalerei, andererseits manifestiert sich darin auch das Bild unserer heutigen Welt des Überflusses und der Unordnung – ein ironischer Kontrast zur Idee der Literatenmalerei, die den Idealzustand vollkommener Harmonie zwischen Mensch und Himmel bzw. Natur zum Ausdruck bringen soll.

Both works by the Japanese artist Aika Furukawa and an 1870 Japanese landscape painting in the Chinese style are a fascinating statement on the theme of entropy as a natural law of the material world. Furukawa's *Lost Colours – 02* (2021) und *Configuration – 30.8* (2018) consist of image collages of folds that she constantly meets in everyday life and has documented in her drawings. The four-meter-long network of folds on the one hand manifests surprisingly strong formal affinities with literati painting and on the other presents an image of our contemporary world of superfluity and chaos—an ironic contrast to the values of literati painting, for the latter is meant to express an ideal state of perfect harmony between humanity and heaven or nature.

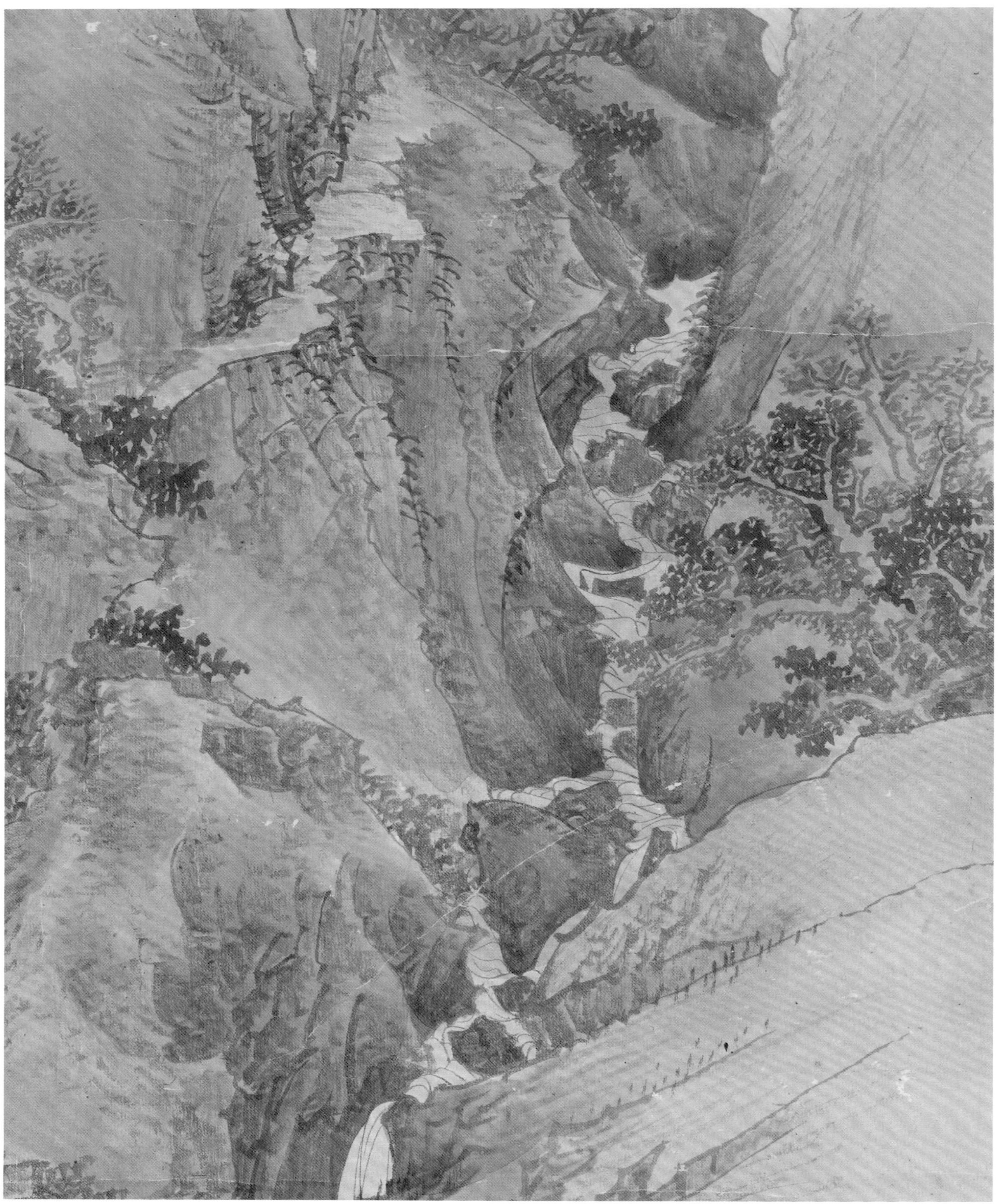

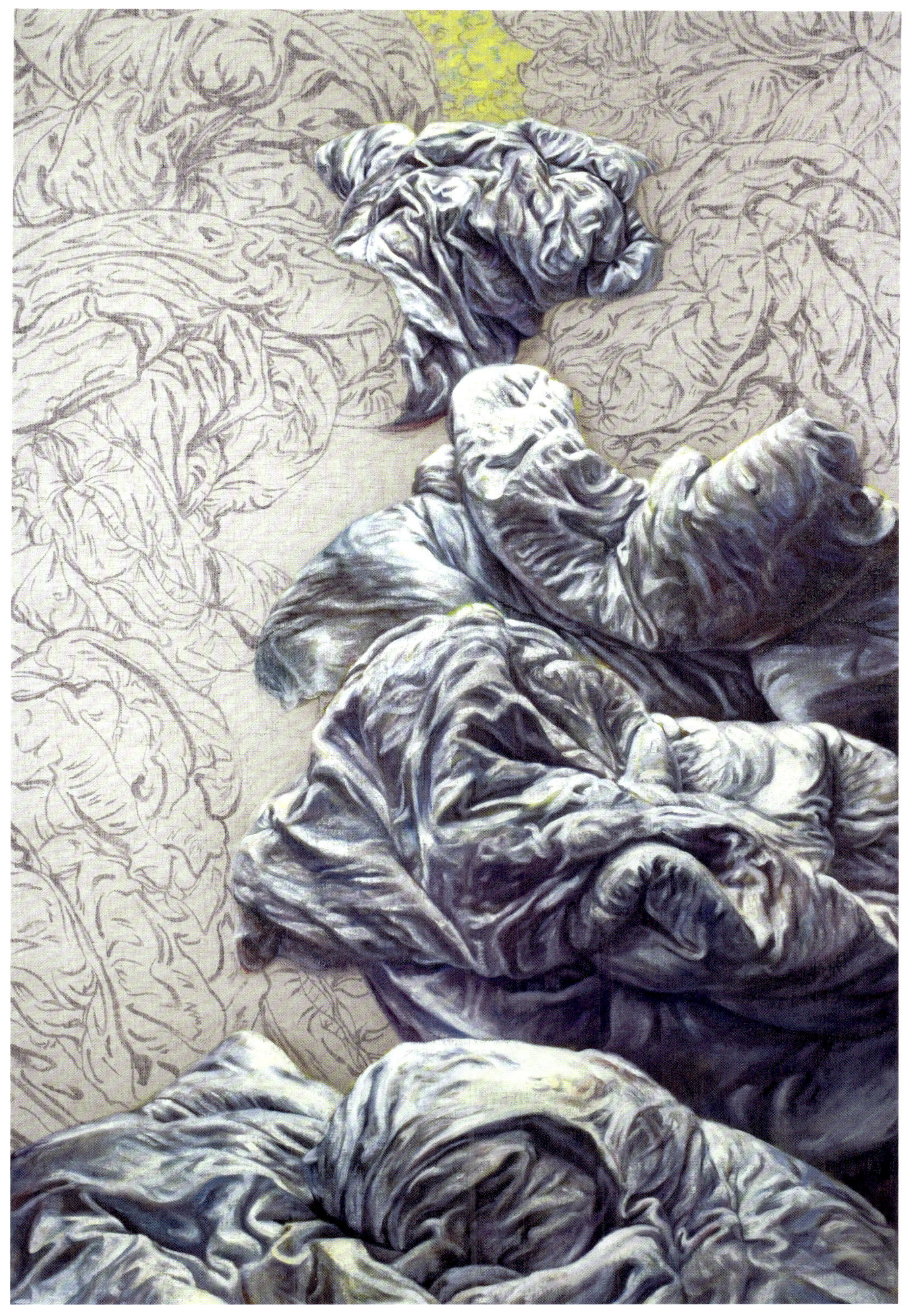

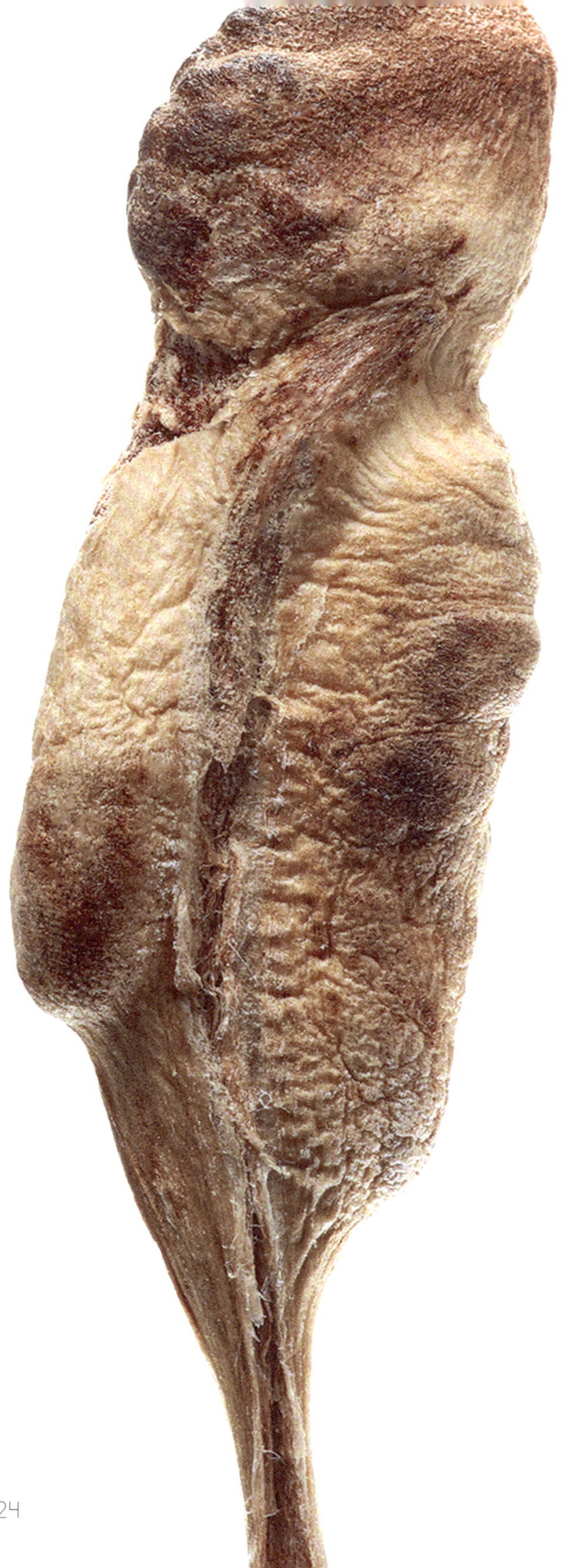

Song Jing
Venus von Wien (Serie von drei Arbeiten)
Venus of Vienna (series of three works)
2019
Fine Art Pigment Print auf on
Premium Photo Luster Papier paper
165 × 110
Courtesy of the artist

Song Jings Arbeiten konfrontieren uns mit überdimensionalen Nahaufnahmen eines undefinierbaren faltigen Objekts. Dass sie jeweils einen einfachen Dattelkern zeigen, ist schlichtweg überraschend. Ein Kern kann verschiedene symbolische Bedeutungen haben: Als Speicher generationenübergreifender Informationen können seine Falten eine visuelle Metapher sein für die Komplexität der raum- und zeitübergreifenden Verarbeitung von gelebter bzw. erlebter Geschichte.

Wird der Kern als Quelle des Lebens interpretiert, stehen seine Falten sinnbildlich für die Prozesshaftigkeit der entropischen Unordnung: Entropie ist ein fundamentales Grundprinzip der Physik, demzufolge sich die Welt der Materie von Zuständen der Ordnung auf eine ständig wachsende Unordnung hinbewegt. Der faltige Kern als physische Manifestation vergangener Milliarden Jahre in kleinem Format ist hier ein Ausgangspunkt für die nächsten (Ent-)Faltungen, die sich zur größeren Komplexität hin weiterentwickeln werden.

Diese Metapher des Dattelkerns und vor allem seine visuelle Reminiszenz an das weibliche Geschlecht offenbaren kritische Gender- und feministische Dimensionen dieser Serie. Trotz des Anscheins biologisch-symbolischer Konkretheit entschärft ihre überdeutliche Sichtbarkeit durch eine extreme Nahsicht das potenzielle Gefühl der Obszönität, enttäuscht aber auch souverän den Blick der Begierde – ein klarer Kontrast zum kunsthistorischen Urahn dieses Bildtopos, Gustave Courbets *Der Ursprung der Welt*. So greift Song Jings Serie augenzwinkernd in die nach wie vor problematische Darstellungspraxis der Gegenwart ein und hinterfragt die Positionierung des Weiblichen im Patriarchat unserer Welt.

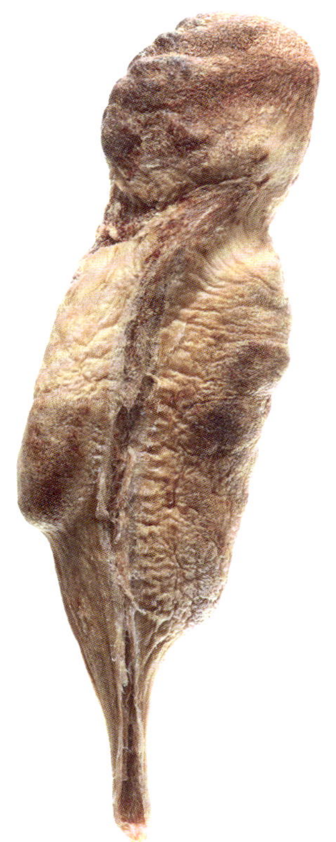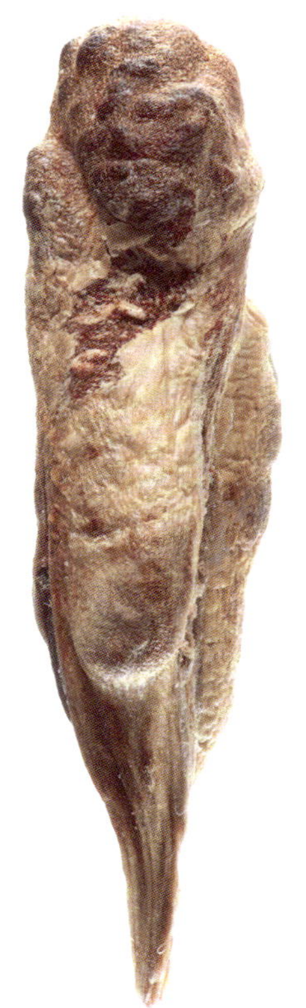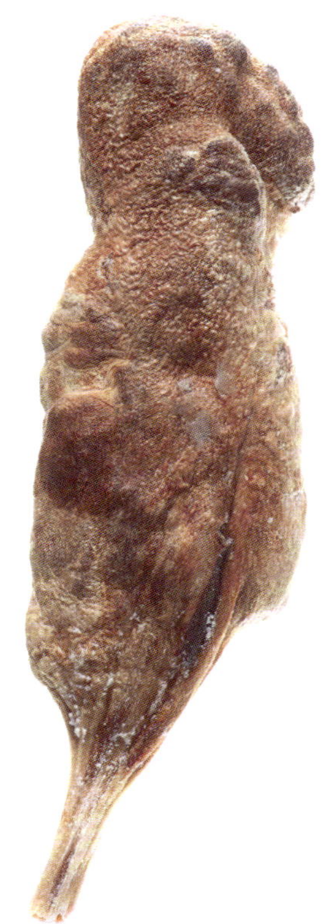

Song Jing's works confront us with oversized close-ups of an indefinable object whose surface is incised with folds. The fact that the close-ups are of simple date kernels is simply remarkable. A kernel can have a range of different symbolic meanings: as a reservoir of information passed on through the generations, its surface folds can be a visual metaphor for the complex processing of lived and experienced history spanning space and time.

If one interprets the kernel as the source of life, its folds symbolize inevitable progress towards entropic chaos, entropy being a fundamental principle of physics, according to which the material world is moving from a state of order towards a constantly growing state of disorder. The kernel with is folds as a miniature physical manifestation of the past billions of years is here the starting point for the next (un-)folding, that will progressively develop towards greater complexity.

This metaphor of the date kernel and above all its visual resemblance to the female sex reveal the critical gender and feminist dimensions of this series. However, despite the kernel's semblance of biological-symbolic specificity, its overwhelming visibility through being photographed in extreme close-up defuses any hint of obscenity while also confidently nullifying any suggestion of voyeurism—in clear contrast to the art-historical ancestor of this pictorial topos, *The Origin of the World* by Gustave Courbet. Song Jing's series is thus a tongue-in-cheek intervention into the ongoing problem of contemporary representational practice, questioning the positioning of the female in the patriarchy of the world we are living in.

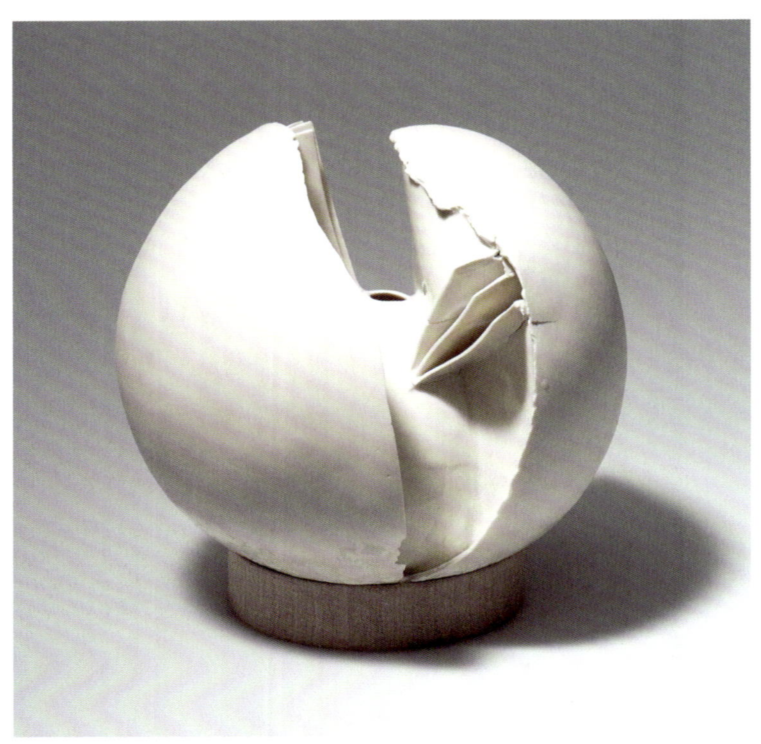

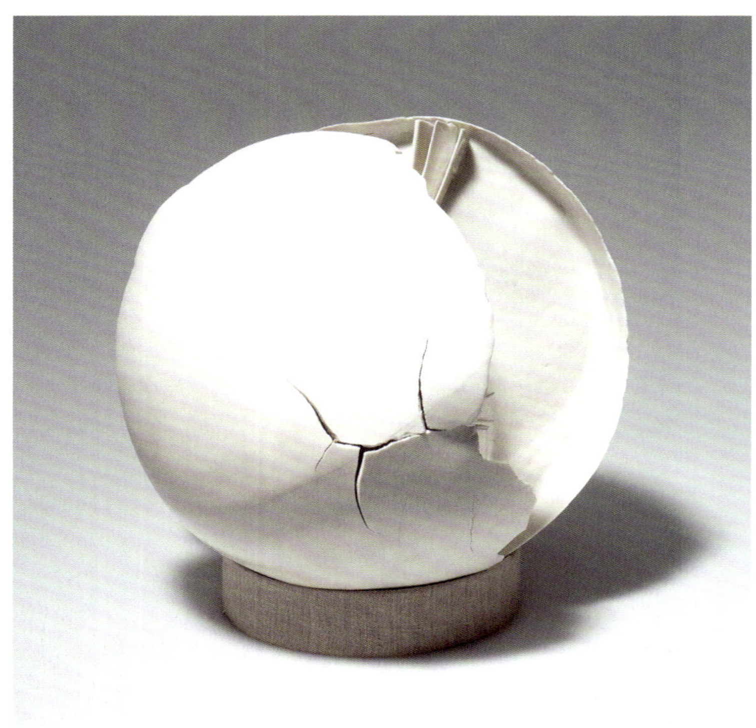

Gerda und and Kurt Spurey
Aufbruch [Departure/
Awakening]
1974
Porzellan, modelliert, unglasiert
Porcelain, modeled, unglazed
ø 26, H 24,7
MAK, KE 9779

Judith Huemer
Scan_24_02_2021 #03, 04, 05
aus der Serie
HEADQUARTERS
2021
Textildruck auf Samt, Unikat
Textile print on silk, unique piece
133 × 186

Courtesy of the artist

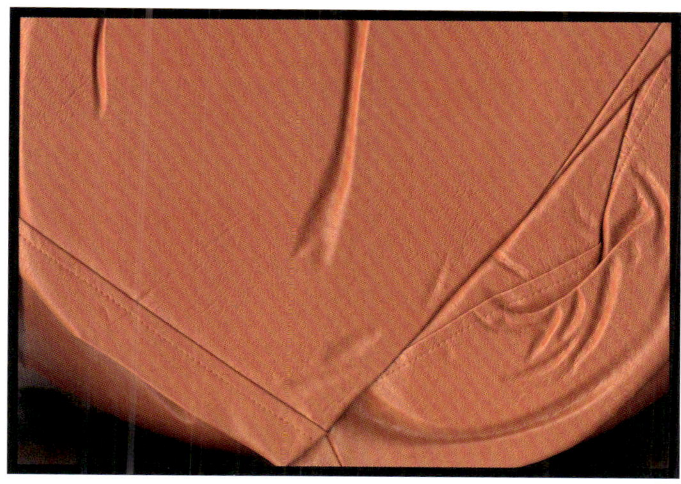

Die Vielfalt der Interaktionen zwischen Menschen und Falten verdeutlichen die Arbeiten aus der Serie *HEADQUARTERS* der Künstlerin Judith Huemer. Die komplexen (Miss-)Verhältnisse zwischen dem Körper und seiner äußeren stofflichen Hülle werden hier erforscht und sichtbar gemacht. Sichere Kontrolle über den Kontakt zwischen dünnem Stoff, Körpervolumen und einer aalglatten Sitzplatte aus Glas zu finden, erweist sich trotz des Versuchs einer mechanischen Sitzbewegung als äußerst schwierig. Äußere wie innere Bedingungen wie Schwerkraft, Luftfeuchtigkeit, Laune oder Motorik bringen jedes Mal andere Ergebnisse hervor. Dieses künstlerische Experiment zeigt humorvoll die Gesetzmäßigkeit der physischen, „faltenlastigen" Welt und stellt zugleich gesellschaftliche Ansprüche an uns und kritische Werte wie Perfektion, Beständigkeit, Natürlichkeit oder Kontrolle infrage.

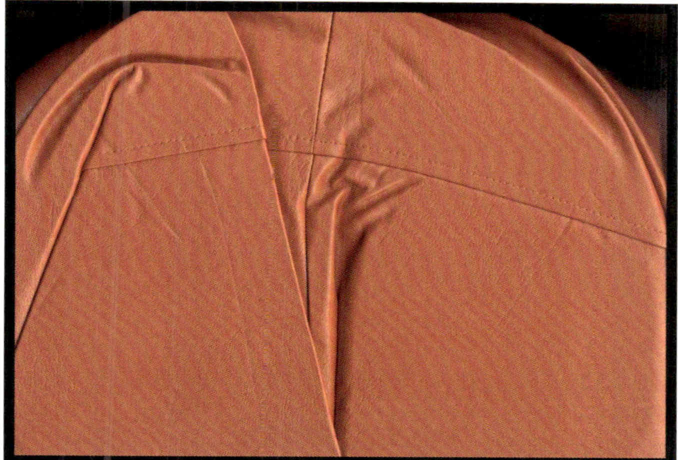

The abundance of the interactions between people and folds is made clear by artist Judith Huemer's *HEADQUARTERS* series. The complex theme of (dis)proportion between the body and its outer material envelope is here examined and elucidated. Exercising absolute control over contact between thin material, bodily volume, and a slippery seat of glass proves—despite attempts at establishing mechanical motion while seated—to be extremely difficult. Exterior and interior factors—such as gravity, humidity, one's mood or one's motor skills—produce a different result each time. This artistic experiment humorously demonstrates the laws governing our physical, "fold-burdened" world and at the same time challenges us socially, questioning critical values such as perfection, constancy, authenticity, and control.

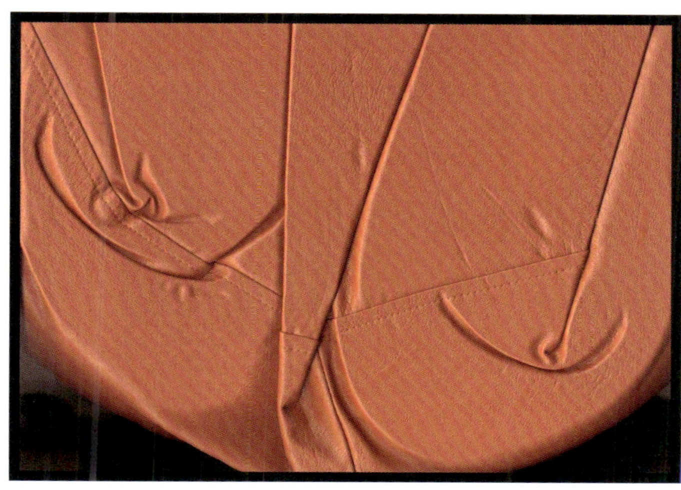

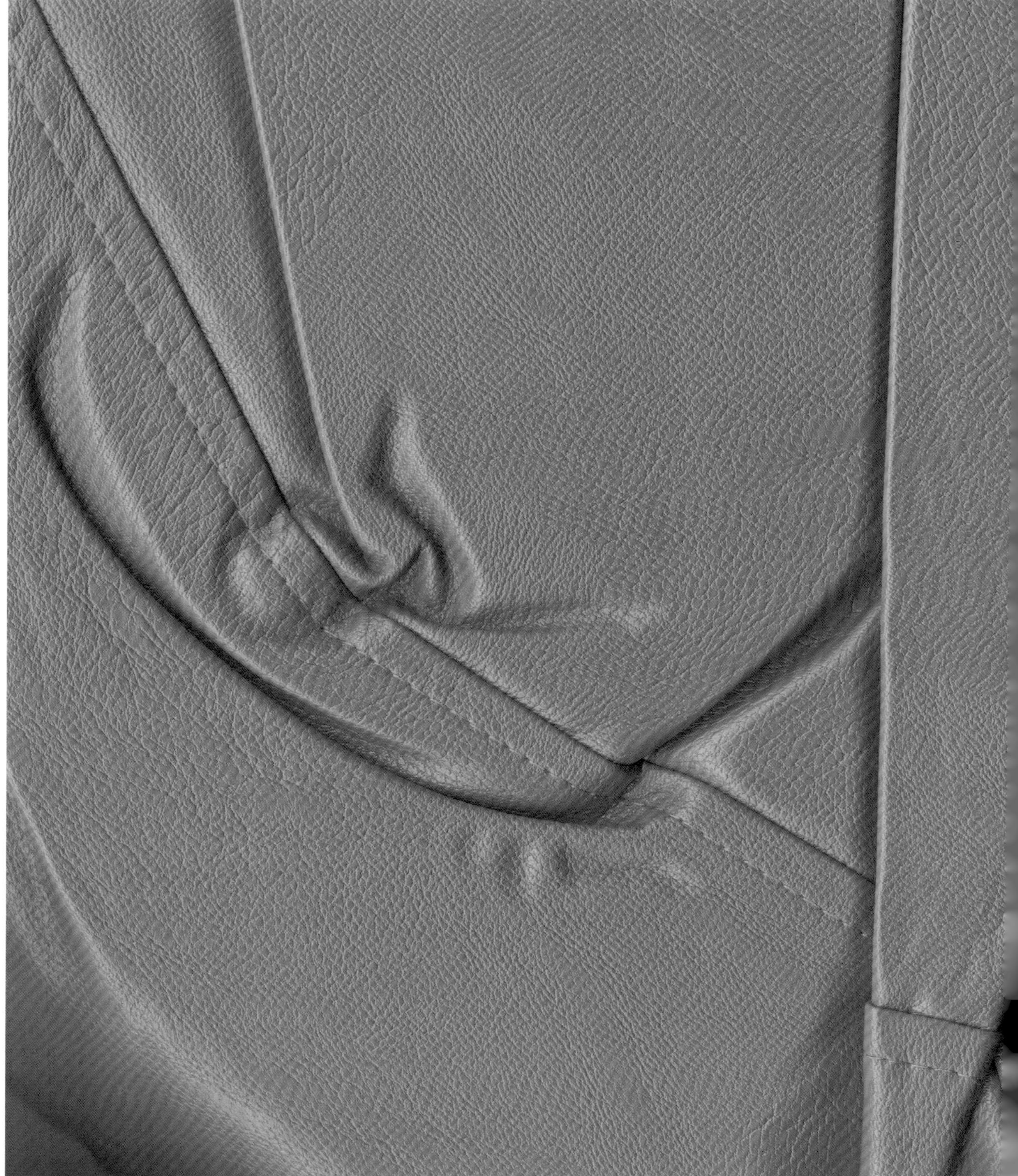

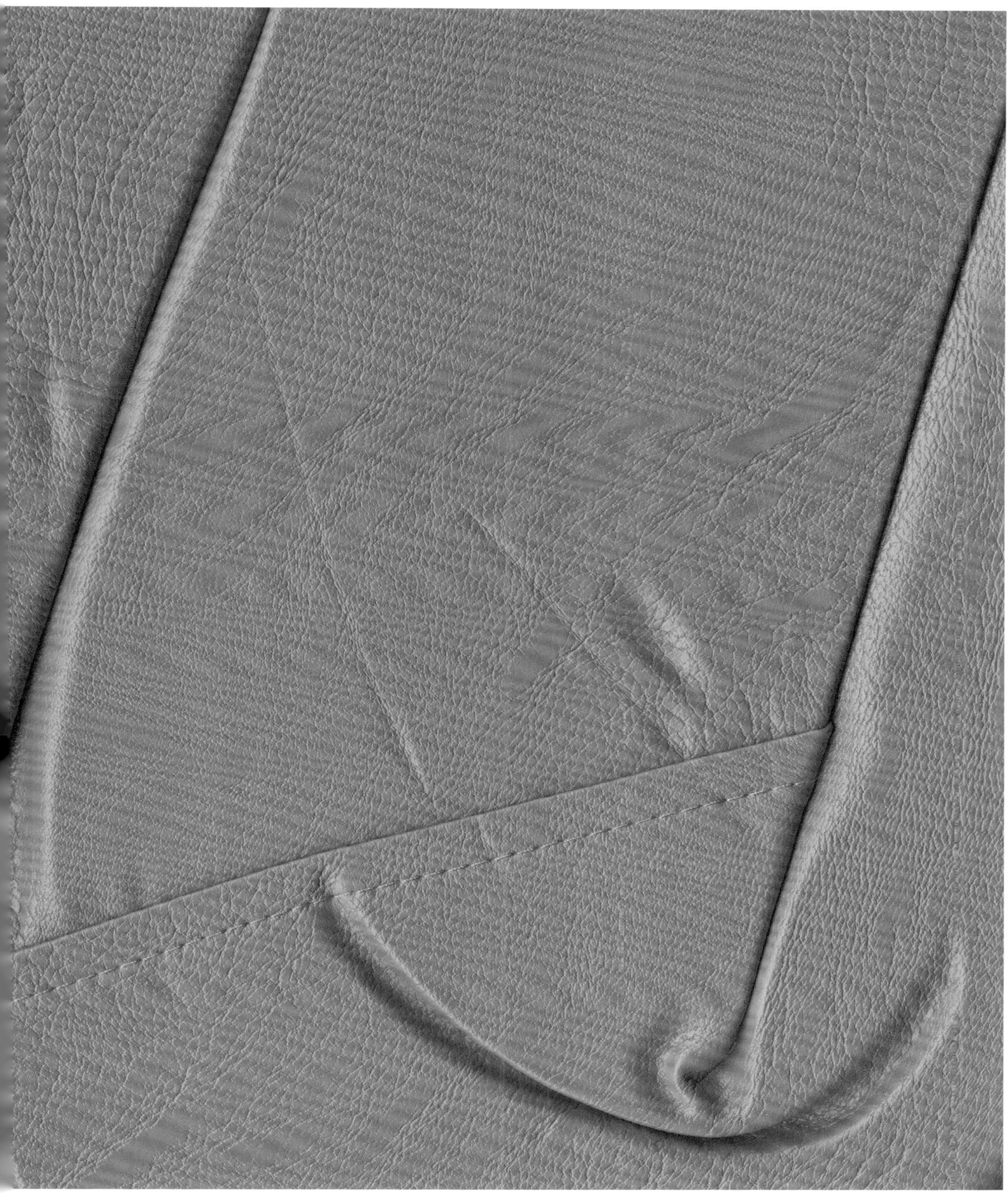

Dieser Katalog erscheint anlässlich der Ausstellung FALTEN im MAK, Wien
This catalog is published on the occasion of the exhibition FOLDS at the MAK, Vienna
1.2.–21.5.2023

© 2024 MAK, Wien Vienna und and Verlag der Buchhandlung Walther und Franz König, Köln Cologne

AUSSTELLUNG EXHIBITION

Kuratorin Curator: Mio Wakita, Kustodin MAK Sammlung Asien
Curator, MAK Asia Collection
Ausstellungsgestaltung Exhibition Design: Robert Rüf
Grafische Gestaltung Graphic Design: Maria Anna Friedl
Ausstellungsorganisation Exhibition Management: Aleksandra Drozdowska

KATALOG CATALOG

Herausgeberinnen Editors: Lilli Hollein und and Mio Wakita
Katalogredaktion und Texte Catalog Editing and Texts: Mio Wakita
Publikationsmanagement Publication Management: Astrid Böhacker
Lektorat Copy Editing: Cornelia Malli
Übersetzungen Translations: Stephen Richards
Grafische Gestaltung Graphic Design: Maria Anna Friedl
Reproduktionen Reproductions: Pixelstorm, Wien Vienna
Schrift Type: New Atten, Noka
Papier Paper: Magno Volume 135 g/m² und and 300 g/m²
Druck und Bindung Printing and Binding: Gugler GmbH, Melk/Donau

PurePrint®
innovated by gugler* DruckSinn
Gesund. Rückstandsfrei. Klimapositiv.
© drucksinn.at

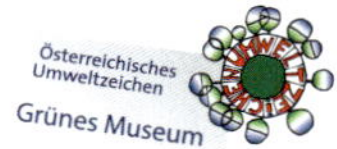

Das MAK bemüht sich in seinen Publikationen
um eine gendergerechte Schreibweise.

MAK
Stubenring 5, 1010 Wien Vienna, Austria
T +43 1 711 36-0, F +43 1 713 10 26
office@MAK.at, MAK.at

MAK CENTER FOR ART AND ARCHITECTURE
Los Angeles at the Schindler House
835 North Kings Road, West Hollywood, CA 90069, USA

MACKEY APARTMENTS
MAK Artists and Architects-in-Residence Program
1137 South Cochran Avenue, Los Angeles, CA 90019, USA

FITZPATRICK-LELAND HOUSE
Laurel Canyon Boulevard/Mulholland Drive, Los Angeles, CA 90046, USA

T +1 323 651 1510, F +1 323 651 2340
office@MAKcenter.org, MAKcenter.org

JOSEF HOFFMANN MUSEUM, BRTNICE
Eine Expositur der Mährischen Galerie in Brno
und des MAK, Wien
A joint branch of the Moravian Gallery in Brno and the MAK, Vienna
náměstí Svobody 263, 588 32 Brtnice, Tschechische Republik Czech Republic
T +43 1 711 36-220
josefhoffmannmuseum@MAK.at, MAK.at

Library of Congress Control Number: 2024943908

Erstmals erschienen bei First published by
Verlag der Buchhandlung Walther und Franz König
Ehrenstraße 4, D-50672 Köln Cologne

Bibliografische Information der Deutschen Nationalbibliothek
Die Deutsche Nationalbibliothek verzeichnet diese Publikation in der
Deutschen Nationalbibliografie; detaillierte bibliografische Daten sind im
Internet über http:// dnb.dnb.de abrufbar.
Bibliographic information published by the Deutsche Nationalbibliothek
The Deutsche Nationalbibliothek lists this publication in the Deutsche
Nationalbibliografie; detailed bibliographic data are available in the Internet at
http://dnb. dnb.de.

Gedruckt in Österreich Printed in Austria

VERTRIEB DISTRIBUTION:

Europa Europe
BUCHHANDLUNG WALTHER KÖNIG
Ehrenstraße 4, 50672 Köln Cologne, Germany
T +49 (0) 221 / 20 59 6 53, verlag@buchhandlung-walther-koenig.de

Vereinigtes Königreich & Irland UK & Ireland
ART DATA
12 Bell Industrial Estate, 50 Cunnington Street, London W4 5HB
Vereinigtes Königreich UK
T +44 (0)208 747 10 61, F +44 (0)208 742 23 19

Außerhalb Europas Outside Europe
D.A.P. / DISTRIBUTED ART PUBLISHERS, INC
75 Broad Street, Suite 630, New York, NY 10004, USA
Tel: +1 (0) 212 627 1999, orders@dapinc.com

ISBN 978-3-7533-0732-9

Alle Maße in cm, sofern nicht anders angegeben:
Höhe × Breite × Tiefe, ø = Durchmesser, SH = Sitzhöhe
All measurements given in cm, unless stated otherwise:
height × width × depth, ø = diameter, SH = seat height

Die Transkription des Japanischen folgt der revidierten Hepburn-Umschrift, für das
Chinesische wird die Pinyin- Umschrift verwendet. Bei der Nennung chinesischer und
japanischer Namen wird der Nachname dem Vor- bzw. Künstler*innennamen voran-
gestellt, es sei denn, die europäische Namensnennung ist international bekannt, z. B.
Issey Miyake.
The transcription of the Japanese follows the revised Hepburn transcription; the
pinyin transcription is used for Chinese. When stating Chinese and Japanese names
the surname is placed before the first name, respectively the artist's name, unless
their European mention of name is internationally known, e.g. Issey Miyake.

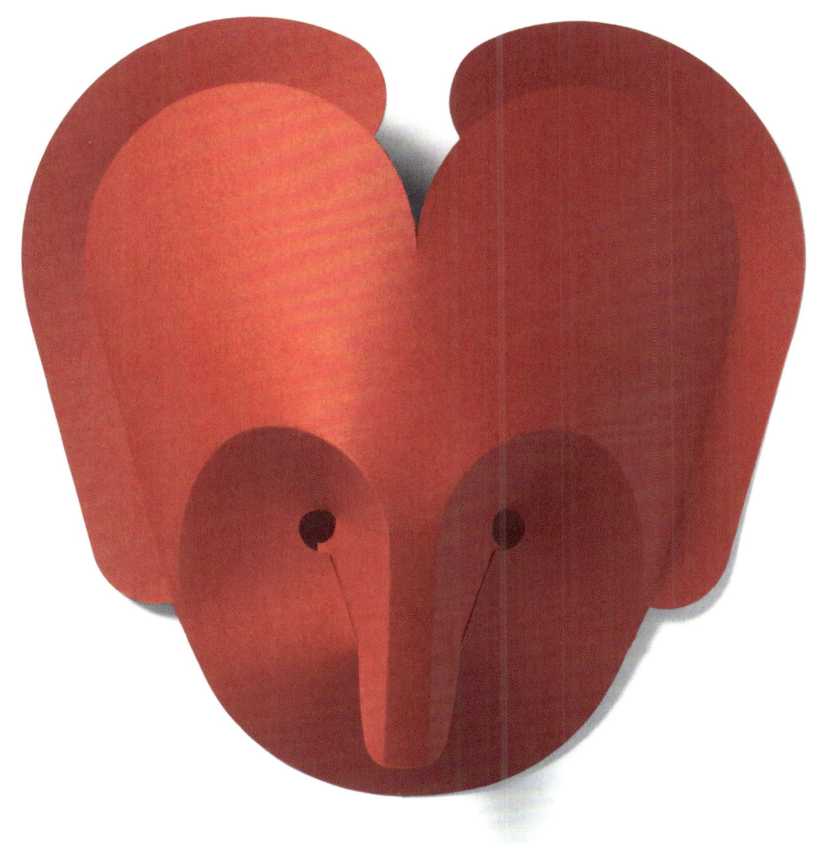

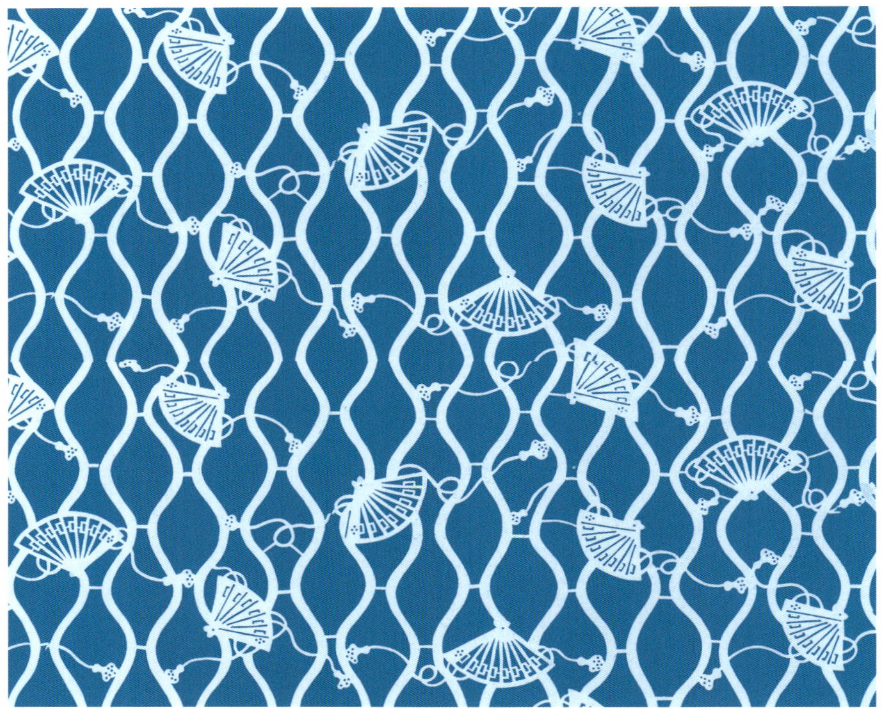

Dieser Katalog wurde ermöglicht durch die großzügige Unterstützung
von Maki Hiroyuki, CEO von Buffalo Inc.
Wir bedanken uns herzlich.

This catalog was made possible through the generous support
of Maki Hiroyuki, CEO of Buffalo Inc.
to whom we extend our deepest thanks.

DANKSAGUNG THANKS TO

Gina Corrigan, Volker Elis, Gabriele Fabiankowitsch, Aika Furukawa, Galerie Elisabeth & Klaus Thoman, Haito Masah ko, Judith Huemer, Stefan Krause, Paulo Mulatinho, Nishida Shatner, Otake Ayaka, Peter Sandbichler, Silke Schröder, Ruth Smith, Song Jing, Kurt Spurey, The Miyake Issey Foundation, Universitätsbibliothek Heidelberg Heidelberg University Library, Weltmuseum Wien, Johannes Wieninger und and Bettina Zorn